LAND AT T

CW01474826

LAND AT THE CENTRE

CHOICES IN A FAST CHANGING WORLD

John C. Holliday

Shepheard-Walwyn
LONDON

First published in 1986 by
Shepheard-Walwyn (Publishers) Limited
26 Charing Cross Road (Suite 34)
London WC2H 0DH

British Library Cataloguing in Publication Data

Holliday, John C.
   Land at the centre.
   1. Land use — Social aspects — Great Britain
   2. Great Britain — Social conditions — 1945-
   I. Title
   333.73′13′0941   HD596

ISBN 0-85683-084-4

Typeset by Alacrity Phototypesetters,
Banwell Castle, Weston-super-Mare.
Printed in Great Britain by
A. Wheaton & Co Ltd,
Hennock Rd, Marsh Barton, Exeter

To Moira

Acknowledgements

Wide acknowledgement is made to academic staff and students, and to professional colleagues who over the years have provided the stimulus for this book. In particular I acknowledge a debt to William Ogden who taught me when I was a student and with whom I have worked for many years. It was he who began our association with many European colleagues in a group which we called Managing the Metropolis, and to whom I am grateful for some knowledge of their countries. To Peter Roberts, who joined this work, and more recently to Ray Green and colleagues on a Royal Town Planning Institute study on the planning response to social and economic change, I am indebted for many discussions about the problems which face our society.

To William Ogden again, to Tim Holliday, and to Michael Yates I am grateful for comments about the book made at an early stage. I am also indebted to many local authorities, especially staff from the West Midlands County Council and Birmingham City Council. In addition many kind people in government departments gave of their time.

Throughout I have been helped and encouraged by my wife, Moira, and it is to her that I dedicate this book.

Contents

Diagrams

Introduction

This book is focused on the problems of England in the context of a rapidly changing world. The message is a simple one. In new global and local conditions, people and institutions are recognising the need to adapt to changing economic fortunes, but they have not seen an equivalent need to adapt their perceptions and use of land which are no longer appropriate to secure the wellbeing of the nation. Britain is generally acknowledged to be the first modern industrial nation, and by the mid-nineteenth century had moved out of a rural and into an urban era. Today the Western world is at a stage which appears to be taking it, along with other nations, from an industrial society of a familiar kind, to what has been called the post-industrial society, although others would call it a new industrial society, while others again, notably the 'Greens,' call for radical changes in the philosophies and economies of the Western world.

To the East, although urban industrialisation is growing, there are different cultures derived from ancient traditions which lead to new conflicts within and between nations, as recent history in China and the Middle East confirm. We are now also familiar with the problems of fast growing populations, starvation, pollution, land erosion and other threats to survival. These have given rise to new arguments about limits to growth and to the emergence of global conservation movements to save wildlife and rain forests and to check the erosion and misuse of land and the destruction of cultural landscapes in city or country.

While the place of land and its ownership are central to political and economic struggles and advance in the developing world, in Europe they are no longer seen in this light. Nevertheless, arguments over green belts, agriculture, and urban sprawl contain within them hidden values which relate to ownership, privilege, power, and myth, both ancient and modern. It is more difficult to expose and evaluate the land issue in the rich countries than it is in the poor. Yet it can be argued that it lies at the heart of human life and wellbeing, and is central to social and economic progress.

The title of this book is taken from an observation by R. H. Tawney that land lay at the centre of the problems of economic and social affairs which occurred in post-reformation England as it moved from medieval to modern society. Prior to the Industrial Revolution, land also lay at the centre of scientific and aesthetic developments in English agriculture and landscape, leading both to traumatic effects upon the rural population as enclosures removed its livelihood, and to one of the few native art forms which influenced the wider world.

Today we are faced with many problems which relate to land: the inner city, industrialised agriculture, power stations, transport, pollution. Yet for the most part these are seen separately from problems of the economy, unemployment, and social welfare. Economic theory and practice in the UK and elsewhere does not accord to land the same place as it does to labour and capital. Why is this? Could it be to do with the place of land and power in British history, not only in feudal but also in subsequent periods? The early political economists in the seventeenth and eighteenth centuries laid the foundations of modern economic thought at the outset of the Industrial Revolution. Their views on land and power persisted into the first part of the nineteenth century, until the rising urban classes wrested some power from the landed classes. In the twentieth century modern economics became well established, and land was seen in a different way altogether: to be 'protected' against urban sprawl, and disconnected from economic thought. These are factors which should be considered, for land and its bounty are the most precious resources and should be conserved and managed for all life. In a property-owning democracy there are still many problems to consider in relation to the ownership and control of our environment.

During the last decade or two, the pace of change has accelerated, and we are in the midst of revolutions of ideas, cultural conflicts, socially untested new technologies, and potential nuclear or ecological disaster. A re-appraisal of land and its use is well under way, but it has not yet developed far in the advanced industrial countries. It is the purpose of this book to try to uncover some of the hidden issues and to consider future directions, for land is a key to many doors. As resources become scarcer and more in need of conservation,

as life-styles change, and as life itself is threatened, so new perceptions are necessary.

How should an approach be made to a re-appraisal of the place of
land in our society? First and foremost it must be said that we live in
an age of rapid and complex change, with human activity operating
on unprecedented scales and in unprecedented ways. Response to the
resulting uncertainty is varied. Some hope to make progress through
well established methods of science and rational argument. Others
intuitively feel the inadequacy of the method and, with the benefit
of television images, take direct action to bring into prominence
questions of nuclear threat, social justice, or loss of wildlife. Others
again show their concern through the way they dress, eat, or behave.

The method is difficult, but it would seem that general observation and deduction need to be combined with more detailed
empirical observation in order to approach the problem. Given the
nature, speed, and uncertainty of change, no more than a broad
sketch of the wider issues can be attempted, so that a subsequent
focus on England can be seen in context at the conclusion and can to
some extent anticipate the needs of the next century.

Part 1 sets out the wider observations on global, European, and
English situations. Chapter 1, Horizons, looks at a range of questions which arise from the merging of old paths with newly
developed phenomena such as global population levels, computers,
and new knowledge. The new paths to be followed are unclear, but
at least we should know how we have arrived, especially as regards
wealth, wellbeing, and land. To reach any horizon from the present
turbulence, we shall have to learn and adapt more effectively, and
discussion of this problem concludes the first chapter.

Although world communities are now bound up more closely
than ever before, each will need to find its own way through the
forthcoming unmapped terrain. Chapter 2 looks at Europe as a new
kind of community, and at England as an old one, in order to sketch
out some of the constraints and opportunities which lie ahead. One
of the new and fascinating areas of study now being developed is to
do with regional and national cultures, the reasons for their particular characteristics, and their effects on human behaviour. To
adapt effectively requires self-knowledge. *What should they know
of England who only England know?*

Although the subject is an old one, the development of social

psychology allows for new insights, and the task of beginning to
know ourselves, why we have arrived, and where we are going, is
now under way. In this process, the structure of thought is a crucial
element. There may be genetic factors which are universal, but the
effects of language and culture give rise to radically different
approaches to problems, not least between Latin and Anglo-Saxon
peoples. Needless to say, attitudes to land, especially to farming,
constitute a central question.

After the attempt to sketch out the wider landscapes in Part 1,
Part 2 begins by asking in Chapter 3 how we perceive patterns of the
world, and in particular how we perceive our cities, towns, and
countryside, their design and the values they hold for us. New action
can only come from new views and new systems of thought and
political will. For centuries social, economic and physical change has
pushed and pulled the locations of people in all lands. As an early
industrial nation, we have gone through much stress and conflict,
but we have also chosen particular ways and means of progressing,
and choices still lie ahead. The argument in Chapter 4 is that we now
face new choices about the distribution of population across our
land, and Chapter 5 goes on to suggest that land reform is necessary
if the economy and social wellbeing are to prosper.

The last part of the book — A Fairer Country — discusses a new
model and structure of settlement within the wider system of
change. Unemployment in cities, the destruction of life and landscape, global concerns with ecological balance, and the control or
ownership of land are intimately related. It is possible to tackle these
problems separately, and such specialisations are necessary, but it is
also necessary to see them whole, particularly if we are interested in a
fair as well as a prosperous society. 'System' is an unpopular word,
but it cannot be escaped. Amongst other things it lies at the heart of
Darwin's, Galileo's, and Marx's theories, as well as at the heart of
military industrialisation. Systemic thinking is equally crucial to
problems of land-use, and that means the relationships of land to
people, wildlife, enjoyment, and survival. Systems are discussed in
Chapter 6, while Chapter 7 attempts to sketch out new patterns of
settlement which might be appropriate for the next stage in our
society.

Although emphasis has been placed on the speed and scale of
change in the wider world, in practice we cannot change our patterns

of settlement very fast. The cities and towns remain, as does farming in the countryside. But the doors which are opened now will lead to new places later on, and it is suggested that unless we open them, the economic and social problems of this country will not be helped as much as they might, with vested interests holding back the new age. Of course, all such openings carry risks; but it is a risky world, and the alternative is stagnation. If we are moving into a post-industrial society we must also move to a post-urban industrial pattern of settlement on our land.

Political process and structure within the United Kingdom are at a new stage and so is the economy. We must not allow the part played by land to go unnoticed in economic and political affairs, whether through vested interests, ignorance, or over-caution. If we ignore the problem, there is a risk of greater social polarisation and conflict as entrenched interests dig in. More optimistically, the traditions of countryside, wildlife, science, and toleration offer opportunities to design anew in ways which transcend the old boundaries.

There needs to be a debate, and the final Chapter discusses four imperatives which cannot be escaped. These are: awareness of a new role for Britain; political approaches; the impact of ecological demands; and finally, fairness, as social justice upon a landscape which fits a new world.

This is not a book about solutions. It is more concerned with new movements and possible outcomes. In such times only a relatively small number of people is willing to discuss ideas and change values and expectations. But perhaps the number is growing faster than we think. It is to those who are willing to explore a path that this book is addressed.

PART 1
GLOBAL AND LOCAL

Chapter 1

Horizons

There is no need to emphasise that for human societies the speed and scale of global events now occurring are greater than they have ever been. Our everyday experience is of third-world population growth, the space race, urbanisation, pollution, and climatic and ecological change. All this can be discovered in the life of a child, who can also learn the language of the computer shortly after that of his mother tongue. Every day this context is widened into a consciousness quite different from that of the past, one in which awareness of other people, systems, and relationships is at a level unknown to most older generations. The discussions and conflicts over nuclear power, for example, quickly widen into debate over survival and health, resources and limits to growth, public expenditure and priorities, private territories and public commons, vested interests and social concern. Changes in industrial structure and levels of unemployment raise questions about work and its meaning. What are the opportunities for millions of young people? Do they see promise for the future?

In such practical situations values are changing. Not only must established views be justified against Greens or the peace movement, but at the same time traditional social and economic institutions are also under challenge. Apart from these structural changes are those arising from everyday attitudes towards marriage and other social traditions. So the number of single households increase, for example; or women earn the money and men stay at home; or both run independent consultancies from their computerised cells set in ecological gardens, places where wildlife is more various than in the industrial landscapes of high technology agriculture.

Individual approaches to the new conditions are thus remarkable and indicative of fast changing situations and values. The large institutions of government and some big businesses may appear to be slow in their ability to adapt, but the launching of space probes has hardly been laggard in conception, design, or achievement. Today, people, groups, nations and international movements operate at such a scale and speed (made possible by telecommunications), that mental responses are to a degree faster and more comprehensive than in the past, just as the mental responses of urban people were once faster than those of rural people. The counterpoint of fast change and the slow pace of traditional life-styles is one of the fascinating if disturbing contrasts in contemporary society, but they are not incompatible. Crafts and home pursuits of all kinds continue alongside the high fliers; and the high fliers have always sought the recreative powers of handwork and nature. Many people engage in both kinds of activity.

Present evolutionary processes are often not easy to discern as patterns quite different from those of the past. Recent and less recent trends are not necessarily a good basis for assuming future directions in art, science, economics, or politics. And the very words we use keep thought on the old rails . . . *plus ça change* . . . but an historical perspective can demonstrate certain changes without difficulty. A few examples must suffice to show the increasing speed of events. It took several centuries to move from medieval to modern thought, from Renaissance and Reformation to the Ages of Improvement and Enlightenment, and so to the Industrial Revolution in Europe. Between the beliefs and practices of the established order in 1750, and the full emergence of urban industrialisation in England, a hundred years elapsed. From the shock of World War 1 to the present day is a little over seventy years; and since 1945, the speed of global events already mentioned has accelerated over a period of forty years, is still accelerating, and is moving towards catastrophe or a new order of things.

The accelerating growth of world populations, combined with material wealth and wellbeing, has increased and will increase the consumption of resources to levels which it will be possible to sustain only by radical changes in production processes or by defining limits. In practice both situations are likely to occur. The rapid early growth of northern populations has now moderated, but elsewhere numbers continue to rise fast. The energy used to support each person in the rich countries is of the order of fifty to a hundred times more than in the less wealthy. Extremes show a much greater disparity. It does not require much imagination to see that the economic order must change one way or another in order to resolve the problem.

The consumption of resources which this use of energy represents for the rich consumer societies, increased by a fair measure of material growth for the poor, poses the problem of how to sustain life in quite new ways. Instead of living off the earth's capital, we shall have to manage with techniques which use renewable resources of energy, land, forests, minerals and much else until they become an accepted way of handling production and consumption. Because of costs and territorial conflicts, each nation is already having to conserve its resources far more effectively.[1]

Knowledge is another area where change has accelerated, both in the numbers of educated and highly skilled people and in the means for communication. This is not only true of science and technology, but also of social science and the arts. The slow development of early psychology through philosophy and literature is now a fast expanding study in which all educated people participate, including children. The nature and extent of individual and social awareness (which is another measure of energy), is unknowable, but appears to have an infinitely greater potential than ever before. In terms of Darwinian evolution and social evolution, the debate is intensifying, and it is apparent that jumps in the process of change (periods of very fast change) are part of the story.

When all this is combined with the manifestation of the so-called new industrial revolution or post-materialist society, it is apparent that whether we call it fast evolution or more or less peaceful revolution, patterns of people, their societies, and their environments are changing with great rapidity. The speed of strategic and tactical response is a first principle of social survival.

Such periods in the past, less fast but equally traumatic, have been associated with war and bloody revolution; they still are in many parts of the world. But after the shock of two world wars and socialist revolution, the advanced industrial countries exhibit characteristics which, while ridden with conflicting interests, seem to have evolved into what many see as pluralist and communicative in style, with a greater tolerance of different interests and, in the face of nuclear war, a readiness to talk rather than fight, however slow the progress.[2] However, unless learning and adaptation can match the speed of other changes, prospects look bleak.

In an accelerating situation it is difficult to adapt effectively. The novice in a canoe on the rapids is likely to drown, and perhaps this is the state that much of society is in. On the other hand, the survivors are those who can learn quickly, adopting strategies which antici- pate rapid change; Japan in the world economy is a clear example. Recognition of the pace and nature of many rapids is an essential prerequisite for success, and if that is the aim, it is likely that many of the conditions which determined past actions will have to change, perhaps more quickly than might be anticipated at the moment. These changes will include perceptions of global and local resources and their use and conservation; the basis for work and social behaviour; and new patterns of settlement and land-use.

Social Development

At the outset it is as well to remember that in a scientific sense human evolution spans a few million years, of which only some thousand present modern problems of urbanisation, military wars, and the dawning of consciousness of the nature of life across the planet. We have now rushed to the point of extinction without knowing how to control the process of advance, how properly to assimilate the variety of cultures in society, and how to control the nature of our evolution in a dangerous industrial society.

There are crucial strands which history has unravelled, even if interpretations vary and aspects are hidden from sight. The divine right of kings, religious wars, slavery and serfdom, democracy and socialism can be plotted broadly on a graph of time and place. Conflicts of power have culminated in two world wars, themselves a sufficient shock to the system to alter the course in radical ways. War and bloody revolution continue over parts of the globe, but in the first Two Worlds the threat is now different, lying in starry-war- eyed thinking and deception, in '1984' and 'Big Brother'. At the same time the demand for rights and justice continues, sometimes rhetorically from the top, sometimes from popular movements, but also in philosophy and the work of the courts.

The stress of new forces on old systems is now translated from regional and imperial dimensions and ambitions, to global space and beyond, so that tensions and conflicts arise in new forms. The structures and politics of the superpowers of the USA and USSR are now joined by those of China and India, by the new blocs of Europe and Africa, and by the rise of religion in the Islamic world. Associated strengths in the form of global and multinational corporations and international finance raise conflicts for Third World development, as well as for the internal harmony of industrial nations. How should these great powers be used?

The problems to be confronted are well enough known: nuclear war, trade wars, ecological disaster, famine, North v South, urbanisation, and pollution. Little of this is confined to regions; most now depends on international knowledge and action. The assertion of power by any bloc over another is negated by the biological consequences of outright conflict, nuclear or otherwise, in defiance of nature's laws.

Few would dispute the identification of the major problems. The issue is how to reconcile them with old structures and attitudes, or with aggressive and intolerant individuals and institutions. The divergence is very great. Yet there are also strong movements towards convergence and progress. The global problems provide common ground. A polluted Mediterranean brings European, Middle Eastern, and African countries and continents round the table to sign a convention of common economic interest, for a sea without fish or tourists is of little use. The polluted Danube flows through several border countries between Russia and the West, a uniting force in more ways than one. Acid rain takes its place with the economy on the agendas of summit meetings. Apartheid is a powerful agent for changing the attitudes of black and white, and so is oil. Despite tension all these have resulted in adjustment to international understanding. The economic interdependencies may have ramifications as important as those of the old slave trade and empires, but the rate at which new attitudes must evolve is a good deal faster. This and the technical apparatus for responding, that is fast learning, communication, and discussion, provide the opportunity for people in power to act swiftly and sensibly, if they will.

If they cannot, then power can be exerted elsewhere. Popular movements against reactionary established groups have been common enough, and there are plenty in evidence today. These are not just the more obvious Peace and Green movements, but also the smaller links between individuals and settlements across the world, between cities in Russia and Western Europe, and between towns in various continents. Linked by telecommunication and with new knowledge, what has been called an 'informational agora' has the potential to challenge the corporation of state and big business.[3]

The influences of such movements are already evident in the softer voices of world leaders, who must convey an image not only of authority, but also of concern, common sense, and moral integrity. Neither false images nor blandishments should be able to fool all the people all the time, although we witness leaders trying hard to do so. Education, much valued as a means of advance, has now provided the globe with a larger number of knowledgeable people than has ever existed before. The nature of politics and representative government is changing in consequence.

The extent of cultural, artistic, scientific, sporting, and tourist interchange also ensures that in all nations certain common values are converging, while at the same time illuminating the desire to maintain individuality and the uniqueness of old cultures. Much is diffused through schools, churches, and other assemblies, providing new knowledge in novel ways, linked to local communities and political leaders.

Within all this movement there is evidence of the emergence of new values, particularly in the rich countries of the world. The causes are no doubt many and complex, but amongst them are responses to global change and the nature of new communication; the extent of education and what Karl Deutch has discussed in his *Social Mobilisation and Political Development* (in simple words, public participation); the security of forty years free of war on the soil of the rich nations; and new levels of material wealth. To these should be added the outburst of youthful vitality and exuberance of the 60s, with its challenge to established values of all kinds. This unique combination of developments has brought what some have dubbed 'post-materialistic values' and others 'the post-industrial society'.[4] Whatever name may be given to the phenomenon, few can dispute the extent of change. As has been the case throughout history, groups of radical thinkers are linking together in an attempt to re-state the nature and purpose of society. Two key concepts are identified by the wide-ranging study of futures carried out by the

Organisation for Economic Co-operation and Development (OE-CD): these are liberation and the establishment of roots. They include freedom from moral taboos, hierarchical constraints, and central control. Independent communities and local decision-making are also sought through the establishment of new roots. Thus social and political structures are under question.

This new enlightenment is a challenging prospect, although some may view it otherwise. As always, it faces the armies of established interests and central power: governments, the military, and all those institutions which combine a genuine desire for stability with a dangerous proclivity to hold on for just too long and so, in the past, inciting revolution. The new age of dialogue, Churchill's 'jaw jaw' instead of 'war war', is accompanied by new kinds of conflict in which key groups are able to dislocate society, as with the blocking of the nation's main roads by the lorry drivers of France. Who knows what terrorist or technical group might hold the world to ransom in years to come?

Dirty and dangerous as the process may be, this is a stage of social evolution which has to be faced. The question of a decent living wage is joined by many new questions about the basis for advance, including interpretations of genuine wealth in a gargantuan, gluttonous, consumer society. Perhaps in the 60s the materialist utopia of the nineteenth century visionaries was almost reached. Yet suddenly it became a mirage, in which the blossoming environment of a rich society melted into a reappearance of poverty and deprivation in the harsh townscapes of the inner city and sprawling shanty towns, and in the sterile eroding landscapes of the world. Material degradation has brought out a new sense of social obligation which, even if motivated in part by the instinct for survival, has also become a spiritual force.

In all this the environment plays both an active and a passive role. It is active in the sense of the fear of famine or ecological disaster, as once it was actively the home of wrathful gods. It is passive in accommodating the demands of modern societies, relatively ignored by economic theory and used as a backcloth to human affairs. Yet to every individual it is his or her home, work, enjoyment and sorrow: the substance of social and personal evolution. Because of its value and wealth-giving properties, it is guarded and held by those who have it, and proclaimed as inviolable property. The patterns of its ownership and use change slowly, except in revolution, yet inexorably they do change, as from feudal agrarian holdings to industrial cities. When the economic and social forces which created the pattern change, and when the environment is seen as an active agent, so change again takes place.

In the processes of change so far outlined, responses by individuals (and thence from the institutions in which they participate) are creating accord or discord within society. It is very difficult to know what to think, how to act, or in which direction to set sights. Some past points of reference, especially the place of land in political economy, may help to put the present into perspective.

Wealth, Wellbeing, and Land

Today's tumult must contain something of the fervour and intent of earlier periods of great social change. It may not be possible to sense the same feelings, but it is possible to recognise some similarities in the extent of turbulence, as old and new orders struggle to survive or establish themselves. Western people have for so long travelled the road of science, rationality, and the growth of wealth, that it is difficult to be brought face to face with moral issues of a different but recognisable kind. They are still set on an old stage, but they are floodlit by new technology and pelted with information in an auditorium in which only the supine do not notice the difference. Unfortunately the audience is also so caught up in its own set of values and perceptions that is is questionable how, and indeed whether progress will be made.

The Renaissance and Reformation drove Europe into a magnificent if tragic civilisation of exploration, war, wealth, art, and science, with strong associations of material and spiritual responsibility. In this process the context of thought and action passed through significant barriers at times when what appeared constant, changed. Notable were such times as those of Galileo and Shakespeare, Newton, Voltaire, and Darwin. New ideas and concepts were thrown into the relatively constant formulations of the place of Man in the universe, while bloody revolutions upset the traditional belief in kingly and princely power. Today it is the speed of change and the real threat of extinction which acts as the spur.

The assumption that science, technology, and the growth of

wealth could solve all human problems had foundations in a world where disease, ignorance, and superstition were the rule. The assumption is still valid as part of social purpose, but as a result of potential disaster and new philosophical thought, there is now strong resistance to a sole reliance on this assumption. There is also an opportunity to review the structures of belief and take account of new conditions. Modern ideas of wealth and wellbeing form one root of any new examination, and must join with other roots, many older, if the new design is to be acceptable.

In our complex global cultures the values of western civilisation are bound to mix and conflict with the values of other and sometimes older civilisations, even if wealth, science, and technological advance continue their onward march. Within the West, one of the roots of the problem of adaptation lies in the growth of modern economic theory, which owes much to Adam Smith, who himself lived in a United Kingdom which, before the Union, had developed a political philosophy appropriate to the new age.

John Locke was a major figure in formulating new approaches, discarding what he termed the old false principles which were concerned with God, kings, and people. In the second half of the seventeenth century, following civil war in England, the rise of Parliament and the dawn of the modern world, he asserted the commonwealth of people. But he also wrote at a time when those without property had no place in government, and when land and power went together. Thus in discussing property in his *Essay Concerning the True Original Extent and End of Civil Government* he tends, while advocating the equality of men according to natural law, to assume that the order of power and land then prevailing would continue without much change. He developed his theory that labour was the important factor in a world in which there was no shortage of land, and he mainly used agriculture as an example for showing how the just division of property arose. Although a utilitarian in one sense, he also justified the absolute right of property owners in another, and helped create the climate in which *laissez-faire* economics led to the success and iniquities of the Industrial Revolution.

In 1776, a date generally assumed to fall within the period which marked the beginning of the Industrial Revolution, Adam Smith, the father of modern economics, published his *Wealth of Nations*. In this he drew on mercantilists and physiocrats, with their concentration on trade and land respectively, and produced a foundation for later economists which formulated a scheme based on the division of labour and a labour theory of value, with the effective use of money and commodities in a market of wages, profits, and rent, set in the context of a nation's taxes and public expenditure. Although he was perfectly clear about the roles of land and rent, he did not pursue the problem of the effects of monopolies in land ownership and rent, even though he was much concerned about fairness and was also the author of the *Theory of Moral Sentiments*.

The concept of a self-regulating market in which the rapid communication of individual actions would provide the best possible way to wealth retains its power in the western world, having been developed in the USA and UK particularly on the basis of considering world markets in equilibrium. This notion, though tenable after the war, is under growing threat today, as relationships between rich and poor countries worsen, and as ecological imbalance grows with world industrialisation. The new monetarism and a belief in some western countries that USA-style market philosophies and practices should prevail, is giving rise to problems of social concern, or unconcern, which in themselves are bringing about new political movements in the search for different philosophies of life. The place of land and property, although recognised by earlier economists, was to some extent distorted by Adam Smith, for Britain was still a nation of landed class rule. His arguments about rights over land (as with John Locke a hundred years before) were naturally developed in accord with the social structure of the day. *The Rights of Man* by Tom Paine contained concepts that were far ahead of their time in Britain, although ready for discussion and partial acceptance in the USA and France. Perhaps the 1689 Bill of Rights, following John Locke's views on the Glorious Revolution, were more than enough for the time being.

Labour, goods, stocks, capital, and exchange of money provided the main arguments for wealth in a market system, although it was evident that land rent was a basis for much wealth, whether from food, minerals, or city estate development. The reliance on 'natural' law was enthusiastically borrowed from the brilliantly successful

works of Newton and others, but when applied to the market
without reference to human behaviour and conditions, it contributed alike to the Irish famine (for government refused to modify
this 'law' by intervention to supply corn) and to the appalling
conditions of the early industrial towns.

In his book *The Power in the Land* Fred Harrison develops the
argument that as a result of Adam Smith's economic theories, land
has been left out of market considerations to the detriment of the
economies of the western world.[5] It is also worth noting that in a
pre-Darwinian age of belief in God, the Garden of Eden, and the
natural rights of elite land owners (and apparently boundless lands
in North America and elsewhere), it was easy to exclude certain
indigenous aspects of rights over land or ride roughshod over the
commons.

With the rise of democracy in Europe came repeal of the Test and
Corporation Acts, electoral and local government reform, and
new philosophies in political economy, based on the associative and
greater happiness principles expounded by Bentham; this led on to
collectivism, socialism, and a new role for the state in the public
interest.[6] The conflicts over rights, taxes, and the ownership of land
which raged in the late nineteenth century and early twentieth
century in Britain subsided as the privileges of the agricultural
magnates were eroded by the repeal of the Corn Laws, the introduction of death duties, and the eventual break-up of the old order
after World War I. Town and country planning then became
the public guardian of a countryside threatened by urban sprawl
and a collapsed agriculture. Land was seen with different eyes, and
became even further removed from macro-economic theory and
practice.

In the USA, that early democracy, the opportunity to deal fairly
with land was thrown away, and the country remains nearer to the
beliefs of John Locke and Adam Smith, as well as managing to
combine religion, the market, real estate, and survival of the fittest
into a highly successful if somewhat explosive mixture. But even in
that large country, there is no longer any easy pioneering of new
lands. In the UK and USA, economics progressed to its present
quasi-scientific form, albeit to include welfare economics and to
recognise the cost of waste in the system, but only recently to get to
grips with urban and environmental economics. Like science, it has

arrived at a point in which new movements and human values question some of the deep assumptions.

A nation's wealth and growth measured in money terms of per capita income or in any other contemporary economic statistic is a long way from Adam Smith. The products and 'value added' which make up today's economic environment are still to do with trade, agriculture, and industry, but there are some quite new elements in the theories of economics. One is the growing importance of land, water, and other 'public goods' which are supposed to be part of the nature of things, and free, but have instead become denatured and costly to restore. Another arises from measures of productivity based on labour and wage conditions which are changing rapidly under the impact of new technologies, and in which age-old dreams of robots are coming true. A third is to do with so-called equilibrium theories and the place of rich and poor countries. It is, of course, possible to shift the symbols in the old economic equations, but this will never satisfy Ayatollah Khomeni or the new generations of people who prefer to return to more truly 'natural' laws, or follow their instincts to survive. The chapter on Buddhist economics in Fritz Schumacher's *Small is Beautiful* reflects wisdoms more ancient than some of the values of modern Western civilisation.

So the new equations are no longer to do solely with rigidities in the labour market, the costs of raw materials, equipment, and other inputs in relation to outputs and profit, but must have added to them the costs of pollution, the costs of developing renewable sources of energy and materials, and the costs of arbitration in adjusting to conflicting and social interests. Nor are they only to do with government measures of public expenditure, industrial production, and the balance of trade. Wealth rests on the fruits of labour, the products of industry, and the ingenuity of those who make money out of money; but increasingly the sums become difficult in the light of possible but unpredictable third world wars or bankruptcies, the costs of urban pollution, unemployment, pensions and health services.

In the *Wealth of Nations* Adam Smith was less concerned with land and its ownership than rent. But rent implies something about the social order which is not what it was. Instead we talk of credit and mortgages, subsidies and imperfections in the market created by green belts or other planning restrictions. This land, in agriculture or green belt, is what wealth enables some people to enjoy and others not, and the public enjoyment of nature has long been recognised as a truly natural desire; more so, for some, than material wealth as measured by the number of objects consumed.

The Commonwealth of Locke is also the commonwealth of land, of public as well as private property. It is not always used and enjoyed with justice in the rich countries, and this is certainly the case in many of the poor countries, although things are changing. The continued search for world markets and world labour drives multinationals into conflict with those who are concerned about the conditions of poor mothers and babies, of tea pickers and other such groups. The power of western wealth is geared to a system which has grown logically and often beneficially enough over the centuries, but which is now probably obsolescent. Efficiency may have to be measured in profits, but it must be combined with equity to produce wellbeing.

The closer inter-relationships of world affairs raise new questions of efficiency, equity, and effectiveness, and are equally pertinent to the International Monetary Fund, Oxfam, the communities of Watts and Brixton, and the one in Brussels. It is indisputable that new wealth is necessary, whether it be created by high or intermediate technology, or by the creative use of capital and the productive use of labour. Does this mean we struggle in a tide of beliefs and ideas which is no longer taking us shorewards?

In a return to basic principles of labour and productivity, the presently wasted labour of the rich countries and the exploitation of cheap labour in the poor are bound to be adjusted within the context of land and its resources, and of the fair distribution of money. Whether this means giving land for people to work in China or Africa, or land and homes to which people can devote the fruits of their labour in the rich countries, production will be efficient and effective only if there is space, capital, and opportunity. It is obvious that there is little of any of these things in a deprived inner city: only surplus labour.

It can be argued well enough that labour is surplus because it is too expensive. The USA labour market is more adaptable, less unionised than the British, and there is new land to take outside the old union strongholds of the industrial cities, something less easy to do in England than it was in the early years of Industrial Revolution, when escape was sought from the physical and social restrictions of the old chartered boroughs. But such arguments ignore the need to recognise the so-called dual economy of high technology and global power on the one hand, and local communities and self-help on the other, both in the first Two Worlds and in the Third. The growth of economic theory and practice has naturally progressed in relation to the problems of the age. In the eighteenth century, the concentration was on land and trade; in the nineteenth and twentieth it moved to forms of industrial production in which operative or blue-collar labour played a major role, and in which national accounting systems were developed for sectors of production. Government financial policies followed accordingly, with certain sectors receiving high state subsidies, and others not. Today the market monetarists work in a world in which the 'free market' is riddled with uneven and illogical interventionist policies and in which local communities at the bottom end of the dual economy suffer as a result.

Today, global economics, environment, and politics face a reappraisal in which land once more becomes a public issue, for both peasants and more prosperous people. The planning of which so much was expected in the post-war world is still, like economics, a necessary means for advance, but it too must undergo change in its precepts and practices. Space and land are factors of growing importance in a world of diminishing resources.

The evidence from advanced urban countries is that wealth generates demands for space, and that transport and telecommunications allow the space to be sought outside the congested city. It requires only a little thought to realise that if modern life is to be based on the use of the car and aeroplane, decent homes and gardens, sports fields and nature trails, and industrial production which requires large ground floor areas to produce cars and food, then not only are urban countries going to use a lot of land, but also a lot of urban things will be seen across the land; industrial agriculture, power lines, radio masts, new windmills.

By all means let us rebuild the cities to be more attractive, and do not waste land, but all the statistics point to an inevitable decline in urban density in the rich countries, while the constantly moving markets in housing, offices, factories and other uses work towards a loosening-up of the fabric, except in the highest value central areas. It is the enterprising and the wealthy who demand the freedom to develop, and there is no reason why they should not develop, even in a small country. To suggest that this urban process (which is evident in both capitalist and socialist countries) can be contained within a nineteenth-century pattern, is no better than suggesting that enfranchisement should be restricted to property owners. The demand for land is an essential part of wealth and wellbeing in rich nations, albeit with a different mixture of uses from that of the agricultural developments of the third world.

This simple model of people, technology, wealth, and the demand for space lies behind the dynamic of changing land-use patterns and the reassessment of current beliefs and practices in economics, planning, and agriculture, to name but a few relevant areas. Unless its implications are accepted, we shall be in danger of perpetuating — worse, encouraging — injustices and inefficiencies which we have it in our power to remedy.

The similarities of urbanisation across the world are complemented by a marvellous diversity of occupation, animation, architecture, plants, life, and landscape. Their conservation is a complex matter (not one of preservation), in which land and property, hard work and opportunity, science, art, and management come together in a pattern of riches and poverty, beauty and ugliness. The knowledge and means at our disposal to create and re-create are greater than ever before, but inertia holds back the changes which are needed to jump the gap between old and new.

In the face of unemployment and recession, there is a good deal of positive response, from individual and community self-help to the operation of the money market and the location of new industrial investment. In spite of much gloom, there is evidence of encouraging rapid changes in attitude and action in many countries, including the UK, if people want to look for it. Unfortunately the new harbingers of social advance, both in market and central socialist economies, are not yet politically accepted or applied, partly because they are as yet too uncertain and partly because their advocacy is linked to old political ideologies and interests which, like all established power, is reluctant to change. In the process, a lot of regressive taxation, land control and other policy is hitting the poor hardest, and holding back development. It is quite likely, however, that some sudden shock to the system might precipitate faster change, or that the accelerating speed of events will do the same. In that event, it is as well to anticipate the possible effects, and to consider a number of strategies before the battle. Some of these are considered in later chapters.

Adaptivity

The struggle to survive has reached a critical stage in the face of accelerating rates and scales of change. Unless we can learn to anticipate more effectively, rather than facing potential disaster too late, there is little hope for survival.

Exploration, invention, communication, and the slow accumulation of knowledge have brought us to the modern world. Trial and error, long-held beliefs, myths, religious and other wars, and methods of science and rationality, liberalism and idealism: all these have provided the way for Western civilisation. However, in the present turmoil of events things are changing. The mind-set of past ages is being questioned. Psychology allows for insights now commonplace amongst those who want to enquire, whether personally or socially. New techniques for future studies are being developed. The new tools of telecommunication, computer and biotechnology are available for better or worse.

The problem lies in the way we use these tools, what we learn for, and how to accelerate the insights into individual and social behaviour so as to match, control and manage the rate of technological change. At the start, the political choices and directions determine the future. The old politics of east and west are under question from new political movements and from the very nature of adaptation itself. The old methods of social learning are fast becoming obsolete. There is no time to wait for solutions, no sense in thinking that a Maginot Line mentality will solve the problems. To learn is to change perceptions. Science and technology have been, on the whole, too successful for our own good. Since computers and space craft are now with us, they must be related to social development. The priority turns to survival by rapid learning, negotiation, argument and persuasion, but not by persuasion through nuclear threat.

To ask where to start is to fall into the Maginot Line mentality. There is no single line, place, or way, and every approach has openings, bars, and limits. There are, however, new conditions for learning. Language and tools allowed *Homo sapiens* to develop. Language and tools remain the keys. The environment for learning today is not only new but also revolutionary, with the inclusion of computers, television, learning psychology, and open information on famine or crime, puffins or presidents. There is some choice, and it is possible to learn faster. One has to move faster to survive if engaging in the world of advanced industrial nations. The bullock cart doesn't suit the *autobahn*. This is not to say that all will or should join the rat race and move fast in all directions. The whole idea is to slow down those who are speeding dangerously, and also to change direction; but this implies new awareness.

The inertia of old methods of learning is by-passed by those who adapt quickly. Of course, specialisms build on the inheritance of scientific and other knowledge and will continue, as in biotechnology, but specialisms are set along the trajectory of past events, and can become forecasts and self-fulfilling prophecies, unconscious of wider needs. The problems of today sorely need more lateral systems of thinking. This is not in itself new; it lies at the heart of discovery.[7] Outside the currently recognised structures of knowledge, a great many ordinary people are creating a network where understanding is different from that confined to old-style specialists of whatever genius.

In its nature, this new knowledge has something of renaissance and revolution, but it rests on knowledge of a different order of magnitude. The new knowledge is also to do with morality. The historic examples of Greece and the Renaissance are examples of new argument and perception in the world of magic, nature, man, and God. The arguments about third-world poverty, just dealings from the rich countries, and wildlife, are no different in essence, but they face us with new questions of limits and growth, power and life, which are newly dressed in old clothes. God, courage, spirit, and morality, as well as science and technology, are all part of the ghost in the new machine, the mind in the brain, and the invisible hand of Adam Smith.

The relationship between belief systems, whether they be of science or of justice, provides the raw material from which we learn to forge new concepts and policies. Shock is a great spur. Two world wars have transformed personal, social, and technological relationships. The new global shocks are nuclear war and ecological disasters, third world debts, and Watergates. For many who watch and listen, globalism is more important than capitalism or socialism; the human problem more important than the political party. The phenomenal speed in the growth of information technology has given to humanity a new tool which has the power to transform social relations, provided the values and directions are rightly set.

At present the process of change often appears to be too diverse for understanding, but there are hopeful signs from a number of directions. A Nobel Prize winner, Ilya Prigogine, has started a new strand of exploration on the basis of linking physical to biological systems within a theory of dissipative structures. These structures, including time as well as motion, are in a process of becoming, and produce energy at periods of instability, so as to create new order. This fits into Thomas Kuhn's theory of *The Structure of Scientific Revolutions* and the subsequent discussion, which assert the case for paradigm shifts rather than for the slow cumulative development of knowledge. [8]

Prigogine's thesis of becoming is perhaps the best way of thinking about the future: a state of osmosis or infiltration within the social fabric; a system to be perceived and to be persuasive. In many of today's decisions over-reliance on numerical trends and established disciplines is discarded for scenarios and gaming. Anyone can join and in a sense that is what is going on. Purposeful development of these new 'soft' technologies is under way. Many multinationals adopt them, employing political and social expertise as well as management and technical skills. Management is thus faced with hard choices based on very new kinds of perception about a harsh world. In the more adaptive governments of the world, such approaches are also used, much more commonly than they are, for example, in the UK, where think-tanks and scenarios are not a normal part of the way of thinking.

The crux of the problem, however, rests in the conflicting ideologies of superpowers, nations, religions, races, and their component populations. Is it possible, without some cataclysmic shock, to speed up understanding and tolerance, to divert energies to peaceful and constructive strategies and away from military and destructive strategies? History to date is of limited value, because the responses which we see over time may suit the age, but certainly do not suit today or tomorrow.

The Brandt Report calls for agrarian reform, free trade, a World Development Fund, and other new global institutions.[9] We are all in it together. Two hundred years of Western industrialisation gave the USA and Europe a technological lead. Japan needed less time; others are catching up, but in their own ways. China's recent renunciation of old dogmas and its combination of state-owned land and private profit will produce different results. The convivial society of Ivan Ilytch enjoys a great variety of cultures, but the inherent conflicts will everywhere make progress difficult. As in all such situations which fall short of war, common ground must be found and cultivated. The power blocs, while confronting each other, are in the process of learning to limit and control the smaller warring nations. The control of war, the balance of nature, the full understanding of economic resources, their use and fair distribution, these are all starting-points.

Stronger political commitments to fairness between rich and poor nations, a curbing of pride and prejudice, and a keeping to agreements may all sound obvious and facile statements, but biological threat and famine can sway people's minds and, placing compassion above ideology, aid the changes which are necessary. The sages have consistently told us that self-awareness is the beginning of wisdom, and the same is probably true of nations and regions. However, we also need to have all the resources of intuition and science used with an open and exploratory mind.

It is doubtful if we shall survive unless the human psyche is exposed and investigated. Jung and Einstein were clear about the need. Ronald Higgins, in *The Seventh Enemy*, also identifies part of the problem under the headings of political inertia and individual blindness; and Immanuel Velikovsky in his book *Mankind in Amnesia* takes us from a realm of pre-history to Aristotle and the emergence of science, to suggest that we have buried our old fears at the cost of likely nuclear disaster.[10]

The other possible disaster, catastrophe in the imbalance of the physical world, is something more easily comprehended and about which rational people can and do act, especially as regards the Third World. But the issue is just as important for the rich countries, for they will have to learn how to manage their own social and environmental concerns rather better if they are to play a leading role in any new order.

The commonwealth of land will play a large part. Indigenous development will have to replace exploitation, whether by trans-national firms or by large land-owners. Personal development and collective responsibility will need reconciling in ways freed from market and Marxist dogma. Conservation must be more than scientific, architectural, and tourist-based: it will need to accommodate techniques which also develop the social fabric, as indeed is happening in much new thinking and action. Creative conflict cannot replace the destructive conflict of race violence and terrorism quickly or easily, but it is more likely to do so if some wider view and stronger help are present.

Historically, land plays a crucial part in the development of a nation. Its ownership, its use, its relationship to structures of authority, work, and leisure are all part of an evolving process. Whether in Egypt or England, the fair and sensible allocation of land and the parallel development of public works and infrastructure for water-supply, roads, and land management, are a necessary partnership in the process of physical, social, and economic development. The ways in which land is owned, controlled, used, and measured, and in which these factors relate to a nation's development, vary greatly. The information revolution is likely to make it more and more difficult to keep secret such facts as, for example, who owns the land in England. There is still no new Domesday Book of any adequacy, but the recent exposure of agricultural malpractices and the destruction of heritage, like the earlier urban destruction, point inexorably to the need for re-assessment. Across the world, problems to do with land form one leg of an unstable system of which the other two legs are people and capital. Amidst a flood of facts and ideas, future sanity depends upon fast learning and fair sharing.

✻   ✻   ✻

This chapter has emphasised a number of changes which will affect the thinking and actions of all nations in their struggle to adapt. The major changes can be listed as follows: first, the accelerating speed and scale of world events; second, the emergence of new social values related to concepts of life and nature, justice and politics, science and economics; third, the scientific and technological advance over the old structures of belief and institutions; fourth, the recognition of the plurality of economic structures large and small, old and new, and the need to reconcile them; fifth, the conflict between centralised power and decentralisation in a world of wide education, fast communication, and political awareness of a new kind; sixth, the growing importance of systems-thinking as a complement to specialisation; and seventh, the need to adapt and learn more quickly and effectively as a result of rapid change.

These seven areas of change and conflict can no doubt be criticised, reduced, or augmented. In a sense this is part of the problem of living in the present age and accepting uncertainty as a fact of life, rather than sticking to such 'facts' as the fairly recent calculations which 'proved' that it was impossible for man to land on the moon. The influence of all these movements on our future is unpredictable. This does not, however, remove people's age-old attempts to consider strategies which aid their success, whether in chess, war, moon-landings, or in the planning of great cities and irrigation systems.

A major problem is that only recently have images of world problems, of leaders, and of others, been so immediately available to people at large. Machiavellian manipulation of the media is to be expected, but it is doubtful whether in the end it will be any more successful than Dr Goebbels or Lord Haw Haw. The propaganda wars now visible on page and screen — pluralist versions of religious painting — are more varied, but different in that people are not as ignorant as they were, and false images can be broken, provided the media are relatively unbiased. Children learn much faster than they used to, and the capacities of the young far outstrip those of the old, as do their values. There should be no fear here. The fear arises from the unfairness of harsh economic policies and the consequent violence.

In schoolroom and in political broadcast the conflicts over content — bias and fairness, openness and secrecy, tradition and new thought — involve us all, but the number of arguments and the amount of information are new in scale. Thus the acquisition and control of knowledge remain the keys to power, and the speed and relevance of what is acquired are crucial for success and survival. While the wealthiest command the biggest resources and wish to defend positions, we can expect old conflicts to continue. As general knowledge grows, so does argument, bargaining, and the demand for participation in decision-taking. Out of this new level of discussion we may expect to see new interpretations of all the old values, but agreement will have to come more quickly than it did over the knowledge of Galileo or Darwin.

Most people will work, given the chance, but they do not have to be employed, except in the sense of being out of mischief. Play is work, and learning can be play. There are widening opportunities in rich societies, but they need socially acceptable structures within which to develop. The concepts of shared work, choice, and life-long learning are themselves part of evolutionary change, and the process is speeding up. It is people and labour, after all, which make economics work. The television is rightly considered in advanced countries to be a necessity of life for many, for it provides the same opportunity as a book. There are good and bad contents in each. Selection is a part of the process of adaptation.

All this may seem excessively optimistic, and perhaps it is. We may go bust. We may continue to struggle with wars large and small, and undoubtedly great conflicts over power and wealth will continue. The point being stressed is not that a utopia lies ahead, but that the means for change are moving very rapidly, in ways unknown before, and amongst participants with quite new values and aims. In these circumstances it would be foolish not to be familiar with emerging trends. The means to knowledge and adaptivity is now so great that, provided we survive, it is difficult not to assume that certain broad agreements for the future wellbeing of people will result. Neither is it easy to see authoritarian attitudes going down well in a new society; they have left many western schoolrooms and industries, and are leaving western international politics.

In a consideration of a small part of the earth, these big questions may seem peculiarly limited in their relevance, and in many ways they are. What can English experience do for those Third World cities which are now accelerating towards populations of 25 to 30 million (the forecast for Mexico City) within a couple of decades: populations greater than those of many nations. The International Community, Europe, England, and all other countries will find their own ways forward, but they will only succeed according to their adjustment of old shells and structures to accommodate new life-movements. If we are at a 'jump' stage of social evolution, as many believe, wits will have to be sharpened on the old millstone of knowledge, justice, and fairness set in a new context of ecology, telecommunications, and the survival of nuclear threat. What effect there will be on the pattern of land-use and settlement is unknown: nor will the Third World necessarily follow the urbanised structures of the first two, for the conditions for social organisation and production are no longer the same. For the present, it is enough to try to follow the fortunes of one small area of land on a small continent.

Chapter 2

Communities

The creation of the European Community and its development from six to twelve nation participation is a step not only towards joint purpose but also away from the idea of nationalism. To this extent, industrial, social, and environmental policies in each member state take on some of the ideals and characteristics of others. The present growth of market philosophies and practices in some European countries goes with new movements in the economy which require more effective collaboration. At the same time, unemployment and social deprivation strengthen the case for joint action in the fields of regional and social policy, and changes in agricultural policy will also become necessary.

It is quite likely, for example, that the traditions of farming will result not only in growing scale and production but also, for the UK, in a move towards the smaller units so common on the mainland. The more obvious attributes of cultural life, whether food or football, are the most easily seen at present. The future may see, however, some of the characteristics and structures of land, cities and social institutions permeating all communities, re-directing old national trends, and at the same time enriching the local variety and opportunity now widely apparent.

Europe

The tide of world affairs has presented a unique and difficult challenge to Europe, and particularly to the UK. To Europe the challenge comes from the diversity of its national and regional cultures, each too small in population and resources to face up to the present and emerging super-powers; and hence the attempt to resolve problems through the Community. Even if the Community were to fail, global situations would almost certainly force other means for co-operation in a small and densely populated area, where economic, urban and other developments are no respecters of national boundaries. For the UK, history provides an even more difficult situation, in which the inheritance of past power and influence have prejudiced post-war attitudes to the mainland, while the Commonwealth and USA demand different allegiances. These latter questions bring their advantages of special relationships (even if turned against the UK's entry to the EEC by de Gaulle's use of them) and might in the long run help Europe as a whole.

For the present, it is Europe which provides the context. The binding forces of Roman and subsequent empires, of Renaissance and Reformation, of Industrial Revolution, of Capitalism and Socialism with a West European flavour, are now enmeshed with the need to face a world of new powers, values, economies and urban societies. The continent has now to face the global consequences of what it began with science and industrialisation, and in the process is throwing up quite new movements of economic co-operation on the one hand and Green politics on the other. The question is: can Europe adapt with sufficient speed to meet the challenges of the planet; and in particular, can the UK, with its traditions of slow, unflappable but often pig-headed and insular attitudes, move towards styles more appropriate to a new age?

Two recent books show how difficult the problem is for Europe. One is the light-hearted but wise analysis of the Europeans by Luigi Barzini, in which he contrasts the imperturbable British, the mutable Germans, the quarrelsome French, the flexible Italians and the careful Dutch, topped with a mixture of baffling Americans. Compulsory reading and consequent self-analysis might go some way to helping all round.[1] The other comes from cross-cultural research by Geert Hofstede, in which West European countries are included with the USA, Japan, and others; in all, 40 nations.[2] Hofstede analyses attitudes to power and hierarchy; to uncertainty avoidance; to individualism and to masculinity. In other words he looks at those deep-rooted attitudes which are so difficult for a nation to change, and although the research is aimed at industry and management, it throws much light on government and politics. As might be expected, Great Britain, the USA and several white Commonwealth countries form one cluster of similar cultures, showing informality as regards power structures and hierarchies (*power distance* is the term used by Hofstede), a tolerance of uncertainty, individualism, and masculine attitudes. Scandinavia forms another cluster, generally characterised by even less concern with power structures and assertiveness, and also tolerant of uncertainty. In contrast, the Latin countries seem to conform to a pattern of strong hierarchy and a greater desire for certainty; but while Italy and some South American nations are seen as strongly masculine, others are more neutral.

Barzini's approach highlights the problem of nations with diverse inheritances attempting to live together in a community. The British have been slow to move and are outmoded in their approach to a fast changing world. The French continue their internal historic and constitutional conflicts between creative individualism and the need for strong central authority. The depth of German feelings, their strength and efficiency, and now their East/West division, all portend new problems, while for the young energies are channelled into such movements as terrorism, peace and Green politics; strength and romanticism thus finding new outlets. The Italians, with their strong internal differences, exhibit a capacity to restore economic fortunes in unexpected ways, mysterious to the bureaucrats of Brussels. Both in the use of factory robots and in domestic pre-industrial styles, success can be gained and old life-styles retained.

The future is difficult and progress seems slow, but the author points to an acceleration of learning through the facility of modern communications. To quote: 'High foreign service officials rarely write stuffy ambiguous notes to each other as they used to, notes that could be read from left to right or from right to left; they now consult chattily by telephone as if they were all in one big city to agree on possible common lines of action, and they call each other by their first names.' Here national space which is often inappropriate and difficult, becomes a new and hopeful European space. Internal divisions can be transformed into a combination of high-level policies and local action. National pride is not always the spur, for there are both older loyalties and more important present problems to face, including the deep spirits of the USA and the USSR.

As Hofstede points out, ancient government, empire, and religion no doubt contributed a good deal to the formation of past cultures. Mutable Germany is in a less extreme position than the other clusters, but northern Europe generally inherits less authoritarian modes of government and a greater stress on equality. Switzerland and Belgium, like all frontier divides, have special attributes, while the Netherlands neatly falls between the Scandinavian and English-speaking countries.

Hofstede poses hard questions around findings which suggest that while growing wealth may be accompanied by more individual, pluralistic, and informal societies, economic decline may work against these trends. Perhaps this explains much in the recent politics of France and England, one decentralising, the other centralising. He concludes with a warning that the inner limits of mankind may be more threatening than its outer limits, thus emphasising the critical importance of adaptivity.

Language, law, and philosophy all accentuate a basic difference in attitude between Southern Europe *(We work to live)* and Northern Europe *(We live to work)*. When it comes to specific issues such as agriculture, the problems are obviously great. Deep-rooted life-styles and economies are joined to traditions of tenure (again different in north and south) and to the stages of industrialisation.

The hard-working and less authoritarian northern countries developed into urban industrial nations earlier than those of the south. The reasons are a continued source of argument, but some amongst them can be identified. Perhaps fundamental are the Protestant Ethic, carrying with it personal and thus freer responsibilities to God; escape from the old constraints on money lending or, as we would now have it, money supply; and hence the rise of modern capitalism. However, as Barzini points out, the Italians have their own viewpoint, and the Renaissance bankers and merchants came long before Protestantism. Also of great importance were forms of tenure in which primogeniture (land to the eldest son) drove younger sons to the towns and other places of opportunity. For the eldest sons, wealth from colonial expansion combined with scientific cultivation, parliamentary enclosure, and stock-breeding could raise levels of food production, while trade leagues, unions, and less authoritarian systems of government aided the movement of goods and allowed for new political development.

Whatever the causes, northern modern industrialisation has led to uncontrolled urbanisation and the necessary early regulations for the health, improvement, and planning of towns; a rise in the economic power of industrial cities; the growth of socialism; strong urban reaction to territorial aristocracies; and the subsequent imposition of hard taxes and the break-up of old estates.[3]

In southern Europe, the process of industrial urbanisation is still in full flood, and a visit along the north-eastern Spanish coast gives some sense of city problems once faced further north. In France, autocratic rule and the particular quality of life of the great age of the Bourbons held back modern industrial development. However, traditionally strong central policies of planning and investment also contributed to post-war industrial success, to join with the continued values of an older civilisation.

Part of the conflict within the Community naturally derives from these different stages of development. Four interlocking facets present problems. Firstly, there are the old values of different cultures, many of which are expressed through attitudes to cities and agriculture. Civic virtues in the old city-states of Italy, for example, are very different from those of England, which is more suburban in attitude, 'suburban' in this context having no derogatory sense. Allied to these values are traditions of formality and informality in the design of cities and landscapes. The perspective and mathematical order of the Renaissance suits a more authoritarian style and accounts for the grandeur and symmetry of French developments in city and landscape. Even at a modest level, the Clos, or rectilinear cottage garden of Normandy, contrasts strongly with the informality of the English cottage garden, while the eighteenth-century English Landscape Movement was in part a reaction to the imposed formality of the Renaissance, in part an escape, after Blenheim, from things French and Catholic. As to agriculture, patterns of tenure conditioned the expectation of life on the land.

Secondly, the stages of economic development are different. So the industrial cities of Northern Europe must be renewed while in the South they are being newly built. In an age of international economies, high-technology, telecommunications, and fast transport, the new urban economic patterns are obviously different. They are larger, more spacious, overlapping, and often subject to the decisions of remote corporations. Each town and nation must adapt accordingly. The association of modern industrialisation with dense urbanisation is in part derived from nineteenth-century models (reinforced on the mainland by the existence of defensive city-walls, themselves a force for creating an animated urban life-style). Today it is more appropriate to perceive modern industrialisation as a mode of life pervading the world and its lands at large, so that urbanisation does not equate with dense cities, but includes much industrialised agricultural land, national parks, and all the paraphernalia of power stations, motorways, masts, and satellites.

This urbanisation is taken as the third facet, notwithstanding its integration with economic development, and agriculture is the fourth. As a result of early negotiations towards a European Community, the Common Market, and agriculture in particular, became the focus of change. In the post-war years agricultural employment in France, Italy, and Spain was still at levels of 30%, 40% and 50%, while in the USA and England it was in single figures. The ancient culture of small farm life-styles, and their numbers, exerted a strong political force for developing the Common Agricultural Policy (CAP), a cornerstone of the Economic Market and Community. It is not surprising that the agricultural budget now causes so many problems. In the meantime economic wealth, despite recession, continues to lead to demands for new uses of land, while the pollution of air, land, water, and life gives rise to conflicting values in relation to the economy and the environment. It is in this context and in political stress that the rise of the Greens must be seen. On the small surface of a limited planet some radical changes of value are inevitable, with local and national economic, urban, and agricultural traditions all under question.

Such a series of changes, which can be visualised as planes or fields of activity, presents conceptual problems of understanding. Time allows each to develop independently, in a horizontal time-trend, so to speak, but also in vertical movement, bringing mixtures and frictions between two, three or four facets: new problems as well as new systems of thought, action and organisation. New systems analysis can allow for some comprehension, but it must contend with specialist knowledge in all fields of human affairs: the arts, sciences, humanities, mysticism, religion, and intuitive knowledge. For humanity at large, it is the perception of these misty yet substantial forms which provide material for a new search, with a need to pin down images and work on them, as Constable did with his clouds.

Through all these considerations flows the changing nature of social structure and behaviour; and the resultant changes in belief and values affect our ideas of material and spiritual wealth, of city and country life. In this process much argument about the economy, urbanisation, and agriculture is in flux. Let us look at these facets in more detail, starting with the economy.

The Community, in spite of some success, currently falls behind the USA with its large home market and technological lead. The failure to create a truly free trade area and to collaborate nationally was perhaps inevitable. Within the Market, the infuriating and niggling processes of trade restrictions over lamb, microchips, and a hundred other commodities and goods have become the counters of bloody-minded bargaining in which the balance of advance and retreat may seem a bit like the battle of the Somme. But, unlike the war, it will go on; and this is a process which we cannot afford to allow to go on for too long in the face of new growths in world power and influence. The Commission has made valiant efforts to point up the problems and needs, and there are practical successes in joint ventures.[4] The Community is strengthening research and development, has a high rate of Nobel Prize winners, and is advanced in the fields of biology and chemistry. Per capita income is high, if relatively declining in the UK, and the challenge of international competition should sharpen the perception of need to improve collaboration and performance. At the same time national cultures exert a brake, and why not? For although economic wealth is a priority, other values run deep in old Western societies. For others again, especially the young, the ends of our economic means are not only to do with money, even if it does remain the major component of exchange, value, and perhaps greater happiness.[5]

The concept of a dual economy may be false, in so far as the whole economic system is inter-related, but there are clear distinctions to be made within the range. Europe's future prosperity will depend upon the development of new industry and services at high levels, and linked to these are the fortunes of smaller firms. The current unemployment in the Community may soon reach 20 million as a result of structural changes and world depression. The attempts of governments to deal with the problem are evident enough, but they also rest on economic theories, data, and policies which are far from perfect, and on questionable assumptions about political, financial, and union power. Some of these are looked at in later chapters in relation to the problems of the UK. No attempt is made here to grapple with the wider European economy, but two new aspects are worth consideration, one the so-called informal sector, the other the use of land and buildings.

The old systems of production are breaking down in the face of technical advance and new structures of finance, organisation, and management are emerging. Sir Adrian Cadbury, Chairman of Cadbury-Schweppes, has put the situation succinctly:

> ... we have to take account of the changes which are taking place in the pattern of employment and in attitudes to work ... a blurring of traditional distinctions between full and part-time work, being in and out of employment, between work, leisure and education and between the formal and informal economies.

The logic of these economic and social trends will lead large firms to break their businesses down into smaller units and to move towards an organisational structure which is more like a federation of small enterprises. Two of the attributes of the small enterprise are that it can adapt rapidly to changes in the market place or in its costs, and that it buys its services in, rather than providing them in-house. In a highly competitive world of slow growth, any business organised on a large scale and with the traditional top-hamper of overheads will lose out against lower cost, more flexible rivals. I would expect to see such companies making each section of their business as independent in its operations as possible and these sections in turn will strip out any activities which are not essential for the continued survival of their own particular enterprise.

The commercial pressure to move our businesses on to a permanently lower cost basis will to some extent coincide with the desire of people to strike more of an individual bargain over their life at work. There will be a demand for annual contracts of so many hours of work to be phased to suit the individual. There will be a growth in self-employment to provide the services which the large units are no longer supplying for themselves — administration, computing, design, and so on. A good deal of the self-employment will come from management 'buy-outs' or from people who used to work as employees of large companies but have now set up on their own. The advantages of this kind of shift in the industrial structure would be that it would give more people greater freedom to organise their working lives as they want and it would provide companies with a competitive market in which to buy the services they needed.

It is relevant to bring in here the overriding importance of the new micro-electronic technology in the changes we shall see between now and the end of the century. Its impact will be nearer to the discovery of a new form of energy than to the introduction of a greater degree of automation in our existing operations ...

The importance of the new technology lies in its ability to make feasible the kind of fragmented organisation I have just described. The advent of cheap, distributed information technology means that for the first time individuals can have access to all the data they require, and to the means of processing it, without being dependent on others at the same place of work. Companies centralised control and administration under the first generation of computers; now they can disperse them as widely as they are prepared to allow.

I see the future of manufacturing industry in particular lying with small units, flexibly managed, largely autonomous, organised on the basis of individuals rather than departments and based on personal contract rather than collective negotiation.[6]

From this situation many things follow, especially as regards home and work environments, leisure, education, and the uncertain boundary between the formal and informal economics. Leisure itself is a large growth industry of a new kind. As a member of the International Monetary Fund has said, in a world of growing wealth and travel, shipping the consumer to the product is no different from shipping the product to the consumer as far as the balance of payments is concerned. In other words, we must no longer think only of the export of goods, but of growing service and tourist sectors.[7] And these include a great deal which relates to old life-styles.

In Italy, Spain, France, and other European nations, it is still common to find the old artisan crafts tucked away in city back streets. They are now complemented by gentrified ateliers within reach of week-end residents and visitors. Neither make large profits, but both provide a working environment more acceptable to many than employment in a large firm. Such enterprise can be, and is, aided by governments, central and local. The success of the USA is in part dependent upon the flexible use of labour in a society created to be free of European guilds, corporations, and autocrats. That such an aggressive and acquisitive society should result presents a cultural problem different from that of Europe, which will have to work out its own salvation.

High unemployment in Europe is unlikely to decline suddenly, but as new work is developed and the economy restructures itself, it is likely to fall. France, typically and usefully, created a new Minister for the Informal Economy. England has a current tendency to follow the USA model, which is probably unsuited to its culture. It is not only lower wages which will solve the fundamental problem, but also the recognition of new economic niches in uncharted fields.

The demand for goods and the supply of money provide the opportunity for using our labour, our homes, and our land. At the top end of the economy it is obvious that economic conditions demand new land, more productivity, better markets, and higher standards; but as the urban conservation movement has shown, these cannot be got by destroying a valuable heritage and building Manhattan in Brussels, as the City fathers and developers tried to do. (This Goliath and its proposed 60 skyscrapers was fought by a David of citizens committed to other values — *L'Atelier de Recherche et d'Action Urbaines* — ARAU).

At the bottom end of the economy examples of self-help are springing up like mushrooms, but the flow of capital and land which should be coming from the financial institutions and the planning process is denied them. Sweated equity, provided it is not enforced, is no more than giving to someone who wishes to build a house the same chance as already exists for a workaholic businessman who, on a pittance of profit, strives to build up a firm. The growth of co-operative and participative ideas is becoming widespread, and much can contribute to the economy, whether at local level, or by growing towards the formal end of the dual economy.[8] Similar questions arise in relation to farming, horticulture and tourism. Can the old small farm life-style be accommodated to the modern economy, giving new opportunities to young people?

At this point, combined with tourism and Cadbury's view of future industrial structures, the question of land-use becomes important. For if the old economic structures are changing, may it not also be necessary to see an accompanying change in settlement pattern, land-use, and planning controls? While it is reasonable to posit a continuation of trends, it may also be that present perceptions of, and control over, buildings and land will not fit tomorrow's society. Already planners are having difficulty in distinguishing an office from a research establishment, or a house from an office or centre of education.

The urbanisation which accompanies industrialisation, our second facet, is not new. It has even been argued that towns preceded agriculture, which may well be so.[9] In any case, the scale of modern demands on natural resources — and of mass production techniques — for food, manufactured goods, services, houses — is such that land is less and less 'natural', and more and more affected by the demands of *Homo sapiens*.

The industrial heartland of Europe stretches from the North Sea to the Mediterranean. This great urban region now faces common problems of the environment which in the last century were confined to industrial cities and relatively small areas. Today, dirty rivers, acid rain, and tourists alike cross frontiers and take their concentrated effects to the Baltic or Caspian seas, removing life and solitude from lake and forest, while nuclear war-heads and waste find reluctant hiding places. The whole Continent begins to assume the characteristics once confined to industrial cities and the coalfields.

The inexorable demands of economic production require new places and more space, while the centres of each nation spill out their influences to overlap with each other. From the Netherlands urban expansion moves south towards Brussels and south-east towards the Ruhr. From Paris it moves along the Seine, south to the Loire, west to the Atlantic and south-east to the Rhône. From the outworn Ruhr urban economies move up the Rhine to join Frankfurt and Basle, while west and south of the Alps are the growing regions of southern France and northern and central Italy. Each nation makes a contribution to the European centre. North-eastern Spain and Madrid provide extensions to this heartland, as does Southern England across the Channel. Beyond are the peripheries of the Atlantic and the southern Mediterranean, where there is space but little income. These movements are not only migrations: much growth is indigenous, especially around world-cities such as Brussels, Paris, London, and Rome.[10]

Two sets of forces are at work in this urban region; the attraction of new spaces for wealthy populations, and the desire to escape from the old. On the continental mainland this escape is from urban areas, made more dense than those in England by the earlier construction of defensive walls. Once walls became redundant, the flood of over-crowded people spilled out of the cities, as it did across the Vienna Ringstrasse, and into the suburbs and beyond, still continuing today. Urban densities across old Europe continue to fall, although past life-styles are reflected in new developments. Expanding Paris rejected the dispersed new town solution of England, instead deciding on six grand new cities attached to the periphery of the old core. Regional variations across Europe are many, but in general populations and work places are dispersing.

Agriculture does not escape industrialisation, and so between the cities the view may become more monotonous and devoid of wildlife. On the other hand, it may develop as a haven of gentrified landscape from which to commute to the city. On the mainland of Europe there is a greater urban population to spread out from the old cities, but also less inclination to sprawl as a result of strong urban traditions. Deeper rooted preferences are also at work, to challenge the traditional apartment life with one of suburban house and garden. The English Landscape Movement is more than *Le Jardin Anglais*. The attraction of the city remains, but it is loosening under the influence of autoroute and airport which provide the where-withal to spin across the green belts, into the hills, and onto the coasts in search of more attractive environments. In the small towns land is cheaper, layouts more flexible, and life often more enjoyable. After all, the city is still there, and some will return to it, for there are always change and movement in the search for opportunity. New areas grow old, habits and fashions change, and old areas become renewed. The process is different now only because the spread is very much more extensive, and because wealth demands space.

Regions vary in their density and wealth according to their stage of industrialisation, their distance from the growing central world-city regions, and their resources, not least of people. The dynamic of growth and wealth lies in the central heartland of Europe, fading to the peripheries of Ireland, Portugal, and the Mediterranean, except for southern France and north-west Italy. The causes are similar to those which led to the growth of nineteenth-century cities and the decline of rural areas. These causes include the synergy which is at work where enterprising people are in close communication, with free market flows of energy and money, and with spaces for new building and activity. With modern transport and telecommunication, the dynamic effect spreads, but not as far as the periphery. In today's European economy France, at the geographical centre of west Europe, is better placed than the peripheral countries, while Germany suffers from its post-war division and its current status as a border region.

The regional policy of the European Community transfers a modest fund of money from rich to poor, but it is only a fraction of what goes to support agriculture. Whether the growth of wealth, tourism, and the search for space will redress these differences time will tell. There is no doubt that although the differential remains high, the spread of urbanisation continues. In the old city rich and poor areas, parks and slums, came together in a limited location and worked as an economic unit. Today the heartland of Europe is a business centre, the green belt a park, the redundant old steel town a slum and the Mediterranean a seaside resort. The scale of urbanism matches the scale of the economy. To bring it nearer home, the small town of Baldock in Hertfordshire is now a service station for the A1, overlaid on an old self-contained market town. So across Europe, large new urban functions weigh on the old, and the fight for *Small is Beautiful* provides for daily conflict over new development.

The demand for land, and therefore the rent and price which it commands, is greatest at the centre. But whereas in the past the gradient flowed from the central areas of government and business, today, although these areas remain as a peak, the gradient falls from wide urbanised regions (such as the area around Paris, Brussels, and Bonn), to Scotland, Spain, and Greece. In an EEC measure of accessibility (that is, attractiveness to high-level economic activity) the cities just mentioned score over 70%, whereas London scores 50%, Switzerland about 40% and Greece between 10% and 20%.[11] What this means is that the phenomena of congestion and high rents, as well as poor housing for the deprived sectors of society, are now characteristic of whole urban regions as much as of cities; regions whose leafy city suburbs are now extended into surrounding small settlements or gentrified landscapes. At the other end of the gradient are rural poverty and a poor work force servicing rich tourists and the retired. But there are also the growing numbers of wealthier active people working independently in the pleasanter climates of the South or in the quieter places of all areas.

It is doubtful whether regional policy directed at industrial investment is effective in providing employment, and whether it is fitted to policies for the conservation of land resources and the wellbeing of local populations. To be sure, capital investment provides some jobs, while national and regional parks protect the more beautiful areas. There are also wide tracts of ordinary landscape to be used for development. But regional policy has its roots in an era of pre-war economic depression and different economic and social structures, while the National Parks idea comes from the late nineteenth-century USA, when the last frontiers were open to the land-hungry pioneers. Whether these ideas and policies are the best for a new age is open to question, whatever the spatial dimensions.

The present more diffuse economy with its mobile life-styles, especially when associated with agricultural land and a declining labour force, suggests that old city/rural distinctions may become less and less valid, and that the problems of inequality between regions and within them may have to be seen differently. This is a problem which is pursued, in relation to England, in subsequent chapters. The European nations are too varied for the application of standard solutions and too many to study here. It may well be that before long the peripheral areas will be better off than the urban cores, in rather the same way that the southern United States are growing while those in the north-east suffer all the problems of an obsolescent environment. Redistributions of aid will always be necessary, but the methods will vary.

Different countries will develop their own solutions according to their cultures and the fortunes of history. Switzerland, for example, a country not often referred to in the texts of town and country planning, inherits a tradition of strong independence in its system of cantons and referenda, while the snow slopes conditioned forest laws to control the avalanche long before the tourists arrived. City management is sophisticated in the handling of anything from taxes to the interior conservation of coffee houses. The Netherlands, fortified and reclaimed from the sea, tends to see much of its planning in terms of physical land and water management, applying old skills to new reclamation projects (old skills once influential for English life along the eastern lowlands), and giving greater value to public works and less to private property interests in consequence. All these matters affect attitudes to land development and the procedures of people and government in reaching decisions.

If the planning of physical environments has been a matter of survival for the Dutch, for the French the planning of economic regions has been a contribution to post-war recovery. For the English the planning of town and country was a reaction to early industrial urbanisation. Underlying all these approaches depths of the national subconscious rise to aid or impede the adaptive process for cities and countries. Faced with their past, they must meet their future. The traditions of philosophy in mainland Europe allow for a searching approach to cultural problems, while English traditions respond in a more empirical way. Neither side can now afford to discard the opportunities offered by the other, as they tackle all the problems of the economy, land-use, city life, and country life.

One of the interesting questions facing European communities is to do with life in towns and country as it has developed over the centuries. On the mainland walled cities were once necessary with the Campagna or chateau beyond amongst the peasantry; in England walls for controlling trade, mostly long since gone in an earlier free market, left suburb and country house more easily disposed about a land of large farms. Today, some in England are discovering the pleasures of animation in the city, while their friends from Paris and Brussels are equally pleased with village and countryside. This is not to say that each side is turning its back on tradition; rather, each is extending the opportunities which wealth and modern transport can bring. The wealthy benefit most, and as their numbers and mobility have increased so much since the war, the pressures on attractive spaces grow ever more. Care must be taken not to allow such a polarisation in distance between rich and poor that, as with distant views of labourers beyond the ha-ha, or in the painting of land-scapes, the social conscience becomes once again inured and blind.

This mobility over the old landscapes and towns has to contend with the roots of human life on the land, with small farms, and the attachment to urban quarters and neighbourhoods. The demo-graphic movements indicate the need for space, and economic power can command it. At the same time traditional patterns of small farms and inner-city communities are evidence not only of out-moded structures but also of valued roots. Thus when EEC Com-missioner Mansholt launched his plan for the modernisation of agriculture in the Six of 1968, the clash of economic planning and social values was predictable. His aims were to secure stable prices, increase production and the size of holdings, and halve the work-force. At the time many said that the plan would create surpluses, be expensive, attack a way of life for the small man, over-centralise control, and offer no security in other employment, as was then promised. The ensuing social and economic conflicts are still resounding around the halls of government, while the voices of ecologists and conservationists are now added. Where now is the city employment? How costly are the surpluses to taxpayer and to Third World agriculture, and what price is centralised bureaucratic wrangling? The 70s have brought even less certainty. This facet, of rural land and agriculture, is perhaps at the heart of the problem. It is still the life source and also has its property connotations, its still live romantic feelings. There is now a mixture brewing ready for the reappearance of past conflicts, but this time within the knowledge of ecology, and a better informed electorate whose representatives are instantly accountable on the television screen.

The variety of nations in Europe does not allow for the same land solution everywhere, but three interacting factors are important: law relating to land, the extent and other characteristics of land, and the nature of ownership. Law is made through the Community institutions and applied to member nations. For example, the directive requiring the preparation of environmental impact assessments (EIAs), will require them to be prepared for certain major developments. This measure was supported by all member states except the UK, being opposed by the British Government and Whitehall (although not by the House of Lords or the Royal Town Planning Institute). Certain people hold the view that the British planning system is adequate to deal with these problems, and up to a point it is better equipped than the French, for example. The European need is one thing, but that of each state quite another.

At present the directives are left for application within the laws and procedures of member states, but the very making of them has altered those procedures, has altered standards, and has altered costs. The directives on agriculture, water, and a host of other common problems, all cause difficulty according to national situations, but, like the findings of the European Court of Justice, they are more or less binding. A good example of the problem of contrasting conditions and attitudes to water pollution can be found in relation to the sea-bathing directive which, though mainly concerned with heavily polluted beaches, has now forced the UK to deal with less polluted ones and has altered the policies and costs of both the Regional Water Authorities and the Local Councils.

The extent of coast in Britain can be contrasted with its small area of land. Whereas the area of France is over 50 million hectares, that of England and Wales is only half that amount. Naturally perceptions are different, as once were the views of John Locke in arguing about labour, land, and property in relation to an apparently endless earth. The results of tidy town-planning control in England can be contrasted with the still sporadic development in much of France, although the land factor is only one of several. Only recently in France have country property owners been restricted from exercising a right of free development of houses on their land, and even now they can obtain permission to build far more easily than their counterparts in Britain. However, the ownership of agricultural land in France or Italy is much more widely spread than it is in the UK. In 1975 there were over 2½ million farms in Italy, and only 280,000 in the UK. The past histories of the Highland crofters and the English yeomen are still, so to speak, live issues in parts of Europe.

Even in eastern Europe there is considerable freedom to own land or to build a summer house in the country. This is a freedom virtually denied to the budding country dweller in England. As a result the price of a rural plot, if it can be found, can be astronomical compared with those on much of the mainland. Combinations of law, land characteristics, and ownership operate to give very different results, but they are all central to the question of life-styles and opportunities both in the countryside and in the city. Green belts, countryside protection, and agricultural subsidies, all provide arguments for containing cities, but they also reduce the opportunities for the less well-off.

Attitudes to land depend on the layers of historical precedent in law, custom, art, and poetry. Raymond Williams provides an analysis of the myth of rural England seen through literature. Barthes strips the illusion of landscape beauty off the reality of tourist life.[12] These veils remain, but they are more transparent to people at large than once they were.

All these intermingled layers, spaces, and views have their reasons and meanings, but structures, values, and processes are changing.

The international bodies of the UN in Geneva, of the Council of Europe in Strasbourg, and of the European Parliament and the Commission in Brussels may hinder nations, but they focus the spotlight on collaboration. The European Economic Association of Communist Countries (COMECON) provides a vehicle for discussion on environment and the economy which allows for new East-West political understanding through technical argument.

The growing series of studies on the economy and the impact of new technology and other international developments draw heavily on the joint expertise of the member states to provide common ground for new policies both on the immediate problems of the economy and unemployment and on the likely long-term impacts of bio-technology. Where the line should be drawn between EEC and national policies is as thorny a problem as where it should be drawn between national and local government. That the frustrations of protracted argument should have replaced the devastation of internal wars, however, must be recognised as part of the price of peace and not as a reason for despair.

Justice from the European Courts and the Commission on Human Rights has served, and will do more, to protect minorities from overbearing national actions, inertia, and the secrecy of government. In the UK growing restlessness over citizens' rights can find an outlet elsewhere, if Whitehall or any other centre of power is reluctant. The strength of local government can also be reinforced through the European Institutions. In the Parliament representatives from most member states are familiar with regional government, leaving the UK in a minority. The current trend to over-centralisation in the UK is countered by the recent decentralisation of Napoleonic powers in France, giving both regions and their major cities greater autonomy. It is unlikely that the UK can continue to ignore local feeling, for even outside the EEC there are strong local forces at work in the democracies at large.

Like the shape of the economy and urbanisation, the shape of government in Europe is assuming some common characteristics. The central and local governments of nation states increasingly learn from each other in questions of policy, management, and planning, and the same can be said for citizen groups. But the localities and small communities are also learning to find new lives within the network of supporting structures. At each step of government and across the ecology of the planet new order is coming into view.

The influences on individual nations seem to be inevitable, whether they come from members of the European Parliament, from legally binding directives from Brussels, from the Green and Peace movements, from the market or the conservation of historic towns and countryside. Participation, planning, new market forces, and styles of government are all open to wide scrutiny across national boundaries, requiring common knowledge and activity. In this new world, will the familiar patterns of cities and towns, of farming and recreation, meet the needs of society and its economy and life-styles? Or should we attempt to see the land of Europe in a new light, not as the cockpit for the conflicting interests of old cultures and of agricultural and urban societies, but as a common inheritance of resources which provide quite new opportunities for its people?

The nations of Europe are a divided family, east and west, but they share an ancient land and culture which are inescapable. While global powers strive to heal the big divide, each side must work with the linkages of social activity, the economy, and the use of land and its resources. The scale of economic production and distribution has created an urban system, including agriculture and tourism, to provide a structure within which new styles of work and leisure, of participation and decision-making, are being crystallised. Quarrels will go on, but proximity forges links in the system.

Negotiations and discussions continue at every level from neighbourhoods to the international bodies at Geneva, Brussels, Strasbourg, and Paris. It may well be that strategies are weakened and investment wrongly located through failure to see the future more clearly. Perhaps the old view of city and country inhibits changes which might release energies and use land in new ways.

This land may be town or country based, but will be essentially urban in its dimension and distribution, suiting different preferences, neither constricting lives to mean spaces and buildings, nor sprawling uncontrolled outside. More sophisticated and equitable controls will have to be devised, within which greater individual freedom can operate. For the present, the focus is concentrated on part of a small island community.

England

The high hopes of the UK in the European Community have not been borne out. If anything, they have emphasised the differences: in the economy, in farming, in political philosophies and attitudes. Yet proximity cannot be escaped, EEC or not, and inevitably the links have grown as those with the Commonwealth have declined. Joint economic ventures, trading patterns, the nature of European urbanisation and many other matters, all within a global context, will push and pull this island along to the next phase of social evolution. Together they will determine the pattern of land and living, towards which new thinking must be directed.

Britain is a small island, its community in some ways insular, and the nature of its historical role no doubt makes it difficult for the natives to see the country as it now is; a small part of a larger Community, which is itself struggling to make its way on the new international scene. Now that the country must rely more on its own resourcefulness, the great question is whether it will adapt slowly, continuing to see things as past agricultural and industrial conditions have made them, or whether with quickening pace new patterns of perception and action will emerge.

In attempting to look forward, it is necessary to look back, and particularly to look back at the effect which the impact of the beginning of the Industrial Revolution had and still has on the country, nowhere more so than in its present economic plight and the state of its cities. For this impact came upon a land which had already formed a character, much of which is still inherent. Some of this is held in common with other people, in particular from the roots of human society before industrialisation, but some is peculiar to this country. It may be that old habits of life and work will reassert themselves for many in a less mechanical and more 'natural' style. After all, enough has been written about the evils of de-humanising industrial cities to make one wonder why we are now so worried about de-industrialisation.

In Europe, England has had for centuries a unique attribute denied to others: absence of foreign invasions. No doubt this has provided some of the psyche of the nation. The invasions of Viking, Saxon, and Norman are a long way off, but their influence upon the lives of the natives resulted in the cultures which lie at the back of our consciousness. Anglo-Saxon history and attitudes may now be a joke, but for a long time they were not. They helped to provide our language, our thought, our ways of negotiation, and our humour. In the same way feudal attitudes remain. The cap is still touched to lord and master. Each of the free cities which turned into rotten boroughs provided, as Beatrice and Sydney Webb have shown, a unique character of government. Bristol and Norwich differ in complex ways: in the make-up of their citizens, in politics, in architecture, and in attitudes to town planning and conservation.

There are also unifying characteristics. The arts and love of city life have not developed as they have on the mainland. Rather, country home, suburban living and love of nature have long been part of life and landscape, and the perception of nature in its widest sense is perhaps different from that of people living across the Channel. In law, philosophy, science, and the arts there are traditions which are peculiarly English. The general views of natural laws which derive from Greece and Rome were conducive to forms of thought and philosophy on much of the Continent which differ from those of England, being what Bertrand Russell described (for Leibnitz) as 'deduction pyramided on a pinpoint of logical principles'. On the other hand, for John Locke and others, 'the base of the pyramid is on solid ground of observed fact', and this observational strength is apparent in a number of fields. Thus the methods of scientific observation can be traced from Roger Bacon in the thirteenth century, while the power of recording detailed observations of nature in sculpture, and subsequent influences in architecture and town planning have been noted by Nikolaus Pevsner.[13] Perhaps from early formative influences came the ways of thought and discoveries of Isaac Newton and the mainstream of British empirical philosophy in the seventeenth and eighteenth centuries. These need no emphasis, and in a contemporary vein the excellence of British science can be measured by the number of Nobel Prizes. The establishment of the Royal Society by Charles II in 1662 marks another characteristic, the close association between science and the establishment, and a later lack of interest in manufacture and engineering, which was left to 'the north'. The dis-enfranchised and dis-established workers of Birmingham and Manchester were another nation to some, until their power became useful to London.

Country life, views of nature, and empirical attitudes of mind are only three pre-industrial characteristics which are still strongly in evidence and to some extent run counter to mainland European characteristics. One at least — science — contributed to the development of a prosperous agriculture which was to raise food production for a growing urban population. Here is another connection with the court, for it is linked to the enthusiasm of 'Farmer George' III. But there is also the connection with class through the gentry, with their large entailed estates and structures of land and power which, while destroyed in one sense by rising urbanisation and political reform, remain in another as part of a deep culture. The thread of class is still an important part of social structure, easily seen in shire politics, in Whitehall and Oxbridge, and in the new conflict with industrial cities. The old antagonisms, both of feudal days and of industrial bitterness, surface again today, but in a new context.

Luigi Barzini, in his analysis of the British, refers to a culture of stoicism in the face of past hardships and of a native intelligence which often does not wish to seem to be intelligent. He also suggests that certain deep-rooted traits so useful for running an Empire — a good intelligence service or the ability to win a Falklands war — are now outmoded in this new world. They constituted one reason for the UK's having ignored the Common Market in a post-war period, when it could have done so much to help. On the other hand, Geert Hofstede's recognition of British individualism will ring a chord with many, suggesting some connections with inventiveness in science and engineering, or entrepreneurship during the Industrial Revolution.

The industrial urbanisation of Britain is a cultural layer sandwiched between the older deep-rooted attributes and all the new things which arise today. This middle layer is at the heart of much of our current political conflict, whether it be between left and right, city and country, or welfare state and market. In 1700, there were only 6 or 7 towns in England with populations above 10,000. By 1801, when the first modern census was taken, London had nearly a million, while Liverpool, Manchester, Birmingham, Glasgow, and Edinburgh were all above 70,000. By the mid-nineteenth century the speed and extent of urban growth had made Britain the first country with more urban than rural people and had led to political unrest and the Reform Bill. With it came a limited representative local government and a new political philosophy of intervention by government in market forces which had created an environmental disaster for the working population of the cities, a disaster which threatened social stability. During the early nineteenth century the call for reform in politics and government was strengthening. Although England had had its Cromwellian revolution, church and aristocracy remained, and individual liberties were not seen in the same light as those of France and the North American Colonies during their revolutions. J.C.D. Clark has recently argued that England remained under the sway of monarch, aristocrat, and Anglican Church until the repeal of the Test and Corporation Acts between 1828 and 1830. Only then, with the Reform Act, was Britain set on a new road.[14] With these changes came previously dis-established and dis-enfranchised citizens, many from the growing northern cities and towns, helping to bring about new political philosophies in opposition to *laissez-faire* economics and landed interests.

The powerful urban reaction against landed interests led to the abolition of the Corn Laws, free trade, the growing base of socialism, and a new class warfare. As new liberties and early socialism came together, old and often corrupt government was replaced by strong new local government on management principles first established by Joseph Chamberlain in Birmingham, and developed to provide initially services of water, sewerage, and lighting, with education, housing, planning and social services following later. Needless to say, Chamberlain's Civic Gospel drew on the power of the Church as well as of the people.

Thus industrial urbanisation created an economic and social structure superimposed upon old values and threatening to destroy them. As socialist and liberal political influences grew in a discontented Europe, conservatives in England became alarmed to such an extent that Lord Milner was driven to suggest:

> There can be no manner of doubt that the institution of private property is seriously menaced at the present time — more seriously menaced perhaps in Great Britain than anywhere else in the world ... If the present Social Order is to endure, it is simply necessary, at whatever cost, to effect a great increase in the number of people who have a direct personal interest in the maintenance of private property.

> There is no bulwark to communism at all equal to that provided by a
> large number of small property owners and especially owners of land.[15]

There were also suggestions for the re-enclosure of villages to help
landed labourers. The urban movement was strong but ineffectual in
a country still industrialising and urbanising. The home-ownership
movement, however, struck a more fruitful vein, one still continuing
in recent Conservative policies for the sale of council housing.

The question of England's industrialisation is one that has been
taken up recently by an American, Martin Weiner, in his book
English Culture and the Decline of the Industrial Spirit.[16] Weiner
argues that industry has really never been accepted into the English
culture, and that successive groups have succumbed to the hegemony
of a civilised *rentier* aristocracy. So for both rich new industrialist
and socialist politician the old values persist. The trading and
industrial classes were looked down on in Victorian England.
Dickens dramatised the evils of Coketown; Ruskin scorned the
tastes of Bradford businessmen, while William Morris and the Pre-
Raphaelites returned to the Medieval past. Nineteenth-century
England was thoroughly discombobulated by the Industrial Revolution, as it swept along destroying old ideas about almost
everything, while in the early twentieth century Thomas Hardy
feared for the effects of the same mechanical influences on the
countryside. He now seems to have been right. To Weiner, however,
the countryside became a symbol for integrating the cultures, one to
be strongly protected, providing a psychic healing factor for a
country torn apart. There would seem to be a good case fo this view
which brings Tory and Socialist, country and urban influences,
together in support of such protection. It is the Common Market
which is now the destructive influence, so it is claimed by some,
through supporting agriculture at the expense of the countryside.
Whether Weiner is right about the question of industrial spirit is yet
to be seen.

The other side of the economy — the financial markets and the
City of London — is a different question. Here the traditions of
England support the likely continuing international strength of the
City. From the time of the Great Fire of London and the victory of
the merchants over Charles II and Christopher Wren, whose grand
new plans were thwarted, and on to the arrival of William III, the

links with the Amsterdam banking system, colonial investment and incoming wealth, the financial affairs of the nation have continued their dominant role in the form of capitalism, consumerism, or any other system based on personal acquisition. When the landed estates broke up in the early twentieth century, investment went into equities. As home industry has declined, investment has gone abroad or back into land. Brussels has been invaded by British property developers. What remains to be seen is whether the use of capital can be applied to create a new economy which not only satisfies the wealthy but also replaces old attitudes to the deprived classes with a more genuinely democratic view of rights to share in major investment decisions as well as to own a house. The question of Weiner's countryside as a cultural symbol now combines with new rural problems, and the market threatens to make as big a mess of the countryside as it once did of the cities.

The economic inter-relationships of money supply, industrial production, and agriculture are now creating a new urban situation. The physical fabric of factory and housing in congested and depressing industrial centres is obsolescent. There is often no room to expand and there is still too little attraction to invest, even if space can be found. When economic competition and hardening arteries are added, it is not surprising to find decline. New spirit requires an environment to fit, and to some extent this is apparent in the growth of small town industry which is discussed in Chapter 4. What has been lacking is an ability to respond quickly enough to the new economic and social situation, and this lack of response may well lie in the deeper rooted characteristics. Another overseas observer, Ralf Dahrendorf, well acquainted with England as Director of The London School of Economics, has recently characterised the strengths and weaknesses of the country.[17] They can be paired. The traditional liberties of England go with a lack of central purpose. The excellence of science is combined with an inability to harness it effectively to industrial development. The continuity of institutions and the solidarity of the nation are strengths, accompanied by the weaknesses of a lack of adaptability and problems of class.

The tolerance associated with traditional liberties has meant that people and institutions have been allowed to go their own ways within reason. Perhaps this accounts to some extent for those excellent scientific traditions. On the other hand, the lack of central purpose can be seen in the failure, outside two world wars, to associate that excellence with an effective and continuous industrial development policy of the kind pursued by Germany, France, and Japan since the last war. Strategic forward thinking requires some of the conceptual ways of thought foreign to British empiricism, and although it would be unwise to push this idea too far, few can doubt the failure of government and industry to anticipate growing economic problems. Even if Mrs Thatcher's government succeeds in restoring the economy, there remains a problem of democracy in a country of class and secrecy.

The Oxbridge, City and Civil Service élites have been, and still are, dominated by arts and science graduates who may combine culture and excellence of certain kinds, but who are not necessarily well adapted to thinking ahead in the fast changing economic climate of the post-war years. In spite of the traditional engineering skills of Stephenson, Watt, and Brunel, that profession has never been embraced by the establishment, or given the status accorded to it in Europe. Neither has technical education had the chance to develop to the levels achieved from a better start in nineteenth-century France and Germany. The lack of co-ordinated planning so necessary for national survival was only too obvious to Lloyd George and Winston Churchill respectively at the outset of two world wars.

The central planning undertaken by Atlee's government after the second world war — planning to some extent also favoured by less socialistic minded people — achieved much but ran into difficulties with market traditions. With land problems, for example, free play of the market and fair play for all were difficult to reconcile. The problem of adapting to turbulence in a fast changing world is seen in the slow moving structures of trade unions and management alike. In the 50s and 60s, what dynamism did exist in industry was eroded by a regional policy which, for example, forced the car industry to divert its energies from the South-East and West Midlands to the old depressed areas of Scotland, South Wales, and the North-West: a laudable policy with a questionable result.[18] Planning as a means to an end was associated either with socialism, and hence damned by conservatives, or with town and country planning, once a great ideal but one which later came to be seen as a destroyer of communities, an irrelevance, or, at best, a protector of countryside from development.

The solidarity and continuity observed as past strengths by Dahrendorf he now sees as being under threat, as extremism becomes more severe with the strain of economic decline, the threat to public services, and the emphasis on market forces. Dahrendorf sees the new marketeers as outside the British tradition, with even less compassion than the old Manchester liberals and less concern for the solidarity of the nation. He is more sympathetic with Tony Benn, seeing him as someone more in tune with tradition (he was after all an aristocrat), but finding Benn's analysis faulty. To Dahrendorf, radicalism with slow change is part of the tradition, but the problem today is that the world is changing fast and Britain is not a fast changing country. Whether the new Alliance of Liberals and Social Democrats provides an opportunity remains to be seen.

But whatever its speed, there are new global conditions which will change the shape of the country. Some of them may fit into traditions, others not, but all will have to be accommodated. These conditions include the harsh competition of the international economy; the reduction of an industrial workforce as a result not only of this, but also of automation; the ecological crisis; the effects of computers and telecommunication; and the new politics of power blocs, pluralism, new values, or a participative democracy.

The renewal of an obsolescent industrial structure seems to be particularly difficult for Britain. Not only is there obsolescence, only to be expected in the oldest industrial nation, but there is also the inheritance of industrial strife transmitted through miners and others, whose roots go back to much harsher and older conditions; and there is the inadequacy of an élite system of outmoded educational values and resulting backwardness. Even deeper are the older traditions of law, class, and land.

New industrial development is taking place nevertheless. Productive industry needs an environment and space to expand which is simply not available in the cities, because buildings are old and hemmed in, or roads are too congested, or other costs are too high. Thus most industrial growth is now taking place in the smaller towns. Space and easy communications are not the only advantages here. Workforces are less unionised, bureaucracies smaller, and the social structure is more heavily weighted towards new managerial skills and easy contacts with other professional services. For families, living, schooling, and shopping are often more attractive.

And, after all, the major city centre is never far away. Much of this new industry has not had time to grow, but some of it will provide wealth for tomorrow. Similarly, within the cities there are many new initiatives, as yet too small, however, to replace the old. The cities are and will continue to be major centres of manufacturing production, but services have long provided the main occupations for city dwellers. The complex definitions and relationships between manufacture and services are discussed in later chapters.

The 'work-led' movement of people is complemented by the 'home-led' movement of commuters. Together they are drawing populations and investment away from the old industrial centres. The impact of this on the geography of the country will be discussed in more detail, but for the present it can be said that the urban pattern outlined for Europe also holds good for England. However, the English city is declining faster than its continental neighbours, in part because it is older and more outworn, in part because the English preference for a life in or near the countryside is traditionally stronger. The strength of new economic growth is still in question, but much of what there is will be generated in new areas, especially within reach of London. It is crucial that the new preferences and conditions should be encouraged, but at the same time more positive strategies for the cities are needed, to restructure their economies and provide services for the less well-off. To some extent this will be done through native wit and the rebuilding of commercial and service functions, but much will depend upon the use of public investment to encourage the interest of private investors in industry, in housing, or in other development. The examples of the London and Liverpool Urban Development Corporations are enough to show the potential in links between public and private sectors in these old dockland areas. The strategy could well be extended to many other old areas, but at present the easy options of green field sites or the allurement of subsidised agriculture and forestry tax havens are allowed to hold sway.

No amount of strategy, however, will overcome the association of rising productivity in certain traditional sectors with declining labour needs. The percentages of people employed in industrial production have been declining for some time, and in North America they have dropped furthest. Many analysts now forecast levels as low as 10% for the future. Thus wherever traditional mass-produced goods are made, there may be no great need for people. The agricultural landscape was once covered with labourers, but no longer. The industrial landscape is following the same trend. Employment in services has gone up accordingly, and few should regret the passing of the manned production line, provided there are other things to do. The immediate problem is that there are not, and with the coming automation of the office, prospects look bleak. Leisure, not only as enjoyment, but also as a growth industry, is an obvious solution in part. The informal economy is another, by which is meant all those activities which are outside those regular measures of labour, wages, and value-added production which go to make up the formal national balance sheets. Exactly how and where all these take place is another crucial aspect of future population and land-use distributions.

Two new sets of global circumstances are suggestive of radical change. One is telecommunications, the other ecological concern. Already home entertainment has supplanted the cinema and theatre for many; education is changing through the innovations of Open University and computer terminals. Now business is being conducted from home, as in the Rank Xerox organisation. Shopping and banking are also beginning to operate from home, and soon it may be the same for medicine. The house, then, into which so much investment is going, becomes more important in the economy and as a resource. Like all resources, it is a commodity of fluctuating fortunes. Like industry, much housing is in our old cities while, again like industry, there is considerable new growth in the smaller towns. Much could go into the villages and countryside for that matter, if planning policies allowed it.

Whether the telecommunications system has the power, which transport has, to decentralise populations remains to be seen. It certainly uses a lot less energy, and if there is less employment requiring commuting, it will be less necessary to travel around. Instead leisure and whatever economy develops will determine preferences for home locations. It is here that ecological concerns may merge with the traditional love of countryside. Already the impact of industrialised agriculture has brought strong reactions from populations, many more of whom now live near the countryside. More widely, the world conservation and wildlife movements come with the development of consciousness about humanity's role on a planet which must be shared with other species and made fit to inhabit. The links with some Eastern philosophies of life, and with vegetarianism, are perhaps significant. All this is creating new views about the use and abuse of land.

An initial view might be that urban expansion should be resisted more strongly and the countryside protected more effectively. This would imply a continuation of post-war policies based on pre-war practices. But the growing mobility of people, the increase in leisure time, the importance of home environment, and the industrialisation of agriculture throw up questions about these policies. In many parts of lowland Britain wildlife is commoner in the towns than in the country. The pollution of ground water supplies, once centred on the cities, is now a problem wherever agriculture has become heavily dependent upon chemical fertilisers. The wider air and sea pollution of Europe has already been mentioned. These new abuses of environment must not only be tackled, but they will also require new forms of international collaboration. Escape from inner city to suburb was one thing, but escape from industrialised agriculture is another. The agricultural community is now having to revise its priorities and come back towards those advocates of farming as a job which includes responsibilities for the stewardship of the land. When these changes are combined with the needs of recreation, of science, of the protection of a rich rural archaeology and history, and the growing numbers of ex-urban residents, then responsibilities for country management will be more diverse, farming will be less protected, and the countryside may lose its symbolic status in Weiner's sense.

Not only must the countryside provide much more than food, water, timber, and minerals, but the city too will have to provide an environment attractive by reason of its green spaces and variety of scene. A cursory thought for any city which appeals to us will show how important are river, hill, garden, and view. The economic and social tragedy of Liverpool has the one redeeming feature of the reintroduction of open space to point the way for other torn cities. If work cannot be found in factories, then it will have to take place in an environment which affords new possibilities for the home, workshop, and leisure. It is the trauma of getting there which is the real problem.

Nineteenth century city government grew strong because the city was the economic powerhouse and the need to provide for services was concentrated in a dense geographical area. Today the economic base and everyday life are spread in a continuous band across the lowlands of Britain and the urbanised regions of Europe. Much of the newer wealth tends to move away from the old industrial cities, leaving the less well-off behind. This growing polarisation is reflected in the political map, with its red inner cities, blue shires, and a growing amount of green in suburb and country. The tensions inherent in the divisions are increasingly ones which central government has to face. In the last century most local finances came from local rates. Today half come from central government. Responsibilities for water, sewage, gas, and electricity, which once lay with local government (and are also heavily dependent upon central finance), are now national.

At the same time, calls for decentralisation and the self-sufficiency required in a world of tightening resources demand action at lower levels. At the grass roots, small enterprises and community groups are encouraging and encouraged; in housing, work, or entertainment, they are learning new skills with computers or with nature in country or city. From the town halls, capital from pension funds and property is being directed towards small and middle-sized firms which promise employment, good products, and sound management. The old cities are still a powerful and invigorating force, and in some of them public and private interests are putting their act together. England has been, and still is, hampered by its conservative centralised banking system and by now-absent owners of big industries, which operate internationally. Thus risk capital from local banks and firms is still a problem for new entrepreneurs, but it is in the interests of both government and the private sector to encourage it, to help in the creation of new work, to provide space, and to avoid riots.

In spite of the conflicts, local democracy is very much alive, and some rapid changes are taking place. The problem is that it does not fit philosophies which developed in the nineteenth and early twentieth centuries, and in which the population, the geography, and the functions fitted into a workable frame which no longer exists. Many of the functions must now be central, while new local functions, in both city and country, are emerging. The district councils in the shires are small but active. The big cities are beginning to decentralise functions to wards or equivalent population groups of about

20,000 to 50,000. Perceptions of local government roles are changing, while from such diverse sources as the scientific ecologists and
the new Ecology and Social Democratic parties come viewpoints to
support decentralisation.[19]

Much of this is echoed in West Europe as a whole, but especially
in the older industrial areas of the north. For example, the City of
Liège is, at the time of writing, bankrupt in a political situation
where the Greens hold the balance of power, yet must work with the
old parties. The stresses are great, but perspectives for the future
come together in a global context which must include a resurgence of
local cultures. The growth of a new high-technology economy, the
ecological balance of wide regions, and the forging of new low-level
economies will impact on the land in new ways.

In *Religion and the Rise of Capitalism* Tawney devotes eloquent
pages to the land question during the Reformation in relation to the
new economic forces and traditional theories of social obligation.
Land, he wrote, was at the centre of both: on the one hand, at the
mercy of an unscrupulous minority in search of private gain; on the
other, at the heart of an attempt to protect the poor peasants and
craftsmen.[20] It is worth asking whether we now also face an
economic and social problem which centres on the land, if we
consider land to include the cities.

To the extent that the main pre-occupation of governments today
(leaving aside defence) are economic growth, unemployment, and
social welfare, there are parallels with the past. There are also
similarities in the sense that present economic forces are of a new
kind, and new social obligations arise as a result of the changing
basis for work, once to do with land, now with the aftermath of a
full-blooded urban industrial revolution. The parallels must not be
pushed too far, but it is worth noting that the same kinds of conflict
occurred at the start of the Industrial Revolution, when Parliamentary enclosures were both a necessary step towards a more
productive agriculture, and a social tragedy on a scale equivalent to
the mass unemployment of the 1980s. In other words, economic and
social upheavals had land at their heart in the sixteenth and
eighteenth centuries. These were also times of great legal activity
over questions of property rights and acquisitions.

What of the late twentieth century? Several differences are
obvious. Today the crisis lies within the city where, instead of eking

out an existence from a small patch of land, the poor draw the dole and may have a number of work opportunities to take up. Levels of education and organisation, together with dense associations of people, provide conditions which allow for a great deal to be done. Land is essential for new economic development, as we have seen, but public interest has decreed that strong controls should operate through planning law and practice. They are not there for the benefit of private wealth and sharp legal practice; or are they? Wealthy individuals and financial institutions are inclined, when things go well, to put a lot of money into land; tax laws, subsidies, and the absence of public controls favour forestry and agriculture of a certain kind, and the less wealthy have few opportunities to enjoy its ownership. Social obligation is partly fulfilled through the owner occupation of property, the creation of national and country parks, and the support of the welfare state at some level or other. At least one legal historian has suggested that there is a paradox in English land law, in that monarchical forms appropriate to an aristocratic state exist in a country which has become a democracy.[21] It must be remembered that land is held by the Crown, not by so-called 'owners'. These latter only have rights, but some of them are exercised in almost feudal ways, as with laws of trespass and the absence of freedom to walk on open land, a freedom possible in Sweden, for example.

The land has become a passive, secretive, and often regressive recipient of social and economic policies rather than an active force in securing future wellbeing. The protagonists of developer and planner replace the unscrupulous minorities of earlier times, supposedly as the champion of economic growth and protector of public interests respectively. Both must be served, but do the arguments really fit tomorrow's needs? Is either the containment of cities or the promotion of subsidised destruction in the countryside a fair policy to adopt? Doesn't the global ecology suggest life-systems as a new active force, and do not people everywhere want a chance to join with equal opportunity in the activities which use land and landscape across an urban country, creating private and public wealth and wellbeing?

In the pre-industrial food-producing and trading era of the western world, land was extensively occupied by agricultural populations. Some sense of this lifestyle is still found in southern Europe.

In the development of industrialised consumer societies the cities became densely occupied while rural areas declined. At the next stage of economic consumption, land and populations are again likely to change their relationships. The wealthy always lead in consumption, both of food and of other goods, but there are limits to greed. The wealthy have also led in the ownership of land, and there are also limits to that. Fred Hirsch has argued that land, good jobs, and other scarcities are what he calls positional goods.[22] In other words, to establish your place in the hierarchy you acquire position, money, and space. This is not only evident from history but as far as the environment is concerned, this is now also part of the pattern of ecology, and is thus linked to human evolution. As we know, the social problem demands fairer distribution. As populations become wealthy and consumption increases, demand for land grows and encouragement of the owner occupation of houses, again a deeply rooted preference, spreads the demand widely, first to suburb and then beyond. Those who are the wealthiest can afford the most and can afford to travel furthest. The land is organised to suit them.

For those who live in the city, as well as those who live in the country, the protection of fine landscapes is an important consideration and an accepted public policy. However, this very attraction lies at the heart of further demand, as in the tourist industry, from those redoubtable Victorians who climbed the Alps or Thomas Cook's railway excursions from town to country, to today's mass visits to stately home and wildlife park. The public domain increases, and the search for seclusion becomes more difficult. Thus areas of Britain which had been losing population during the whole of this century, were beginning in the 70s to gain once more from new residents, some admittedly retired, but others working and travelling, both in the tourist industry and in other new sectors.

In one sense there are no limits. Countryside population densities can increase in Europe, going back to what they were in earlier times. Much industrialised production has reduced its need for manpower, and some services will go the same way. But as the home and its environment become a more important component of life and activity, the search for new social and economic opportunities will, literally, change ground. Modern society should not allow a repetition of Tawney's observed land conflicts as a result of stress between economic development and social obligation. But if not, what will this mean for a modern society in which food and industrial production are relatively assured?

Presumably those worst off will either be kept docile through the benefits of present oil revenues and expected alternative future wealth; or they will demand something better, and natural justice will demand that they are offered the opportunity. For many this opportunity will still lie in the city. For others, it may be seen to be outside, but still urban in nature. Indeed, 'urban in nature' is a phrase which highlights the paradox of the problem we face.

If wealth continues to grow, will land needs continue to spread further afield, or can the cities themselves be restructured to provide for new needs? Or, again, does such re structuring overlook possible new opportunities in rural areas? It is probable that the answers to these questions are positive, although perhaps in ways not presently envisaged. The skeleton of a new pattern is already being put together. Motorways, airports, and fast-growing small towns supplement old industrial structures. The economic pressure-points raise new demands in line with modern communications and life-styles, as well as in accord with old preferences and attitudes. Consumers face threats of a de-natured land and make new demands for a balanced life. Ordered land use, planned urban containment, and agricultural support are too simple in concept to meet the complexity of needs which will reconcile all these changes and to meet the multiplicity of demand and the injustices of divisions between rich and poor. To manage the resources of the land for wider social benefit must surely be to fit economy to ecology, new life to new structures, and the whole to a form which is seen to be appropriate for the next century.

PART 2
LAND AT THE CENTRE

Chapter 3

Perceptions

English traditions and culture have given rise to deep feelings about the countryside. These contributed strongly to the growth of the modern town and country planning movement, and now give rise to extreme and sharply conflicting views about new 'villages' (that is, new housing on green fields), and other development. Each case is argued at a public enquiry (except for some recent examples such as the Channel Tunnel). However, the deeper questions of the benefits or divisions which land policies bring to society, the ownership of land in Britain, the relationship of attitudes to social class, and survival itself — these are questions that are rarely discussed. The English way tends to preclude such discussion, wait for the riots, and then act.

Feelings run deep, but their origins are not much thought about. If we are to adapt effectively, we shall have to become more aware of them. Some aspects were raised in the previous chapter, especially in relation to monarchy and class. But in the wider public consciousness there is a sometimes surprising inability to understand relationships between land, economic success, and social wellbeing. Eyes which do not see and attitudes which do not change have always held back social evolution.

What is seen in a kaleidoscopic world are patterns which vary all the time, and yet they must provide some order and structure for everyday life and survival. The search for order in disorder lies within us all, stability and uncertainty being in the nature of man and his environment. It is obvious that the patterns change, and yet it is difficult to adjust the vision from one to the other, not to see the sun as moving and the earth as still, even though we know the facts of the situation. The eye which sees allows the brain to perceive and then perhaps to understand. This is Blake's seeing through the eye —

To see a World in a Grain of Sand'. To see the camouflaged insect on
a branch is to perceive life, but to see its function in the scheme of
things is understanding. Sun, insect, painting, landscape, all carry
with them cognition, which itself depends upon the language of
genetics, of the spoken word and the meaning of the word.

Land is no different. It has been seen and understood through
history in different ways, and will go on being seen in new ways. It is
one purpose of this book to suggest that we mostly look at it today in
ways inappropriate for solving present problems, for fitting the
needs of a new society. From Galileo to Darwin, from the Romantic
Movement into an urban industrial world, and from east and west,
the view has changed as the knowledge has changed.

Who sees? It is the individual at work in discovery, whether it be
Copernicus or Cézanne. It is the individual searching for a new social
order — Calvin, Rousseau, Marx. The need for agricultural
improvement in England was linked with the name of that
eighteenth-century propagandist, Arthur Young. The need to respond to urban disorder was linked to philosopher Jeremy Bentham
and social reformer Edwin Chadwick when reporting on the condition of the labouring population in Britain. With these individuals
come the ranks of the civil service, unions, professions, landowners,
courtiers, bankers, and all the structured and vested interests of a
society rich in texture, varied in perception, and every now and again
forced to take action in riot, revolution or reform, because what is
seen does not fit social evolution.

Today nuclear threat, ecological balance, the peace movement,
Friends of the Earth, materialists, post-materialists, and the young,
all focus new eyes on old patterns, defending, rejecting or seeking
compromise. Science, so long the hope of mankind, is itself in
question, not as a means forward but as the only sure means
forward, a means needing reassessment in the light of Thomas
Kuhn's work and the debate which it has sparked off. The origins of
modern science and its progress cover several centuries, yet within
the next few decades we are likely to see fundamental re-appraisals
of its nature, no longer 'objective' in the old sense, but as part of a
process of human evolution not yet clearly understood.

It is dangerous to use historical example without great caution,
but it is worth asking whether relationships of people, land, and
capital in the context of time can offer any insights for the future, if

only to increase awareness of the way in which interactions take place, and to question whether present uncertainties have characteristics in common with the past. If we look at recent accumulations of wealth, the use of land, and the fortunes of people, certain patterns can be discerned. In the UK these broadly correspond to three phases: agricultural improvement in the eighteenth century, urbanisation in the nineteenth, and suburbanisation in the twentieth. Each phase comprised a long spell of preparation before take-off into fast growth and a gradual levelling off before the next phase. This is the S curve *ʃ*, with each stage building on the previous one.[1] Of course the curve can also dip or fall to decline or catastrophe.

It is in the period of preparation that perceptions of change take place and provide social readiness for more rapid change. The eighteenth century in the UK was an age for the improvement of what we now call infrastructure; the rivers, ports, and toll roads. After English and Scottish Union in 1707, and Marlborough's victory at Blenheim, came a long period of preparation under the stability of Whigs and Tories in unison. This was also the great age of the essayists, who in discussing the nature of society prepared the ground for the acceptance of new social structures.

The accumulation of wealth from colonial and other trade coincided with early scientific stock breeding and crop rotation, while the unimproved state of an old agriculture of open field and common land, with a peasantry reminiscent of the Middle Ages, was attacked by such protagonists as Arthur Young and William Marshall. The landed gentry and the new money allowed for the perception of new possibilities in improved rents and in the production and distribution of food. By 1750, the time was ripe for the massive Parliamentary enclosures of the East and Southern Midlands and of parts of Yorkshire and East Anglia. This, the largest ever exercise in English rural planning, so vividly described by W G Hoskins, affected four million acres and incalculable numbers of people.[2] In the Augustan Age, landowners were also able to create the famous English Landscape Garden, a symbol of liberty as well as an evocation of the classical world, as temples graced the park enclaves, separating the wealthy from the labourers in their new agricultural landscapes.[3] By 1780, the conjunction of science, land reform, food production, flying shuttle, spinning-jenny, steam engine, textile factory, and clothing production, had set society off on the rapid climb into a new consumerism and the Industrial Revolution.

At the same time the seeds of preparation for the next phase were being sown in two broad fields. One was the Romantic Movement; the other utilitarianism, socialism, and public welfare. As Goethe, Blake, Wordsworth, and Beethoven pursued the search for a better world through their individual genius, Bentham, Mill, Cobbett, Owen, Peel, and Chadwick trod the path from which they perceived the plight of the people and the looming problems of urban industrialisation. The process cannot be simplified, and yet the main strands of thought are clear, and in many ways run together: on the one hand an intuitive and artistic search for meaning, on the other rational measures to accommodate social and economic change.

Now capital accumulation was growing in the industrial cities rather than on the land, through making, and exporting. Indeed, barring fair parliamentary representation, human welfare and the environment, it grew to such an extent that political, health, and housing reforms were forced onto a central administration conceding power to a rising local government. This time land reform went against the territorial magnates, with compulsory purchase of private land for the public necessities of sewerage, clean water, and housing. By the mid-nineteenth century, the principles of public interest in an urban society were established, the corn laws repealed, the foundations of full enfranchisement and education laid, and some control over the harsher economic forces established.

At the same time, Romanticism had evolved from the picturesque of the late eighteenth century to Pugin in the following century and the architectural battle of the styles between Gothic and Renaissance, with Brunel and iron functionalism thrown in to spice the mix. As Dickens and Mrs Gaskell enlarged on the perceptions of city evils for the new industrial middle class, Wordsworth in old age opposed the railway and common noisy crowd coming from industrial Lancashire into the Lake District, and thus helped lay another set of foundations, this time for the National Trust and eventually for the Council for the Preservation of Rural England.

The preparation for suburbanisation grew from two strong roots, one deep, one shallow. The deep root lay in the perception of the right of people to a home environment in contact with land and life, with food, toil, song, and joy. The shallow root was the immediate response to the appalling housing of the cities, a response begun by religious and philanthropic men, in garden suburbs and villages, and then taken up by early building societies and co-operatives. The problems of a post free trade agriculture, death duties, and finally the Great War, led to the relative collapse of the old estate structure, and to a flood of cheap land easily reached by suburban rail travel. As the wealth of the nation grew, the emphasis, once on the land, and then on the industrial city, inclined in its physical outcome to suburban housing, cars, and a wealthy and more leisurely consumer society. As the houses, cars, cafes and petrol stations spread, the romantic and rational were formalised into a system of town and country planning culminating in a programme of national parks, new towns, green belts, and state supported agriculture after the Second World War.[4] The new order was a tidy perception of national land-use in an urban society, with the establishment of principles for stopping undesirable development without paying compensation. These principles were not applied to agriculture in a period of post-war food rationing and at a time when new urbanised industrial threats to the land were not expected.

Each of these phases — agricultural, urban, suburban and land-use planned — can be identified broadly with new perception, preparation, growth, and stabilisation. Each phase of change was accompanied by social distress and conflict: in sequence, the dispossession of smallholders, the deprivations of the early factory workers, and the collapse of the old rural order, completed after the first world war. But through the later phases also came the broad movements towards socialism and public welfare, to peak after the war, to be sustained in the swinging sixties, but to be challenged once more by the market and by the distress of unemployment, riot, and divisiveness.

There is no intention in this historical sketch to do more than identify certain elements in the change of perceptions and in subsequent action. The history of England is particular and, given its role, it is not surprising that internal perceptions of a post-colonial world have been slow to change. But global events now force new economic policies and new values. Might these also require new perceptions of the use of land?

Urban Country

The brave new world of post-war growth ran out of steam at the same time as new perceptions of spaceship earth and its life began to grow. The image of world populations and their economy and ecology came into focus not, perhaps, as a structured pattern, but at least in primary colours on a globe. The period for adjusting to these perceptions has contracted into a time very much shorter than the years which spanned the early growth of science and industry, the motives for which are encapsulated within an even longer era of West European thought and development. History will tell whether these perceptions of space and time were in part an illusion, or whether the newly perceived problems of a space-age society took on board an understanding which, vague at first, was soon to become a clear view leading to a stage in human evolution quite unknown before.

Whatever the case, it seems likely that new generations will have to use the land and develop social and economic relationships in ways which go against the many traditional views and interests now so deeply held by those established groups who control daily events. In an attempt to throw some light on the realities, this section looks at four areas of current concern in England: urban growth and the loss of countryside; the market for development; food production and the land market; romanticism and sentiment.

There are three ways of perceiving urban growth. One is to see the growth of modern industrial society as a whole, not just the growth of cities. In other words, the whole land of the advanced industrial nations is devoted to urban societies and will continue to be so, whether the land-use is for factories, industrialised agriculture, or national parks. This concept of urban society provides an assumed background for human development which, interacting with biological factors, will determine the future use of land. The other two are the measured amounts of development, and the perceived influences of this development. The measured amounts of urban development have been catalogued by most advanced industrial nations, and show, for example, that urban land occupies 15% of the Netherlands, 8% of the UK and 3% of the USA. The rate of urban land use growth in the decade of the 1960s was around 1.0% a year for the two small countries, and 0.3% in the USA. 1% of 2 million urban hectares in the UK is of course much less than 0.3% of 28 million in the USA: 20,000 against 84,000.[5]

If the figures are confined to urbanised regions rather than nations, the picture is different. In England over 20% of the south east region, and more in the north west, is developed; and these will become yet denser, as will other urbanised city regions of the rich countries. The new infrastructure of roads and airports provides the access for development which is very difficult to resist on economic grounds. Whatever is said, the M25 around London is likely to pierce more holes in the green belt.

All these measured quantities are mere statistics. The third way of perceiving urban growth is through the influence which development has on our feelings and understanding about the environment. The views of roads, power stations, masts and aircraft, whose ambience is urban, directly affect whole stretches of countryside and indirectly tell us something about the future. These perceptions of urban influence, and those relating to industrial agriculture, raise opposition, override the knowledge that these essential things must go somewhere, and give rise to desperate local attempts to get them anywhere but the particular locality sought. To see urban growth as the development of our society, as physical development and as the cause of feelings about all this development, are three ways of perceiving change.

The second area of concern is the market for development which, under Adam Smith's invisible hand, is not so easily perceived as a whole. The individual buying a house undoubtedly sees it, but once in it, he tends to confine his view to such manifestations as the local garage and supermarket to which his market purchases of petrol and food contribute. For over sixty years now successive Ministers of Housing have been saying that the housing problem will soon be solved, or is already solved, implying that everyone will have a decent home. Yet the market continues to throw up new demands for new houses, leaving undesirable ones at the bottom end to be occupied by the estimated 15 or 16 million relatively poor people in the population of the UK. Are they to stay there always, the children in overcrowded schools and the houses in mean streets? Let us hope not. But if not, then new structures will be needed and they cannot all fit into the old city. Many millions still wait to get into something better, and presumably a free market for a free people is there to do the job.

For the majority who are more fortunate, there is the surge of leisure activity into the countryside and the spread of small towns and villages. Around these, the wealth of owners ensures that horses and rare breeds of sheep and cattle can be grazed, deciduous woodlands kept, and wildlife encouraged. In Hertfordshire roughly a quarter of the county is devoted to such uses in what can be termed 'gentrified landscape'. Of the other three quarters, one goes to industrialised agriculture, one to building development, and one to uses such as water supply and public open space.

This mixture is not, of course, the result of a free market. It is the result of earlier markets and public interventions, the latest of which has been the post-war concept of planning in the public interest, and a tidy view of town and country. Today government pressures for green belt development by private housebuilders and their associated supporters show the potential conflict of interest and the difficulty of dealing with a problem both physical and economic in character. The views are too simply drawn for a satisfactory outcome. A shotgun marriage is not likely to convince either partner that so simple a solution will work. The complexity demands new perceptions of town and economic planning.

Three post-war attempts to meet the problem of reconciling the market forces in land with the desire to secure public benefit (the last being the Community Land Act), have foundered on the interests of political ideologies and pressures. Later chapters will explore new possibilities. Suffice it for the present to argue that perceptions of the land market will have to change if society is going to progress.

This is partly a question of townscape and landscape and partly one of economics and public expenditure. Perceptions of the former have broadened very fast over the last decade or two, representing a stage of social learning equivalent to that of the essayists and novelists of past centuries. As an example, the Arts Council held an exhibition on *How to Play the Environment Game* at London's Hayward Gallery in 1973, and a Penguin of the same name by Theo Crosby, was published at the same time. The *Game*, as part of the game theory popular at the time (and long influential in war and politics in less theoretical ways), provided insights into the causes of change, of victory, and of defeat. Equally, perceptions of the inner-city and metropolitan problems were beginning to persuade economists and politicians that new priorities and policies were required; but there is much yet to surface in the minds of most people about the causes of these problems and the ways to tackle them.

The third area of concern, the problem of food production and the land market, is a political and economic one of vested interests and distribution, not one of land shortage. In the USA farmers are paid to keep land out of production, and in Europe there is concern as to how large areas once cultivated can now be used. On the one hand land use planning in England works on the presumption that agricultural land should not be developed; on the other the land market takes it out of production and lets it be used for gentrified landscapes, horse grazing, ecological conservation, and recreation. The planning control of development for agricultural reasons is in part fictitious. It is true that it saves good soil from concrete, but it is impotent to prevent a farmer building a pigsty in the shape of a bungalow, as has been done; or to prevent land being taken out of production for uses not legally defined as 'development'.

None of this is written to suggest that UK agriculture is not a vital part of our economy and landscape. In large parts of the country high quality soils, developed and cultivated over centuries, produce essential food very efficiently. In other large areas the traditional patchwork of enclosed fields, wood, and copse remains both productive and beautiful. In the hill lands millions of acres are farmed and provide beauty and solace for those whose usual environment is the city. Many of these areas need conserving, supporting, and encouraging far more than they often are. But the policies of the Ministry of Agriculture, Fisheries, and Food are unsympathetic to hill lands and conservation, while the payment of grants or compensation to farmers who aim to destroy wetlands or other scarce resources is quite inequitable when compared with the controls and absence of grant or compensation in urban areas. Neither are enough opportunities being taken to help new entrants to farming or to help rural communities and services.[6]

England is coming round to new policies as the situation gets worse, as it once did with the cities, but neither the absence of controls, nor their bureaucratic imposition, would seem to fit the needs of tomorrow. Later chapters discuss alternatives, but before

any can be effective the perception of land as a whole must shift from
a town and country division to an urban landscape which meets
broad social needs. Lest readers envisage a country spattered with
bungalows, the examples of Switzerland, the Netherlands, and
many other European landscapes can be looked at to see that
attraction takes many forms. England must develop and conserve its
own beauty; but if it is to be democratic, people will first have to
understand the social basis for land use in the historical sense of
wealth, property ownership, and protection. Although the public
domain increases, there are big questions against some of the values
attached to property and town planning law, or the lack of law for
agriculture and country planning. Romance and sentiment seduc-
tively cover some of the problems, while vested interests hide others.

Why uncover them, when it seems so beautiful as it is? Why
bother to look at the Impressionists, when there are Raphael,
Leonardo, and Rubens? The questions go deep, relate to early
structures of thought and language, and cannot easily be answered.
Some of the arguments for perceiving the world in new ways are
already accepted, whether economic or conservationist and ecological. The economic impact is with us; the ecological will not be
long. When it comes, will there be an opportunity to deepen
perceptions about urban lands and their use for people? Or will
Weiner's thesis of the English countryside as a cultural symbol hold
good? There are some sound reasons for believing that it will not,
that the symbol will be seen for what it is, and that the emperor will
be revealed without his clothes. The young will understand that land
is for life, not for vested interest, and that growing and developing
must be nurtured in and on the land. Self-awareness and knowledge,
both intuitive and scientific, are likely to see through romance. True
sentiment and not picture-postcard sentimentality, combined with
learning and political skills, seem more likely to prevail than a set of
planning controls or a farmers' union.

And so, lastly, to romanticism and sentiment. Most eighteenth-
century travellers found hill regions fearsome. Dr Johnson was
sceptical, but he, Burke, Gilpin, Wordsworth and others explored
nature; and subsequent greater safety, travel and appreciation turned
fear to love, love to sentimentality, vulgarised by mass spectacle and
crude pleasures. It was as well to stop the flood by Weiner's symbolic
act; but this was surely to give time for mustering new strategies.

The time is now passing fast, and new kinds of destruction are already present which can, must, be halted. Sentiments strongly held are now being transferred from past interests (Chiswick and Stowe, Lake District and countryside), to new concerns: the world's wildlife, plants, and forests; nature in the city as well as in the country; an environment both urban and still, in many countries, rural. With automation and the next economic surge, more people will wish to live in touch with nature, while work is likely to be more fulfilling and more widely diffused within populations and across the land. If there is a human factor which feels the power of nature, it is in all human beings and is the counterpart of that other factor which pulls societies together.

The perception of countryside in urban society contains very deep rooted feelings against which there is little rational appeal. It also contains perfectly well understood desires to maintain the assoc- iations of power and land, reinforced by a protective planning system. The combination of these feelings and powers may be irresistible. On the other hand, the evidence suggests that new perceptions are growing and that, as nineteenth century landed powers and *laissez-faire* political economies gave way before the forces of urban industrialisation, so the new landed powers and urban containment may give way to urban forces which encompass the landscape as a whole. The fear of despoliation at present holds back change. But the new perceptions coming about through ecolog- ical change may well find a way to reduce that fear and to make fairer the powers which presently control the land.

Design

Design has no easy definition. It is an activity dependent upon the condition of society in various places and at various times, so that its purpose and significance is always changing, sometimes slowly, sometimes rapidly. As a learning process its ultimate achievements, appropriate for one age, cannot be repeated for another.

The word 'design' is used here with reference to building and landscape structures made by people for their own use and enjoy- ment. The design is inherent within the social structure. The authoritarian rule of Pharaoh, king or dictator produces strictly ordered symmetrical vistas and grand buildings. Such development is often associated with the ownership of land or with special powers. The same can often be said for emergent nations and their symbols: Brazilia was conceived and designed in a brief period of inspiration. Greek democracy and the Italian Renaissance produced the more informal arrangements of classical Athens, Florence, and Siena: shared rule and the free genius of the artist creating the dramatic settings which symbolised the aspirations of the time. Brunelleschi's great Cathedral dome retains its power of inspiration and presence. Other social structures create their own designs. The ruling élite of seventeenth and eighteenth century England produced the Georgian squares of London and the classical country house set in a landscape of temples and nature as an evocation of the Classical World. For the masses there were tenements, hovels, cottages, or huts. Only wealth and nature can afford great constructions.

The components of design are simply stated. For building structures they are the necessary land; the use which is required; materials and their technology; costs; the enjoyment of beauty and drama which they create; and the learning, discovery, and achievement of client and designer. For landscapes they are the natural structures and materials of earth, water, plants, and associated structures, whether farms or follies, windmills or temples. The association of structures and landscape is the key to designing environment. When nature dominates and is respected, artifacts and agricultural patterns become part of nature. If man attempts to overrule or ignore nature, the design suffers. Ancient Greek and Italian cities respected and complemented nature.

The ownership of or control over large areas of land allows for big designs. Versailles, the rural and urban estates of the English aristocracy, and modern council housing areas, have all been subject to grand designs, which have succeeded or failed according to quality, economic pressures, and changing social structures. Versailles survived a revolution and remains as a symbol and useful place for government and tourism alike. The Russells' Bloomsbury Estate survived the economic pressures of a growing London by virtue of strict management and control over the use of property, something the neighbouring Foundling Hospital Estate failed to do. Later pressures have eroded some of Bloomsbury and the other great West End estates, but the character is retained, and the Georgian buildings are adaptable. Some modern council estates will also survive as attractive and useful places. Others will go as a result of ugly rigidity, untested technology, and poor management.

Individual ownership in modern democracies results in different patterns. These may be accommodated in large designs, as in Welwyn Garden City (for special reasons to which we shall return), but they are more likely to reflect attitudes to a free land market and the ability to obtain cheap services. In the UK, town and country planning has exerted particular controls in response to early industrial growth and later countryside intrusions by ribbon or other sporadic development.

Because technology changes, new design problems are always being faced, and of course designers develop new technology. Abraham Darby's Iron Bridge led on to Brunel's Paddington Station. Steel frames, elevators, and the restricted plot ownership of the land produced the USA skyscrapers. The Italian Futurists perceived city design as a technological problem, and the shape of the ideal cities of the Renaissance was in part a response to problems of societies at war, so that walls and streets took on certain forms. Le Corbusier's ill-fated statement that a house is a machine for living in reflected technological idealism.

The use of such a machine did have certain advantages over the old load-bearing wall structures, and resulted in the so-called curtain walls (glass hung on concrete and steel) of the modern tower. These were flexible up to a point, inhuman in scale, but able to house the office workers who provided the labour for the service functions of a modern city. Be it railway train or insurance business, new social activities need new structures.

The question of enjoyment and beauty is more debatable. History establishes certain designs as significant, creative, and symbolising the ideals of the era. So the Parthenon plays a continuing role in aiding an understanding of the civilization of Ancient Greece. Scarcity adds to the perception of value, and so the wider community is prepared to pay for the saving of monuments, even whole cities such as Venice. The symbol becomes all-important, but people's values and interpretations are so mixed up with architecture and landscape that design changes its meaning.

In landscape the question is both easier and more subtly difficult. The beauty of landscape is now established in the Western world, but only after a long period of evolution from the Italian Renaissance, and it is still something to be protected. On the other hand, the significance of landscape in Eastern religions and philosophies for long ages symbolically determined the siting of cities and led to such creations as the gardens of Kyoto in Japan. It is significant that the eighteenth-century English Landscape Movement embraced the ideals of Greece and Rome as well as the philosophies of the Far East (although to a much lesser extent) as transferred, for example, by William Chambers to Kew Gardens. The traditional love of nature in England found a sympathetic chord in older perceptions, and certain natural symbols have diffused unconsciously, as with the rock gardens of every other suburban house. The values thus attached to gardens and landscape are very powerful, providing the cultural symbol identified by Weiner as a healing medium after the strife of the Industrial Revolution.

In a democracy such symbols are now strongly protected by the people, not only in landscape but also in architecture. Those who look at or work in the buildings are public judges, who subject architecture to mass observation and thus, according to Thorstein Veblen, render it more or less inoffensive. Veblen was writing in the context of conspicuous consumption in a nineteenth century leisured class in the United States, but the statement is valid today.[7] Prince Charles' comments about the proposed extension to the National Gallery in Trafalgar Square on the 150th anniversary of the Royal Institute of British Architects reinforce the point, but also emphasise the differences between the two democracies. Present-day planners and their political masters must consider the public, and architects often dislike this form of social control. But society and technology are now always on the move, and forms of control or standards of taste in a democracy are very different from those of an oligarchy or a professional élite.

In the Industrial Revolution coherent design was lost in a welter of change. This was hardly surprising in view of the speed and extraordinary range of conflicts which ran on through the nineteenth century. Design could not keep pace with the scale and speed of urban growth or with the new values which accompanied factory life, the pace of rail travel, the clearance of slums, or attitudes to health, disease and sanitary reform. Art was separated from science amidst a plethora of conspicuous consumption: conservatories with exotic Eastern plants, splendid public parks, pinnacles, terracotta tiles, and shiny bricks (a change from the Georgian materials and better able to withstand industrial grime). The traditions of estate design, a very profitable investment, maintained some order and control in London, Bath, and Clifton in Bristol; but further north individual haphazard development resulted in urban chaos. Control was lost as competitive landowners and developers struggled to make their profits.

Ideas of architectural design were fought out in the battle of the styles (Classical and Gothic in the main), involving the most basic feelings of morality. Pugin and Ruskin fought valiantly but mostly in vain in a world of new economics, new politics, and new values, unable to perceive a way out except by reference to earlier ages. In the cities, town halls were temples; in the country, water works were churches.

It is not surprising that all this confusion should have brought about three broad reactions: the advocacy and creation of garden suburbs and cities; the modern movement in art, architecture and design, and the protection of the countryside. A return to basics was inevitable. *Get rid of dirt, overcrowding and disease. Get rid of Victorian vulgarity and extravagance. Protect what nature has provided.* The results were the suburb and new town; the steel, concrete and glass tower; the containment of towns and the preservation of countryside.

These simply stated reactions were the outcome of deep conflicts in a society which grew rapidly in size and wealth; in which democracy and socialism were evolving; where economic philosophies and power were shifting; and where the body of society was rapidly developing and differentiating to meet the challenges of a new world. In the turbulent currents of the age clear vision and the means to achievement had to rest on very basic considerations. Thus the builders of garden villages and cities returned to the idea of cottage and garden for the English working man (Scotland was always more of a tenement urban society), with low rents, food plots to help during poverty, light and air in the rooms, and clean water, both practical and symbolic of purity and new life. The land for these developments was either provided by the wealthy philanthropists behind the movement or came from the work of early building societies and other associations of less wealthy people. Today we live with perceptions of design inherited from this past era. The regulation of uncontrolled growth passed through the stages of sanitation, housing, and planning as chronicled by William Ashworth, and discussed in later chapters.[8] The idea that physical control could solve urban problems remains in post-war legislation for town and country planning, and in the expectations which many people had from a profession also seen to have failed by allowing tower blocks and destroying communities.

The modern movement, so sensitively heralded by Charles Rennie Mackintosh in Glasgow, became a designer's way of leaving the past behind and stripping work down to essentials. But whereas Mackintosh worked successfully on a small scale, the large problems came with the wider aim of harnessing the techniques of mass production to the common good. From the Bauhaus and Le Corbusier came the ideas for clean uncluttered surfaces and geometrical shapes which applied to furniture as much as to central Paris. The artists' vision applied directly to the city has long been both an inspiration and a disaster. At the same time traditional Beaux Arts classical grand manner designs were continued in city and home, with concepts of proportion, scale, mass, and vista widely influencing both central Paris and the architecture of public housing.[9]

It is easy to criticise with hindsight; to lambast the high flats and the nasty terraces. But in the context of slum cities of the 1930s, 40s and 50s it is also easy for anyone who cares to investigate to find the reasons for rebuilding and for the mistakes. Amongst these reasons were political perceptions of the desirability of housing more people near their home ground; there was also the government's attitude to land values, compensation and subsidy, which encouraged the building of high flats, first on expensive city sites and then anywhere, and allowed such sacrilege as the juxtaposition of new towers with Worcester County cricket ground and the Cathedral. In addition, there were the literary attacks on sprawling soulless suburbs, the countryside protection movement, and the strategic food and agricultural land arguments. This was the social basis for urban design. The contrasts of view can be seen in the designs of Harlow and Crawley new towns: one a modern study of new architecture and public open space; the other traditional, cottagey, creepy Crawley, as its critics call it, nearer to Letchworth and Welwyn Garden City, the early new towns of England, and to the English spirit.

In spite of this attachment to nature, landscape design has made slow progress in England since the eighteenth century, although in the sense of gardens and parks, as distinct from wider landscapes, new designs emerged out of the Pandora's box of exotic plants flowing steadily into the conservatories of the gentry or of the municipal parks superintendents. The latter were and still are avowedly populist, some would say vulgar, certainly not sophisticated. The former were strait laced into classical forms, or ran in riots of rhododendron along such romantic contours as Cragside in Northumberland. Only the genius of Paxton tried to unite a new world of plants, glass, and iron into a different vision.

In landscape nothing equivalent to the modern architectural and planning movement emerged. The reasons were partly, of course, the nature of dense urban growth and partly patronage and the old rural ownerships and uses of land. Agriculture and the country estates, although subject to economic and social fortunes, continued in their old ways. Nature did the rest as a rural backcloth to urban life and could remain as a unifying force. But as urban influence has spread and agriculture industrialised, so a new need has emerged. In the 1950s and 60s two women, Brenda Colvin and Sylvia Crowe, spelt out the problems and possibilities of design for an urban landscape of industry, power, roads, and the new world of telecommunications. This wider vision has yet to be recognised by the public, accommodated within the idea of an urban landscape, and linked to new questions of conservation and ecology.[10]

These questions about urbanisation, countryside, and the ecology are not new. They were faced by Frederick Law Olmstead and others in the USA during the last century and partly answered by the designs for Central Park. In England another thread of new art and science came after Paxton in the work of Gertrude Jeckyll and William Robinson, both advocates of design with nature, and in affinity with those knowledgeable and sensitive farmers who traditionally worked within the laws of conservation. Urban people were not much involved with these questions directly, facing as they were the enormous problems of the city. It was only as gardening, rambling, and countryside pursuits developed that contacts with nature were renewed by most of the population; and it is only recently that the threat to our landscape is recognised as a social question of ownership, economic production, financial subsidy, and lack of control and design. It is not enough to look at one or other side; to create national parks, establish footpaths, and take care with the design of power stations, however valuable all these things are. What needs to be seen is a modern nation which must either come to terms with past and future or continue in decline. And coming to terms means knowledge about land ownerships, the distribution of wealth, and opportunities for work.

The new conditions for thinking about design are a growing urbanisation; the new technologies of communication as well as of bridge-building and modern windmills; the erosion of environment and the rise of conservation; the ownership of land and houses; and the means for production. This is not to talk of socialism or capitalism, but of a democracy threatened by extremist and out-moded views.

There are grounds for hope. At a domestic level more people are becoming involved in the design of their own environment. Even in the late 60s, for example, the rehousing of people from old terraces into new flats in Byker, Newcastle-upon-Tyne, was done through discussion between architect and residents by the setting up of a 'shop' for ideas and consultation before the new building was finalised. Those who participate in a design are much more likely to accept its final form, and the new Byker Wall, as the sinuous line of flats is called, was fairly well accepted.

The basis for design is changing. The imposition of new forms requires more preparation of the public ground than in the past, but it need not be less exciting. It can be an act of drama, but like good drama requires a sense of human psychology and expert execution. Tolstoy considered the springs of art to lie in the basic actions of rhythm, song, dance, and sculpture. Today we see these actions in folk music, street drama, gable-end murals and other happenings. The Pompidou centre in Paris accommodates such needs. This community creativity extends to building down below the level of the jewel architecture of rich clients and expensive constructions. School children examine the problems of building in the town, or plant gardens in the city.

The whole exercise of public participation is a development which, while mainly used by those knowledgeable about the system, is not only to the advantage of the better-off. Television and individual learning are fast extending the realm of public concern beyond wildlife and historic houses. Environmental education is another widespread development across Europe and elsewhere, instilling understanding and responsibility. Soon this will feed into the adult dialogue and argument which takes place every day over proposals for development.

At the top, traditional assumptions are challenged everywhere, from those of the nuclear power industry to those of the British food and farming industry. They are of course related within the economic structure. As the public understanding grows, the maintenance of myths becomes more difficult, for as in the nineteenth century, the mess and unfairness demand a return to basics. Only with a clear view of society can a new design emerge which meets democratic and not oligarchic needs. Then urban landscapes may be designed to meet wider democratic needs, more basic than sight-seeing, and less élitist in perception and management. The global problems of food, famine, pollution, and conservation will continue to impinge on local perceptions and actions. Life may be perceived as a whole: an Eastern rather than a modern Western viewpoint, infecting attitudes and behaviour towards such diverse matters as vegetarianism, nature in the city, and organic farming.

There is no need to become too philosophical. Already government, the NFU, and the influential Country Land Owners Association have executed their U-turns, partly as a defensive manoeuvre, but partly in recognition of genuine needs. When the recognition can link rural land and landscape to the conservation of architecture and of communities, new designs for environment could come naturally. Structures depend on their relationship to land and social values as much as on the creativity of designers. Inherent conflicts can be constructive if open to view, as Kenneth Clark pointed out in discussing the public appraisal of sculptors working in the yards of Renaissance Florence. Great irrigation works can create wonderful landscapes, but they are bound to affect personal prospects. Judgement in a participative society requires much argument about such problems, with the forging of new canons of design and fair compensation to the individuals who suffer from development. When society faces up to these questions, design flourishes in new ways.

Land Values

The perceptions of land value fall into three distinct domains of thought and action. The most fundamental sees the world as holistic; it is both ancient and modern, spiritual and scientific. From Eastern philosophies, through Classical concepts of nature, to Darwin and present-day ecological conservation, the ultimate value is life in association with a wider unknown presence in space. The second domain comes from concepts of the market and economics. Money exchange is the mechanism for dealing with land, which is bought and sold like other commodities. In Adam Smith's day land seemed limitless and presented no apparent problems for the wealth of nations.

The third domain has arisen as a result of conflicts between the first two. Nature and the landscape have long been perceived to contain values above the market place. In the USA, for example, that land of market freedom, the national parks movement led to the protection of scenic areas, and Central Park within the commercial towers of Manhattan symbolised the importance of nature for city dwellers. From these and earlier perceptions of landscape value in Europe, China, and Japan came modern movements for the protection of landscapes and places of scientific interest. All the values attached to parks, green belts, architectural and scientific conservation, come within this area which we now call the public interest. Today, the separate domains overlap so that the individual spirit, the biosphere, the market, and the public interest relate and conflict as sets of values attached to land.

The reality of value does not exist except in the beliefs of certain groups and in each individual philosophy. It is the reality of political and financial power which confuses perceptions of value. Thus the food industry in Europe and the USA exerts influence to persuade society of its wholesomeness, advertising good meat and red apples which have lost their natural flavour, are artificially coloured, or even poisoned; and the energy industry advertises power lines across the countryside in association with an electric oven. This is the hard sell of a consumer society.

If other social interests conflict with agriculture or power lines, or if free choice is modified by subsidising homes or transport, or by the planning control of development in green belts, then prices alter, and hidden costs and benefits occur. Once this happens, perceptions of true value are made complex through ignorance or assumptions which are at best confusing and at worst unjust. There is also a lag factor, so that people come to expect a payment which no longer represents fair value. Complaints about the cost of home helps today may relate to the wages of servants 50 years ago. Fishing licences and car parking charges are two very sensitive areas where lag is in evidence, and where many refuse to pay more than a fraction of the real costs of stocking rivers and maintaining roads. At the same time perceptions of value relate to profusion or scarcity. The rich now enjoy eating salmon, whereas servants in the past refused to eat it more than four times a week. Access to land is perceived in ways particular to the country. In Sweden all can walk over fields provided that no damage is done to crops. In England the laws of trespass and the blocking of footpaths reflect more selfish and aggressive attitudes to land use and its enjoyment.

The facts, distributions, values, and myths associated with land present a difficult problem. In what follows we shall look at the nature of the market, at town and country planning and the professions, at research work, and at some attempts to change perceptions through law and practice. Our first consideration is of the market. The buyers and sellers are dealing in land, houses, offices, factories, and other saleable properties. Today's house price will depend upon whether you live in Wigan or Westminster. Since North Sea oil began to flow, office rents in Aberdeen have gone as high as they are anywhere in the UK, except for the City and favoured areas of the Home Counties west of London. In the nineteenth-century rush to build and invest in railways, the engineers, landowners, and promoters fought to develop or preserve land, and large profits were made, and estates were conserved. The necessary private acts of Parliament required easy access to the lobbies, which included the engineers who established their headquarters in Westminster. Their Institutions are still there, near the House of Commons.

Investors in land and property know where expectations lie: for example, around motorway junctions, places where the bastions of green belt and countryside protection have to be strong or crumble in the face of potential high rents and land values, the so-called hope values. Although the 1982 average price of agricultural land in England was something over £3,000 a hectare, values in the proximity of cities and towns are very much greater, rising to six figures where permissions for development are forthcoming. Housing land in desirable southern pastures exceeded £50,000 per plot in 1984, whereas in the Gorbals of post-war Glasgow, or the Bronx, New York, it was virtually worthless, and today also there is no market for some poor urban areas. This is a result of the mixture of multiple ownership, the political actions of residents and local authorities, blight, and the high costs of site development. Adjacent city-centre rents can be astronomical, and it is this contrast which has created all the argument over plans for the South Bank of the Thames. In a wider context, 1981 office rents in the City of London were £25 per square foot on the eastern fringe of a bulge of lesser but high rents of about £5-£10, which took in Worthing on the south coast and tapered off along the M4 to Bristol. Only eight other very much smaller areas in Britain reached £5, and they did not include such traditional giants as once proud Liverpool and Manchester. The industrial map is more even, but the north still lags well behind the south.

These values as much as anything prove the pull of London and its region, and reflect the perceptions of those who wish to locate and invest in the right places for financial success. They simply illustrate what the evidence of research confirms for all major international centres. In Tokyo figures are even more dramatic, but some countries are not so dominated by a single city. Germany and the USA have their centres spread more widely, and both are countries which have developed on the basis of regional powers. Within cities, traditional gradients of value relating to distance from the centre are disappearing as urbanisation spreads, a fact returned to in later chapters.

A second group of interests concerns the professionals; engineers, town planners, valuers. They mostly serve developers or local government, although more and more are working with communities to defend minority interests. In the UK planners are seen as having a 'town and country' prefix, but elsewhere in Europe this is less the case; architects and economists may assume the title more readily; the distinction is due in part to historical circumstances and to the importance attached to professionalism.

Those who have skills in building or estate development are one band of planners, those involved with budgets and investment another. Current practice is bringing together members from both groups, for it has become clear that the problem of a declining city, for example, cannot be solved in isolation. Investment on the land is to do with the use of the land, and neither historic rents nor historic land uses may apply any more. Individual choice in the market of money and land, combined with road transport, has taken many industries out of the city, leaving much old industrial land over-valued and unwanted. Naturally, landowners, both commercial and domestic, are reluctant to reduce their prices, and professional valuers resist any shift in their perceptions. Many towns are now valued more as traditional centres of commercial and shopping activity, entertainment, and animation, than as centres of industry, which are tending to grow in new places where space and good communications are more easily found.

As we have already seen, the emergence of formal values amongst professional people comes from wider perceptions of need at par-ticular times, whether in the age of the Romantics or during the Industrial Revolution. Many of the values held by those who support the protection of the countryside in England can be traced through three stages: an eighteenth-century stage of the recognition of natural and scenic values; a stage of formal protection in the late nineteenth century and the first half of the twentieth century; and now a third stage which embraces countryside conservation. The concepts of such values are essentially broad, but they imply a social recognition of land values outside the market place. Owners no longer have free rights over land, nor does the 'economic' argument always rule.

Research to establish the mechanisms in which market and other values interact to produce patterns of land use falls into categories which offer different interpretations of reality. Scientific research in the empirical tradition of Northern Europe and North America has established a body of knowledge which rests on measurements of such variables as land use, accessibility of resources, and costs of transport relative to type, distance, time, and congestion. This factual knowledge can explain why land has been used as it has. More recently, and especially since the advent of the computer, theories of explanation and prediction have enlarged the knowledge of urban systems. Such scientifically based observations and theories are limited when political factors and the absence of 'soft' data (for example social values) are considered. There is also the problem of the speed of changing events which makes the cry, 'We need more research', of limited use.

Another school of research has paid more attention to relationships between the distribution of wealth and development. It is common knowledge that all cities have their good and bad areas of high and low land values. Much of this can be attributed to market choices in search of an unspoiled environment. For example, London's West End and its continuation west to Richmond, and south to Brighton, can be seen in relation to the attractions of an environment which includes the Court as well as the landscape. When land-ownership, wealth, taxation, and subsidy are examined, political influences on change become easier to understand.[11]

Future policies will in part depend upon the knowledge and understanding revealed from the secrets of old chests and new filing cabinets. The present campaign for a freedom of information act concentrates mainly on secrecy about such policies as those of defence and nuclear power; but it is likely to spread to questions of property ownership, one of the crucial areas of survey currently unavailable to planners of the environment. The recent requirement for local and other public authorities to keep a public register of unused land owned by them is not complemented by any such register of private land. Amongst the problems of fair valuations are the artificial book-values of much urban land and the consequential high costs of purchase and compensation.

The way in which some odd valuations are made is well illustrated by recent negotiations for land on the Duke of Westminster's Grosvenor Estate round St George's Hospital at Hyde Park Corner. As a result of an eighteenth-century covenant, the Estate recently obtained rights over some of the most valuable land in England in return for a pittance. The covenant was not challenged by the Secretary of State responsible for the Hospital land, but as a result of protests, a later additional transfer of land has cost the Duke over £6 million, and also benefited the taxpayer. As another example of the problem of reconciling private and public interests, Government has recently decided to pay Fountain's Forestry Ltd £120,000 to plant conifers at Creag Meagaidh, one of the rare haunts of the golden eagle. While these are not simple questions to deal with, fairness and the public interest demand a more open approach on the whole question of private and public costs and benefits.

The problem of political power and the use of land is central to the market and to the fair distribution of wealth. On the face of it, Conservative administrations and local councils work with developers to secure changes through the marketplace, while Labour intervenes to bring benefit to the less well-off, both in promoting the compulsory purchase of land and in controlling development. In practice marketeers tend to go for subsidy and tax policies which favour those with property such as large estates of forestry and agriculture, while interventionists work to direct resources towards the less well-off through such policies as public housing and rent control. But because the workings of the land market are imperfectly understood, anomalies abound and conflicts are by no means easy to unravel. Labour has not opposed green belts, although these tend to work against the less well-off who are trying to enter the house market. But then in principle labour may prefer to see fewer private owners. The Thatcher administration has attempted to allow new private 'villages', each of 10,000 people or so, within London's green belt, and such a move might, if associated with better and fairer inner city policies, help both the economy and inner city residents. But at the same time it rouses the fury of well-heeled conservationists, blue as well as green in politics. Such crude attempts to aid the private sector and so damage green belt policies are not the way to deal with people and their land.

A combination of ideology, traditions of adversary politics, and a lack of analysis and open discussion keeps perceptions locked up in old compartments. The same can be said of the profession of town planning, which ought to be making things more explicit and open to wide judgement. But town and country planners are mostly employed by local authorities, and so are constrained in their ability to present wider and more open views.

During the second world war, at a time when planning was approaching its zenith, and the welfare state was being conceived, a battle took place in Whitehall between marketeers and socialists over rights of owners, the value of land, and the interests of the public. The story has been told by Barry Cullingworth in an official history derived from government papers, which include those of the

Cabinet Committee, set up in August 1940, with the aim of looking at a post-war European and world system, and particularly at the economic needs of nations and a social structure to secure equality of opportunity.[12]

A reconstruction committee set to work, with the Cabinet favourably disposed to the principle of planning, but it soon ran into problems of land-ownership, compensation, and betterment (the increase in private gain as a result of public works such as new roads). It was perhaps significant that some of the earliest recommendations came from the Ministry of Agriculture, asking that all good land should be maintained. This brought a question from Mr Atlee as to whether the same principle should be followed for the mines. Churchill also put in an oar, writing for powers to compel 'recalcitrant, obstructive or merely incompetent country authorities to do what is necessary in the larger interest'. There was recognition that a good social and economic land strategy was equivalent to a good war planning strategy. The questions of land values and compulsory purchase, compensation, rights, and control over development and betterment, were argued back and forth until late in the war. Agreement was eventually reached to control all new development, to extend compulsory purchase powers, and to set compensation levels at 1939 land values as a standard, but not as a ceiling.

The issue of development rights over land and of state land-planning in the wider sense of a public resource for the nation was not resolved, and it was left to the post-war Labour government to attempt a solution, a 'solution' which removed all market incentive from land sales by imposing a tax of 100% on gains. The result was a drying up of activity. New compulsory purchases of old urban areas were now possible at 1939 values and operated for inner city redevelopment. By the late 1950s, however, the new financial provisions of a Conservative government returned values towards market levels. Thus new school playing fields became more and more expensive, and today a council wishing to buy a private open space, perhaps a playing field attached to a redundant factory, might have to pay £50,000 an acre in an urban area. Hence the provision of open spaces in cities is very difficult, and many existing ones are being developed. With regard to a gains tax, subsequent legislation left Britain with a development tax of approximately 60%, a solution similar to that operating in a number of European countries, but one that was abolished in 1985.

The control of urban development without compensation still remains if an owner wishes to go beyond any legally defined use, and the definitions are currently under review. The owner would be compensated only if he were refused the continuation of an old use. In other words, you can build a house on a plot where one has come down (subject to detail), but not necessarily a high block of flats. If you are refused the house, you will be compensated, but not if you are refused the flats. Cases can be complicated, for there are many regulations and interpretations, but the principle remains. So far agriculture has escaped control altogether, except that on sites of special scientific interest (SSSIs), control can be exercised but at a normally prohibitive rate of compensation.

So some advance was made, and some newly gained ground lost. What are the lessons to be drawn? Firstly, in a mixed economy private gain is central to the economic engine and includes the freedom to use land seen as necessary for the job. Secondly, urban owners were no longer free to develop and profit by speculation, even if their land was ideally placed on a main road, and it seems that this control will remain. Permission for new development rests with the local authority, with allowance for appeals and other categories of procedure. The issue depends on an evaluation of market needs and the public interest. Speculative sales of land take place, often at a high price and in the expectation of higher values to come (hope values). Though planners may be thought to be under the pressure of bribery, few are brought to court. Yet the gain on five acres of land allocated for housing in a good location might well be £250,000, subject to capital gains tax. The lesson here is that corruption in an old sense is rare, but that the war-time Cabinet's view of a social and economic structure to secure equality of opportunity is now a thing of the past, with land policy weighted heavily in the direction of market forces. Thirdly, the exclusion of agriculture from control can no longer be seen as an equitable policy, one where compensation is assumed to be a right.

Just as significantly, public policies executed through land-planning allocations and controls have ensured that select places are kept select, and that only the well-off are able to buy their way into them. Further, restricting the supply of land raises the price. In the

light, or darkness, of the inner city problem, this is a social difficulty
which has still to be met. In 1945 it was met by new and expanded
towns, public housing, and the welfare state. Since then levels of
owner-occupation, of both houses and farms, have risen a good deal
and hence have provided both a stake in the land and a static
dimension to settlement patterns. But the market is always alive,
justice is always around, and new values, laws, and practices may
soon emerge.

At the end of the last century the question of securing public
benefit from the development of land was a major political issue.
The nettle was grasped by Asquith's 1909 Liberal Administration,
but the sting released the hold, and, as we have seen, the same
problem occurred in mid-century.[13]

Two individual figures have been influential over the same
period: Ebenezer Howard, writer and the builder of Letchworth and
Welwyn Garden Cities; and Henry George, American advocate of
land taxation, a cause espoused by British Liberals at the time.
Howard succeeded in creating the modern British New Towns
movement (starting with Letchworth and Welwyn), one admired
and emulated elsewhere, notwithstanding its failure to achieve one
of the founder's central aims, which was to plough profits back into
the community (this is still the practice in Letchworth) and also to
help cure the social problems of great cities.[14] Perhaps the main
lesson was that political will could exchange old perceptions of
central cities and the 'laws' of the market for new ones of wider city
regions which, changing as they would have been anyway, could be
planned at a regional scale. Another shift in perception arose as a
result of the planning and creation of what was only the second post-
war fully pedestrian UK shopping precinct, at Stevenage New Town
(the first being in blitzed Coventry). Opposition from traditional
retailing and estate valuation lobbies was defeated, as much by
public outcry as by architectural defence of the plans.

Henry George's thesis has still to be tested against economic
theory, as Fred Harrison has attempted to do.[15] It is probable that
speculative land investment does harm the economy, but no good
way of dealing with the problem has yet appeared in Western
countries, although China's new combination of state-owned land
and private profit suggests that other ways are possible without
resorting to the Russian example. We return to these very difficult

questions later, together with the problem of rates, which are a main form of local taxation in many countries, but which are under suspicion in the UK as being unfair and ineffective.

One other name should be mentioned, that of Patrick Geddes, Professor of Botany at St Andrews University, sociologist, planner, and visionary, who was also a contemporary of Howard and who would have been entirely at home today, but was out of his time then.[16] His strengths were systems analysis, human ecology, and community self-help, expounded when mechanistic futurists, modern technology, and the modern movement were the mode. His values were in accord with those other perceptive people, the French Impressionists, whose paintings and concern with the physics of light and colour as well as with the lives of ordinary people in parks, streets, seaside, and countryside raised questions about the new democracies.

In many ways Geddes is more relevant today than either Howard or George. His concepts were of systems which included the fundamental and holistic viewpoints mentioned at the outset of this section. With public interest now changing, a new force for critical appraisal is present, one concerned with the ecology of man and his environment and with the justice and injustices of present market activities which make an impact on communities and the land.

In his book *Business Civilisation in Decline* Robert Heilbroner writes of Schumpeter, a conservative theorist, as follows: 'For Schumpeter, however, the villain of the piece was not an expected failure of the economic machinery: it was the underlying cast of mind characteristic of a business civilization — rational, calculating, sceptical. Such a mindset served capitalism well when its rise was opposed by the 'irrational' privileges of an aristocratic order; but once in the saddle, Schumpeter maintained, this critical intellectuality would be turned against the pretensions of property and would reveal them to be as empty as those of nobility'.[17] The questions of land and property, capitalism and socialism, cannot be dissociated, and it is the 'mindset', the perception of market and public policy, which has to change if progress is to be made.

The insistent demands of the modern economy are a central theme of this book. If the environment and life are to be rescued, the values attached to land will have to move away from both market and socialist philosophies, for at present industrialisation advances regardless of political bent. Something more fundamental than the pulling of levers on the old juggernauts of power is likely to be needed, and it can only come from changes in social values. The perceptions are changing quite fast, and as with the discoveries of science, they will change the directions of society. Whether they move fast enough remains to be seen.

Instead of seeing city and countryside as quite distinct things, it is increasingly obvious that they are becoming so closely related in space, time, and use that old distinctions are hampering a fair and open view of choices and opportunities. Urban England is, in one sense, the whole land, to be used more or less intensively for its people. It is no longer a land of large and dirty industrial cities or pit villages on the one hand, and beautiful agricultural landscapes on the other. Of course, old urban areas continue and their communities can enjoy them if work is available; and likewise, beautiful landscapes remain under caring hands. But the scale of the international economy and the values of conservation and ecology require new distributions of use, new designs in buildings and landscape, and new evaluations.

The symbolism of town and country is deep-rooted and powerful. Like other symbols, land is not necessarily amenable to numbers or logic, and can be powerfully evoked to maintain certain values. In England land is not extensive, and pressures are strong. But the same pressures have been able to remove open space and beauty in the city, where there are also strong symbolic positions of other kinds. The solution of such problems is one of the more difficult tasks confronting the country, but one which must be faced fairly.

This chapter has been focused on land and the way it is perceived and used. Needless to say, such a view is only part of a much wider set of changes, notably those to do with the social institutions of family, law, and government, with social security, and with concepts of work, employment and leisure. It is not to be expected that any partial view can do more than be seen to interact with the wider landscape of human affairs. The modern civil service, local government, and mass employment in factories developed in the late nineteenth and early twentieth centuries. Two wars and the pace of technological change have now created a social environment in which everything is uncertain, but in which, until the system is seen in new ways, progress will be difficult. Whatever the place of land, we can no longer afford to hide questions of use and values behind veils of secrecy, or to treat land and its design as divorced from the issues of labour and the use of capital. So much is happening that new structures for new lives are bound to become clear before too long.

Chapter 4

Choices

The problem of choice lies at the heart of personal life, and the present uncertainties and conflicts in British society reflect problems associated with the variety of views held. During phases of transition, such as the one we are in now, choices are more difficult simply because the outcomes are less easy to see. If we stick to old and well tried ideas, perhaps all will work out in the end. If we make radical changes, there may be failure rather than success. In the end, however, we exercise our vote in response to political programmes, and the choice of programmes depends upon party perceptions of priorities.

Before priorities are established, evidence for their popularity and validity must be clear, and at present, although 'Green' movements are in evidence, land as an issue does not come into the category of social or economic policy. Yet it may be that land is one key to the successful opening of new opportunities for work and wellbeing. As has been discussed earlier, history shows the crucial role that land has played, and with new economic forces at work, it seems very probable that it will do so again. In a country where 60% of our homes are now owner occupied, where many people are in regular contact with the countryside, and where concern over wildlife grows, grass root political pressures may well demand changes which are seen to be fairer and necessary, not only at home, but also in relation to Europe and the Third World.

The dawn of the modern age raised new and fundamental questions for church and state, art and science, but the pace of argument and change was slow. In the flood of later Western industrialisation came new doubts and choices, but once a course was set, the values of scientific and technological progress held sway and determined the form of modern urban industrialisation. Today humanity faces fundamental choices again, but now the pace of change requires faster decisions, and these are likely to set the pattern for the next century.

The uncertainties introduced by ideas of limits to growth, by threats to the balance of the biosphere, and by the rise of power blocs in the Middle East and Asia are joined by uncertainties about the meaning of science, progress, and life; and while these may not be new, they now exist in a context where new perceptions are emerging and new patterns of development will appear. Uncertainty is compounded by the rise of democracy and the social mobilisation produced by high levels of education and the new freedom of information which telecommunication, like the book, offers to all. The old political parties are having to face new internal and external rivalries, the old cities are threatened, and traditional strategies and defences crumble under expert scrutiny or technological failure, as in the case of nuclear reactors. These are not to be compared with early railway disasters; the stakes are now too high to brush away as part of the price of progress.

The system of politics, power, and the use of science and technology remains strong, but under question. There are broad new choices emerging, partly as a result of new problems and partly as a result of wealth creation and the ability to produce food and manufactured articles easily, mechanically, and with the greater choices offered by such developments as computer-aided design. The possibilities ahead provide wider choices of life-style, home, work, and culture, but it is difficult to be certain about particular directions. Hence the emergence of scenarios and future studies, not as predictions or trends, but as possibilities laid out to aid social choice. Trend forecasting, whether it be for water, energy, or housing needs, has proved a limited and often faulty and misleading means to choice, and we search for new ways. At the same time, research grows in methods of choice and of risk analysis, both in the political sphere and elsewhere.[1] These aids to choice can be exercised when perceptions and possibilities are wide open, and they are necessary when scarce resources demand careful investment decisions.

One of these resources is land, and because it is limited and under growing pressures, decisions about it become more important. Since the nineteenth century regulation and control over building land have been increased steadily, and planning inquiries have been one of the major vehicles for public discussion about such things as power stations and roads. But their limitations have become increasingly evident as public questioning has grown, and frustration over the limits to discussion has led to anger and even violence. On reflection, it is absurd that decisions which lie at the heart of social development should be taken as the result of a planning inquiry. For the present, let us put aside this way of choosing, and look at more fundamental questions, returning later to the planning process.

The free market remains as a powerful concept, most of all in the USA, in which individual access in a competitive environment is assumed to maximise welfare. However, as many people fail to survive effectively in this system, state regulations and an essentially utilitarian philosophy of social welfare accompany the market. In Europe the social welfare aspects are stronger, the market less dominant. When it comes to land, the differences between the USA and the UK can be seen in the extent of use, of waste and dereliction, and of the role land plays in the economy. Because land is a safe investment, it attracts the rich, who divert resources into 'land banks' against the day when development profits can be taken, or private environments can be protected and enjoyed.

In the UK the stronger controls which have developed on the basis of a consensus over the protection of countryside are now being lessened by Government with such developments as enterprise zones and the proposals for simplified planning zones. But, in addition, the pursuit and encouragement of market forces, strongly influenced by the USA, is leading to large private land purchases, high prices, and growing difficulties for those without much money. These trends are accompanied by housing policies which favour owner occupation, and planning policies for the containment of urban areas and the 'protection' of the countryside. This protection is in part a fiction, for there are virtually no planning controls over agriculture or forestry. The subsidised market or tax havens of these land uses do not necessarily contribute to a public welfare policy which takes account of choices for young farmers, and the promoters of wildlife and other activities. The whole question of how the land is used and for whom, how planning and property laws operate, who gains and who loses, has now become an urgent one, and choices have to be made in the political arena, choices which provide some general agreement apart from the amalgam of individual investors and those who represent the public interest. There is no such political consensus at the moment, and the multiplicity of interests makes it very difficult to see how one might arise.

The broad elements of individual freedom and social contract are reconciled by an acceptance of law and practice according to political philosophies of rights and justice. In Western Europe a relatively stable political environment suggests a continuation of social democracy in which the pendulum of market freedoms and social control will swing across broad spans of time. At present the trend towards market choices holds sway; so let us examine individual freedom of choice.

If a cave-man had been asked where he would choose to live, it would be in another cave, although perhaps in a different place. The choice of the medieval labourer on the land would not be much greater. When the growth of cities offered new employment, wider choices appeared, and when the growing middle classes of clerks and shopkeepers in their grimy nineteenth century town terraces were suddenly offered, through cheap train travel and the semi-detached house, a chance to cultivate their gardens, the choices opened out still further. The factory, the office, and the conditions of employment still regulated work, but there were wider opportunities for changing jobs and improving one's lot.

With the growing specialisation of productivity in the economy, choices for some are now getting wider, but for those without jobs they have narrowed. While standards of living have gone up, it is questionable whether choices have widened for those who are at the bottom of the pile. To be sure, there are no starving peasants or children down the mines, but the poverty trap experienced in a poor dwelling today offers little in the way of escape. The relative nature of poverty may allow that a television is now a necessity of life rather than a luxury, but in providing a television in an inner city room, instead of the peasant's rural environment, has society offered a greatly improved choice? Not to go hungry is a clear gain. To be crowded at the centre of fifty square miles of bricks and tarmac can be considered a loss. The environment, as well as the television, must offer a choice. If income is low, choices are few.

To enlarge a little on market choice and its absence may help to identify the issues. Those who have money command a wide choice of increasingly specialised goods and services, homes and workplaces. The individual will make a personal selection, trading off choices between, for example, a cheaper home in the country with expensive travel to work and a more costly town house with low travel costs. Schools, shops, and other facilities also enter the equation, and in the wider search for a good place to be, the market throws up a range of environments to suit those pockets which have something in them.

As the economy becomes more specialised, new kinds of job and house appear to offer a long ladder of opportunity for the adventurous. Once the house is bought with a tax relief mortgage, a substantial sum of currently untaxed capital is assured, so allowing for the accumulation of other capital to spend on cars and other personal goods, travel and leisure within a wide geographic area which is perhaps international in scale. There is nothing new in these motivations, but there is a widening choice of work, house type, consumer goods, and specialised entertainment.

Those outside this more prosperous market have no capital, are dependent upon subsidies or rent relief for their accommodation, and cannot afford to travel far. If they live on a new outer estate, the journey to hospital and city centre is expensive, and this is why public transport fares are such a crucial matter. It is one of the ironies of modern life that as technology grows more sophisticated, the poor become relatively more deprived of services which were once cheaply and easily reached. With the dispersal and loss of jobs, it is less easy to get another nearby. Even a relatively well paid secretary in central London will find it difficult to obtain a decent home within a distance over which travel costs can be afforded.

Over the centuries, charity, philanthropy, and government aid have recognised the obligation to provide firstly the means for life itself, such as food and shelter, and then better homes, education, insurance, and the whole panoply of the welfare state. Not only are these services offered, but the wider consideration of a decent environment (and perhaps a more contented and productive work force), stimulated the Quakers and others to build garden suburbs, and the government, fifty or sixty years later, to build new towns. Whether private or public in origin, opportunities for the wider enjoyment of life were offered, but in the case of government they were bought at the cost of subsidies and of compulsory purchase of private property, for the perceived interest of the general public.

Behind these personal and social choices lies the economic engine which generates wealth and consequently the use of the land. The investment decisions implicit in production and its location created the industrial city, just as trade and commerce created the earlier commercial city. In this the availability of land was crucial. In the early stages land could be found easily at the edges of growing towns, or used to support high buildings within their centres. But as space for work and machines, for rail, road, and air traffic has grown, so the choices of location widen beyond the old confines, and indeed are impossible to keep within them as populations and demands for space increase. The interaction of work places and homes has always been a crucial determinant of settlement patterns. The new factors of increased industrial-cum-agricultural productivity with less labour, rapid communication, the computer or work-bench at home, growing leisure, concern with the countryside, all set the scene within which new choices will have to be made.

The timing of public and political response to social need in relation to the market is an uncertain one. When do collective market actions, with a strong counterweight of social obligations in an active economy, require public response which controls excess and provides for those who have been left behind? Are there cycles of economic and social activity which can be discerned as important influences on the processes of change?

Economists have recently been much attracted to the long cycles first described by Kondratieff in the 1930s.[2] Starting with the beginnings of the Industrial Revolution in England in the late 1780s, he traced periods of about 50 years, 25 of growing prosperity, 25 of decline or relative stagnation. Having experienced high growth between 1945 and 1970, the industrialised nations are now in a down phase which may well last until the mid-nineties. There is an interesting and perhaps quite accidental relationship between these cycles and those of social reform. At the start of the economic upswings in the late 1840s, around 1900, and again after the last war, there were equivalent social movements in the UK: in the 1840s the reaction against *laissez-faire* economic policy and the beginning of the period of government regulations in public health and housing; in 1909 the reforming Liberal administration which introduced new measures of social benefit; and in 1945 the Socialist welfare state. If this indicates no further social reform until the end of the century, things look bleak for the poor, and certainly current policy offers them little hope. But this is an unproven link and perhaps an irrelevant digression.

Nevertheless, the choices of individuals and the actions of social institutions have led us in certain directions which are indicative of future trends. In the eighteenth century, an age of improvement and near feudal attitudes, the economy, accompanied by science and discovery, led England not only to land reforms through Parliamentary enclosure, with consequential worker distress, but also to greater food production. In some ways, however, the workers slowly gained. There were new opportunities to earn money in the growing industrial towns, and at this easy stage many moved to and fro between town and country, as they now tend to do in the urbanising countries of Africa. Other choices were also wider, both in consumer articles such as textiles and pottery, and in all the ancient attractions of the city. But as exploitation in housing and working conditions grew in intensity, distress of a new kind emerged, political perceptions changed, and government regulation of the market came into force. Positive freedom required a balance of negative freedom: the control and security which allowed for personal protection and new opportunities.

At the same time, wealth continued to grow, and new kinds of choice appeared in the market. The railway provided opportunities to live in spacious suburbs and commute to work, or to go further afield to country towns and villages. Those with a sense of social obligation developed garden suburbs, while friendly building societies provided money for many to buy houses. Humane standards of living became a perceived public need, and slum clearance and council housing resulted. This is not to impute pure motives to public authorities. Some of the impetus, as with Napoleon III and Baron Haussmann in Paris, was to rid the inner-city quarters of poor, unsightly, and often degenerate humanity, making room for commerce, new streets, and the creation of a grand image. Nevertheless the broad social movement is clear: more space, better houses, parks, education, insurance, and security.

The post-1918 boom into a car-owning suburbanising nation brought with it the wider effect of sporadic countryside development in an era of depressed home agriculture, cheap land and inadequate planning controls. The industrial anarchy of the early nineteenth century was in danger of being replaced by the individual anarchy of private house ownership and the use of the car. Again public opinion built up, condemning not only sprawl and ugliness, but also poverty and squalor. The mood of the late 1930s was ready to endorse a post-war Labour government and a new effort to widen choice for the less fortunate. Free medical treatment joined free education; new towns provided jobs and accessible countryside; depressed regions were also offered jobs; coal mining and railways were to provide a proud public service. The vagaries of the house market were strictly controlled and agriculture resuscitated. A new, clean, tidy public vision replaced anarchy in the market place.

It is now forty years since the post-war mood for strong government intervention. In the 1960s the choices in a wealthy society seemed to be freer than ever, and produced not only a tremendous growth in teenage consumption, but also the planned dispersal of city populations to expanded towns a hundred miles away. To go from London to Kings Lynn in Norfolk, encouraged and subsidised, was to be offered a choice even more dramatic than that provided by moving to a new town. Population was expected to increase by 20 million between 1965 and the end of the century, and new cities were envisaged on the wide estuaries of the Severn and Humber. Yet by the mid-seventies expected new populations and new cities had vanished from sight, and by 1980 unemployment was soaring. The struggle was on to find any kind of choice at all for the millions out of work and on social security. The televised choices of the rich could only exacerbate the frustrations of the poor in the 1981 riots, and the threat of more communities struck down by market forces could only encourage a militant stand to protect the threatened coal mining settlements.

In the ups and downs of economic prosperity and decline, certain long term trends stand out. The overall variety of work has grown both in kind and in location, as part of an increasing specialisation of social and economic functions in the evolution of society. The variety of available homes is a function of related changes in technology, design, transport, and communication. The steady growth of wealth is part of the process (whether or not the distribution is fair), extending the range of choice for an even greater number of people. The accompanying growth of leisure time extends choices still further, some in pursuit of sport and recreation, some in learning and the arts, some in voluntary work at home and overseas. The women's movement and changes in the institution of family have been liberating forces for millions and have certainly extended choices for many previously trapped within old social conventions. In the mixed economies of Western Europe, the integration of market forces and government policy becomes even more essential if prosperity is to be combined with social progress.

If so much has happened to extend personal choices, are there no trends the other way? Some of the largest have been touched upon: limits to growth both material and ecological, and the post-materialist values which, while including freedom and liberty, reject a surfeit of consumption. While limits suggest unwanted constraints, post-materialism suggests choices towards a simpler life-style implicit in the advocacy of intermediate technology, self-sufficiency, and social concern. The two types of trend can be seen as moving together: one forcing an economic change of direction towards some self imposed restriction on consumption, the other representing some broad social choice, and both converging towards a different life-style.

It is not incompatible for both types of trend to occur at the same time, as material growth and wider choice continue. The computer and television can exist perfectly well in a settlement which uses intermediate technology for heat and waste-disposal, with local home learning and medical diagnosis linked to central high level systems. Wealth can provide a new range of life-style choices sensibly connecting a high-tech economy to an ecological environment. The more unpleasant constraints of a police state, with erosion of democratic freedom, or of limited nuclear war, are not forgotten; but if vigilance and survival fail, the arguments of this book are worthless.

What then are the issues which restrict or enlarge choice? Put simply, they are wealth and its distribution, land and its use, and the exercise of political power. A geography of all three issues is not easy to describe, for even the apparently most justifiable 'open' information, that is, the ownership of land, is not available. But even if it were, together with wealth locations, the political power conflict remains and is at the heart of all issues. To extend a simple view, changes in the power structure are likely to result in changes in the distribution of wealth and the use of land. Redistribution of wealth does not mean a move to egalitarianism, but rather a shift in distribution, as, for example, from the eighteenth-century landed aristocracy to the nineteenth-century industrial cities. In this sense it is not difficult to sketch out the geography and consider the issues.

The wealth, the land, and the power can be polarised between any deprived inner city location and an attractive surrounding environment of old agricultural settlements and productive lowlands; or between an outer council estate and a prosperous suburb. In one are the bulk of those without work, on social security, and in poor houses or flats; in the other, a predominance of car-owning workers in more spacious settlements. There can be little doubt that if the poor and unemployed had the choice, most would join in the search for a better environment, thus increasing the demand for land outside the city and high quality quarters within it. But, in addition, and in accordance with economic specialisation, we should expect a widening choice in the market of job types and home locations. Where might these lie?

It has been noted already that between the wars collapsed agricultural land values and lack of planning control led to urban scatter in the rural areas within easy reach of the city: the stockbroker's Tudor in the 'cocktail' belt and shack development in poorer localities. Since 1945 a policy of planned containment and agricultural support has concentrated any new development in or around small towns, or within the confines of the big city. As we have seen, the choices were nevertheless increased, except for two: the choice for the isolated home in the countryside, and the opportunity to start on the farming ladder. The first was stopped by planning policies (which included consideration of service costs, for example); the second by agricultural policies which were associated with growing mechanisation and the scale of production. The resultant high costs of land for development and farming have reduced the choices both of individuals in the market and of those public authorities which are looking for opportunities to help the disadvantaged, both at work and at home. In other words, the market, plus planning in the 'public interest', plus vested interests in agriculture (also in the name of public interest), have contributed to a difficult situation in which land costs combine with economic decline to perpetuate the old patterns and limited choices. At the same time, the adverse ecological impact of the new agritocracy suggests that the present curtailment of choice will be followed by severe threats to its existence. In this situation let us look next at the opportunities and possibilities which could be found.

The Widening Opportunity

Current economic problems, changing values, and the limits-to-growth argument tend to obscure the steady growth in wealth and personal consumption that has taken place this century in the rich countries of the world. By almost any measure the majority have benefited. Higher wages, more spacious homes and gardens, the amount of food, the number of goods such as clothes, cars, telephones, washing machines, televisions, all are measures of growing wealth. Recession or not, the mechanisation and higher productivity of manufacture continues with computer and robot, while the potential global demand is enormous. Wealth, however, is poorly distributed and cannot all be measured. Post-materialist values are to do with other qualities of life, while social obligation demands that material standards for the poor should go up.

What are the wider opportunities for the UK in this situation? Firstly, if wealth continues to grow, then so will material standards for the less well-off, with consequential choices in the market for homes and goods. Pressures will erode the still large areas of poor homes and environment, while encroaching upon pleasanter places. Growing leisure will have the same effects, while economic differentiation and the need to work will also result in a continued search for new kinds of working environment.

A second possibility is that the workings of international politics and the economy will force the smaller and weaker of the rich countries to look much more to their own resources, with a reduction of opportunities to profit from world trade. In this event, support for social welfare would become more difficult, and the resources of people, their native wit, their land, and their capital would have to be used with new ingenuity and purpose. While this might not be a widening of opportunity for some, it might be for others. The rich would be less rich, but the poor would have to find or be given ways of contributing to the economy. Realistically, it is difficult to imagine that they will not set out to improve their homes, to produce domestic goods and services, and in doing so to seek capital, property, and land which fit their demands. If the argument that too much is invested in homes and not enough in work places proves correct, and more rented accommodation comes on to the market, there are large numbers of people who will inherit the capital locked up in freeholds and houses, and who will wish to use it for new purposes in new places. Workshops may have to be put into suburban gardens, while new homes and land may be required outside urban areas where a self-sustaining alternative economy could rely more on intermediate technology, with new forms of supply for heat, energy, and other essentials. There is a good deal already happening, and the editors of *The Ecologist* have presented a model of this life-style.[3]

A third set of opportunities arises within the limits-to-growth arguments themselves. There are many sides to this set. One assumes finite resources of minerals and other necessities, with a consequential need for rich countries to cut consumption and to restrain developing countries from excessive growth on the Western model. This would lead to the approaches mentioned above. Another side is explored by Fred Hirsch in his book *Social Limits to Growth*.[4] In this he points to such finite quantities as time in a person's day, the number of satisfying jobs, and the amounts of attractive land, calling these latter 'positional goods'; all these impose limits on personal and social opportunities. These social limits are equivalent to the physical limits relating to pollution or overgrazing. Unless all moderate their demands on the commons, the situation is not sustainable.

Like many others, Hirsch calls for a recognisable social ethic to be added to the personal ethic. Here again opportunities are presented, but of a different kind. If material wealth and growth continue (a point of view held by most as necessary and desirable), people may be forced to reconsider the way in which positional goods are to be shared, for the pressures will increase. Like the growth of socialism, there may have to be moves to enlarge opportunities by restraining the workings of the market, but not in the old ways. Central and collective state education, health services and subsidised housing may be replaced by decentralised local social organisations, a situation seen as desirable from many political viewpoints, and one that is also practical in the light of the possibilities offered by telecommunications and easy access to high-level services by local communities. The argument of *The Ecologist* also pursues the idea of a decentralised political model. These alternatives are not mutually exclusive; they could run together, providing alternative opportunities according to choices of life-style. In every case new approaches can be made. Alternatively a passive *status quo* can be the choice, one unlikely to bring hope to many. Other possibilities arise from the nature of economic development and the use of information technology.

An interesting viewpoint on the economy comes from Jonathan Gershuny in his argument about the industrial and service economies.[5] Having examined the arguments of a move from an industrial society, based on economic growth to a liberal, post-industrial service society, he refutes the idea that services will grow to replace industrial employment. A close examination of the statistics of employment and occupation (not the same thing: a manufacturing firm employs a person whose occupation is a service such as accountancy) leads him to suggest that service occupations are growing as specialised sectors within an economy of increasing industrial production. Apart from education and health, marketed services are not a potential growth area, and even education and health could decrease. The reasons for this and for the continued importance of manufacture are that intermediate services within the whole process of manufacture are growing and that much manufacture is directed towards final consumption of goods — washers, power tools, computers — in the home. The economy, in Gershuny's phrase, is the new service and self-service economy. In this process the home becomes ever more important.

The implications of this for land use and work patterns is potentially enormous. The trend greatly reinforces the opportunities available as a result of the Englishman's traditional love of home and garden, and DIY can include food production and other extensive land uses.

A number of other changes lend support to this thesis. The growing influence of women in society brings greater attention not only to equal opportunities but also the value of people's work at home. The television and video have already taken over a percentage of leisure time, and the amount of learning time is also increasing, both formally as with the Open University and some school learning, and informally through the wider range of public interest in history, wildlife, science and other subjects. Credits in education are joined by credit cards, and computerised accounts will soon influence shopping habits more strongly, while more spare time and flexi-time will encourage the trend for working at home which is already well established. In an ageing society, and with both centralised medical advice and decentralised local help, social care may well develop more strongly in relation to home activity, much but not all of it voluntary, and with less formal social work from outside.

As Gershuny suggests, social innovation may bring new forces of investment in services so that, for example, rather than a heavy investment of wages for social workers, there would be capital investment in communal buildings and equipment to be used by a community served by a combination of paid and voluntary workers. This kind of approach answers other questions which he raises about isolation in a too highly self-serviced home.

The Town and Country Planning Association has recently turned its attention towards new communities in an era when new towns may no longer be established. It has been joined by Telford New Town in Shropshire and the district authority of Wrekin in a plan to set up a new community on 225 acres of land at Lightmoor in Telford. The idea incorporates principles of self-determination in the planning, layout and building of the community; principles of joining the locations of home and work on one plot of about an acre, allowing for workshops, cultivation, and husbandry; and principles of financial benefit accruing to the community. It is a practical step towards a self-service economy which, if successful, could well lead to a rapid and wide adoption of the idea, with consequential new demands on land as well as new attitudes to local government, financing, and design.

The distribution and type of work-place and home are always changing, and in the past have been related to agrarian and manufacturing economies with work in field or factory. These distinctions and ties are now much weaker. Not only is there less concentration in a certain place (village or town), but there is also less emphasis on a certain type of home (cottage or terrace). The forced mobility which took Cornish tin miners to Durham pit-villages and rural labourers to urban centres is, of course, related to centres of employment. A reduction in such employment and an increase in other forms of work and leisure combine with home investment and a lack of rented property to reduce mobility. Are most opportunities then to occur only where people live already?

The land/factory situation which provided much of the earlier employment is now gone or going. The commerce and services of the town remain but are under some threat from developments in telecommunication and the self-service economy. While high level central urban activity will remain, the increase in leisure at home and in the countryside will emphasise the role of suburb and more outlying districts in the distribution of work. One present trend is towards the South, the other towards the spacious surrounds of the old cities. Added to these movements and to the influence of leisure activities are the preferences of particular groups, for example, the growing numbers of retired, and the wishes of some of the young to enter farming. Given the productivity and industrialisation of high-level agriculture, and the existence of much gentrified agriculture, there are good reasons to assume that new dispersed patterns of employment would not work against productive agricultural interests in the wider economic sense.

The opportunities arising from economic differentiation which were extended to workers at the time of the Industrial Revolution, and subsequently in full urbanisation, must not now be seen to reside mainly in those old cities. If the choice is extended further, it becomes a choice across urban England, not just within the town; a choice to live on 'the land', in a village, or in a small town. For the poor, only government intervention can offer that choice. The present strong movement of the better off away from old cities results from a dislike of obsolescent dwellings in obsolescent environments. In place of these, planners, architects, and developers have unfortunately built some new ones which are themselves now ready for demolition, especially those soulless flats to be seen across Europe and to a much smaller extent, in North America and Australia. There is a lot of this poor housing to be replaced, as in Glasgow, where estates as big as new towns stand grimly about the city.

While estimates for defective housing show a slow reduction in numbers in many areas, there were still over two million in England in 1981, and the number in need of repair is going up.[6] These do not include many houses which are in obsolescent environments or which are unpopular in themselves. So there will be a continuing demand not only to improve the unfit, but also to get rid of the unpleasant.

All this adds up to a large rebuilding programme, whatever the future economy. But what should be replaced or renewed? The 1970s' movement away from mass slum clearance to the improvement of older houses came about partly because the worst of the nineteenth-century slums had gone and partly because there was community resistance. There were also strong economic arguments for this switch of emphasis, as well as the movement for the conservation of areas with architectural quality. In addition, changes in the population structure give rise to new demands; for example, the growing numbers of single-person households (whether young, old, or separated) make the conversion of Victorian villas to flatlets a profitable and land saving business.

The computing of all these variables keeps a large number of developers, planners, housing officers, and demographers at work. Some claim great shortages of land, others the need to use the wasted areas of our cities. There is broad agreement about the need for some new land, and much is tacked on to expanding small towns. At the same time private developers have been encouraged to build or renovate in the inner city, thus raising the proportion of good houses and the well off sectors of the population. Such gentrification also lowers densities of housing, for the better off can buy more space, overcrowding is less, and land demand elsewhere increases.

In all this we can discern a very wide variety of home types and more individual choice, though not of tenure. Since the second world war, the number of private houses to rent has fallen from over 50% of the stock in England and Wales to under 15%, partly as a result of rent controls imposed to prevent exploitation, partly through the incentives to owner occupiers, and partly from the development of the public housing movement. The so-called third arm of the Housing Associations contributed something to private rented homes, but as is the case with council homes, sales to occupiers are now part of recent political philosophy and action. There has been much criticism of the lack of rented dwellings on the grounds of reducing choice and labour mobility. Co-operative movements — much used in northern Europe — are other safeguards against exploitation and constitute one way of extending types of tenure. Collective tenant action in shared blocks or condominiums, both in Europe and the USA, suggest other possibilities, as does also the new experiment in Telford by the Town and Country Planning Association. It seems likely that social and economic change will bring rented property back into favour, safeguarding tenants in ways other than through rent control law, while allowing for an economic rent to be charged.

Another absentee from the field of choice is the new rural house. The wealthy are taking over the attractive villages and converting farmhouses and barns, but the past inclination to build an isolated house, perhaps with a smallholding, has been virtually stopped by the planners. A policy of containment prohibits such untidy things, and there are some genuine problems with services, although these are not as difficult as is made out. There has long been a cry to stop the depopulation of rural areas; it is still heard in many uplands in the UK and is even louder in marginal lands in parts of Europe.[7] Here especially work on the land is vanishing, and with it go people, shops, and schools. But the cry of those who opposed Commissioner Mansholt and the EEC agricultural policy is remembered. Will there be alternative work in the cities if agricultural employment is reduced?

Most European countries have policies to help declining rural areas, and most are concerned with small local manufacture, related to resources of food, timber, and the leisure industry. There is still considerable potential in these, for leisure and tourism grow particularly where there are new opportunities opening up in the development of biotechnology. While the balance of work is still overwhelmingly in small town and large city, it is growing in the former at the expense of the latter. In other words, it is spreading into less densely urbanised areas. This creates new demands for services, for homes, and for part-time farming and other rural occupations. These are questions more fully discussed in the following chapter.

With mobility of transport and the opportunity offered by telecommunication, very large areas of land are now freely available as potential workplaces. The process is one of interacting opportunities for homes and work; of the accessibility offered by transport; of sufficient populations to support local services; and of capital to develop new structures. It is fair to say that the opportunity for selecting the locations for capital investment is greater than ever before, particularly as the infrastructure of motorways, electricity, and other services now forms a network which covers the land.

In post-war Britain, when the public mood for improving old settlements was so strong, there was much argument about the merits and demerits of investing in old places or in new. On one side was the belief that the 'social capital' (represented by cinemas, shops, or community life) of old areas should be used; on the other the conviction that a clean break was needed to establish higher standards. In the cities overcrowded and often appalling houses and workplaces forced attention on to a new town or outer estates programme. The attempt to retain some part of the old communities failed. High flats could not house a happily balanced population; factories in old, and then in new areas, closed doors. The attempt to match homes and jobs was also thwarted by growing mobility. After the war, in the mining areas of County Durham, all new investment was guided to the two new towns or to selected 'key villages': a policy only to be overtaken by growing car ownership. This ensured the continued life of dormitory villages without working mines but within commuting distance of town work.

Today people vote with their wheels and move out of the cities to more attractive environments. There is no doubt that without planning control new settlements would spring up, creating a demand for services. The old equations of trying to balance homes and workplaces, of reducing journeys to work, and of retaining old 'social capital' are now suspect. The attempts to bolster old conurbations in these conditions are foiled by falling employment and a preference for the greener areas outside. Of course the old areas will retain very large populations, slowly improving living conditions, and, especially, giving more elbow room. However, with much fixed investment going elsewhere, and less into the city; with high productivity and falling labour needs; and with new and more attractive areas within easy reach becoming a pattern for both manufacture and office development, the old arguments now look fragile. There is a process of de-investment going on in the city as a whole, one calling for radical changes in perceptions of need.

So what are the new arguments? At present there are few. The basis ought to lie in the new structuring of work and the growing importance of homes; a far better use of people's willing labour; a better ecology of land use; more effective direction of capital investment; and the abandonment of old perceptions about agricultural protection and industrial cities. The disastrous results of untrammelled urban and industrial market forces in the nineteenth century can be recognised as a sad lesson in human affairs, with the swing to socialism as a necessary corrective, but one still unable to control the economy and support welfare at high levels. The failures of no planning and of over centralised planning have led the more far sighted nations to mix the two policies within a framework of strategic thought directed towards the international economy, together with local freedom within certain planned guidelines. The management of such affairs is a skilled task for which many governments are unfitted and which many people and institutions are unwilling to recognise as necessary. This problem is considered later. For the present the question is whether the time is now ripe for change in the face of a new emerging economic and social structure and a combination of threatened landscape, a growing polarisation between rich and poor, and the need for a fairer use of resources.

Time for a Move

For those who can afford it, a move is always on the cards: a new job, a new house, a holiday. For those with energy and enterprise, even if they lack wealth, there are always opportunities. For those with neither wealth nor youthful energies, there is inertia, alienation, the poverty trap, or a combination of all three. Any moves for the last group are difficult, if not out of the question.

There is another dimension to choice, which is not to move. To stay where the roots are felt and where continuity is established. If economic forces do not dictate a change, then why not live life where it is, especially if home ownership and a self-service economy point in that direction? There is no doubt that for reasons of inertia, the existing location of settlements and owner occupied homes, and economic deprivation, a great many people will not move. But a few figures indicate the other possibility.

Between 1971 and 1981 London and the other major metropolitan areas of England and Wales lost nearly one and a half million people. Liverpool alone lost 100,000 (16% of its population), and Manchester a similar number. The gainers were the surrounding country areas; the South-East outside London grew by half a million, the South coast by a quarter of a million. In general, small towns and rural areas gained everywhere at the expense of the cities, and the southern at the expense of the northern regions.

The dynamic behind all this was a combination of new employment and housing areas, especially in more spacious and attractive small towns, together with good economic locations, airports, motorways, and accessibility to world markets. These areas are the thriving part of the economy, together with City business and the financial institutions, but the movements also include, for example, a large number of retired people, as in the South-West. There are obviously limits to such changes, but, given the number of job losses and poor houses in the cities, the limits are not yet reached.

Within all this, there are fuses burning. One points at the needs of the deprived. Public recognition of such needs is weak. One authoritative estimate puts a figure of fifteen million on those living in relative poverty in the UK, and thus lacking choices.[8] (A figure confirmed in July 1986 by a survey from the Office of Censuses, Population and Surveys.) In alleviation there is a modest inner city programme of £350m per annum (1985), compared with mortgage relief and exemption from capital gains for owner occupiers of about £5 billion. Market and government moves have increased the distance between haves and have-nots. The riots of 1981 were sparks which as yet have ignited neither an explosive mixture nor the public conscience. This fuse is pointed at the old cities and it may burn faster as a result of present right-wing and centralist tendencies against left-wing city strongholds. Another fuse is burning in the opposite direction, towards the countryside. This is connected with publicly subsidised market forces in agriculture, on the one hand giving to the rich corn-lords and depriving the smaller farmer, especially in the hill lands; on the other, raising alarm amongst an ecology and wildlife minded middle class, resident in village and small town amongst growing prairie fields. European action will affect the timing of this one. There is a third fuse within the social fabric of defence, police, centralisation, information, and secrecy. This points at democracy and freedom wherever it is. It is made more dangerous by the declining economy and the lack of adequate social responsibility.

These seem to present a classic formula for unrest, conflict, and

eventual change, whatever the state of the economy. Some ex-
plosion of political force and moves to redress wrongs may come.
Alternatively, the characteristic stop-gap fudging of British policies
may restrain anger and hopelessness. In a fairer society, there seems to
be little doubt that some positive action will be needed to quench the
fuses and capitalise on the possibilities offered by new technology
for wealth creation, for wide information, for decentralised power,
and for co-operative effort. Just as important is the creation of a
land in which old city and country perceptions can be broken down,
allowing an urban people to attend to the cultivation of their
gardens without destroying the commons. In other words, there
will be a need to seize the opportunity to spread habitation more
widely, more fairly, and with new international and local skills
effectively joined.

This would require policies of positive resettlement and the
restructuring of old settlements, using the new unemployed resources of labour, much of it young, some of it older but skilled in
management. Capital would need to be aligned to this labour
potential for the creation of new wealth, both in the inner city and in
agricultural areas. Much of this provides argument for the rest of the
book. Before concluding this chapter, a word needs to be said about
the physical and social geography of present patterns, and the forces
of inertia they represent. Two arguments against any new approach
can be made: that there is plenty of space within our cities and towns
to accommodate all future needs, and that resistance from established interests will be so strong that the cause is hopeless. Firstly, let
us consider the present urban fabric. Chapter 3 has already looked at
the steady annual growth of land use and demand, not only in
relation to acreage but also as a perceived urban influence over the
countryside. An attempt was made to show that perception is an
important part of this process, and that perceptions can change. The
influences of a fall in agricultural land values, combined with a
relaxation of planning control, have also indicated what might
happen as a result of personal choice for particular life-styles.

So it is not enough to measure land in cities and allocate so many
people to the acre. It is true that there are very large suburban areas
which could accommodate many more people. As with the conversion of Victorian villas, back gardens could be used for small new
homes or workshops. But no one who bothers to walk around the

high-density post-war council flats of European cities can doubt the potential for rebuilding on a more humane scale, with less inhabitants per acre. In the small towns, pockets of open land are filled in, again reducing demand outside. But, as we see every day, fields at the edges also continue to be filled with houses. Eventually this kind of expansion could stop, and it would be possible simply to re-cycle the land within the urban fabric so as to accommodate new needs. What this does is to cut out the choice of living outside the urban area; but it is obvious that many would opt for this latter choice. To the potential young farmers, at present kept out, can be added those interested in protecting and conserving the rural heritage, those involved in the leisure economy, and those who are country dwellers at heart, content with an acre or two to grow some food. Perhaps the biggest demand of all, however, would come from those commuters who have already converted all the old barns, and would be glad to build anew in similar quiet locations. At present, with urban containment and agricultural protection, choices are being limited by those who already live in the countryside and who argue against development, often using public planning policies for private interests.

What is being said is that many people in urbanised countries would prefer to live in the country, as did their forbears. This is an assertion which has some evidence behind it, but cannot be proved. The market reflects such a desire, but land values and planning control prevent its wider satisfaction. Plots of land in desirable village locations may now cost £50,000 before the house is even begun. Land values in desirable parts of cities are also high, but with wider freedom of choice these values would be spread more thinly. It is scarcity which pushes up the price; or, in the case of agriculture, protected markets and guaranteed prices, a situation which urban power once before destroyed (witness the Free Trade Hall in Manchester), and which international forces could destroy again. It is also true that the market leads and stimulates the desire for market town and country residence, but underneath, the economics of space (discussed in the next chapter) suggest an inevitable growth of demand outside the old urban areas.

The resistance from protection interests is also inevitable and continuous. The fiercest post-war battles were concerned with attempts to house big city 'overspill' in surrounding counties.

Cheshire and Worcestershire fought protracted public inquiries to keep out the populations of Manchester and Birmingham. Part of the opposition was opposition to any developments; part was opposition to development to house the working classes of the cities. The former part continues every day in local planning inquiries for new housing, nearly all of it now private. People seek to protect their environments, naturally enough. The latter part has virtually ceased as new public housing declines in volume, what there is being mostly within the cities. Any new attempt at such housing in the shires would certainly cause an outcry.

The shires are likely to be safe from urban invasion until the economy picks up, or a left-wing government attempts some new public policy, or a combination of reduced agricultural support and relaxed planning controls encourages new moves out of the cities. One other possibility is the growth of support for the decentralised small settlement of the ecologists, a theme taken up by the Town and Country Planning Association in its New Prospectus.[9] The Association began with the ideas of Ebenezer Howard, founder of the British new towns movement, and the creator of Letchworth and Welwyn Garden City. It has steadfastly advocated policies of decentralisation, and the New Prospectus arises from the problems of tensions in the big cities, an over-exploited natural environment, and the loss of self-determination.

There is no doubt that Disraeli's Two Nations are again becoming emphasised as a result of economic recession, divisive political policies, and a growing polarisation between rich and poor which is reflected by incomes and the places in which people live. The growth of socialism and the welfare state was an attempt to narrow real income differentials. The planning of post-war housing was an attempt to improve the environment. Today the welfare state is creaking, and the streets of London's new towns are just as likely as the inner city to house the poor — although in fewer numbers. Nevertheless, gains have been made; and in spite of the moves towards private education and medicine, a recent survey has shown that many people wanted more public money spent on those services and were prepared to pay for them.[10] The new towns have been successful as financial investments and, on the whole, are good places to live in. The choices have been extended.

One of the more divisive symbols of class was the council housing movement, once necessary, now perhaps on the wane as houses are sold to occupiers and re-vamped to look different. Many see the growth of owner occupation as a drain on investment which could more profitably go to industry, or as an unwelcome narrowing of opportunities to rent property, thus reducing choice and mobility. There is almost certainly a need for a widening in choice of tenure, and although a deep rooted individual preference for ownership is widespread in Europe, there are also large scale co-operative ownership movements, which may well grow in this country. Co-operatives also fit better the concepts of political decentralisation and self-reliant communities. While the cities have already demonstrated the possibilities of such movements, the extension of choice requires other locations, as well as other tenures, and some of these would be in country areas, associated with new work. It is not necessary to see the work as employment in factories. Rather it would emerge in new ideas and construction (themselves generators of economic activity), and in small enterprises of many kinds in the fields of information, learning, the arts, sport, and leisure, as well as in high-technology and craft products. The old model of economic and social structure which emerged from widespread urbanisation is not the only base for new opportunities. The more difficult task of defining policy to fit emergent change is what will eventually have to be tackled.

At present we have a complex problem made more difficult by old perceptions of need. National economic policy is depressing demand, although the well off home seekers and new industrial and leisure developments continue to move out of the old areas. Developers are seeking new land, but supply is carefully controlled by the planners to avoid sporadic building and possible waste. The new investors, by choosing to go outside the old areas, require new services such as water supply and health, with a consequential smaller investment (some would say disinvestment) in the once proud industrial cities. Strict public expenditure controls cut back on such public works as housing improvements, further depressing the old areas and encouraging moves away or closures. The rating system as a means of local independence becomes more difficult in consequence.

The calls for greater public expenditure come from the need for jobs, services, rehabilitation, and new construction. Such an injection of activity is resisted by Mrs Thatcher's Government on the grounds of the need to restore the national economy. At the same time demands from the wealthy continue to grow strongly, for land no less than for any other commodity. If more public expenditure were accepted, this would accelerate demand both within and outside the old area. It will not be concentrated on inner cities and public housing, but will work its dynamic way into wider situations, for new employment will mean more money and a stimulus to house and car ownership.

Who should benefit then, and where? If the emphasis were to shift to the less well-off, through tax relief or subsidised jobs and homes, it would generate activity in the old areas some of which would lead to new demands for space in home, workshop, street, and car park. In this process waste land could be reclaimed and old property rehabilitated more quickly than at present, the eventual results being pleasanter environments and perhaps new demands. But to suggest that all this can be contained within our towns and cities ignores or denies two things. The first is that there is already a very strong demand outside, as is shown by the high price commanded by any land sold for development. The second is that this demand, while controlled, is controlled in ways which restrict choice; for example, agricultural interests control entry into farming, and planning controls development in the countryside. Young farmers and others with initiative are restricted. Yet the growth of small 'rural' firms of all kinds is taking place quietly, and on the whole, unobtrusively. Some people are exercising choice, but the strict controls on public expenditure and land are holding back development in certain ways while encouraging it in others. The deprived urban areas continue to go downhill, but the wealthy take over the wider landscapes for private use.

This combination of affairs shows the wish to meet wider needs, and the need to open up land use. In other words, it shows different priorities on expenditure and land. The means to this end is difficult, but not impossible. It requires new structures of taxation and subsidy, tenure, law and procedure. These are discussed in the last section of the following chapter in the light of more evidence as to what is happening on the land.

Chapter 5

The Case for Land Reform

In 1939, the fear of air attacks and the growing problems of the large cities led a Royal Commission, the Barlow Report, to conclude that the strategic, social, and economic disadvantages of the great industrial concentrations constituted serious handicaps to the nation's life and development. It went on to recommend the dispersal of industries and populations from these areas.[1] The environment for life and work, much of which was constituted in the nineteenth century, was seen to be unsuitable for the twentieth. Half a century later, researches into the decentralisation and decline of the old conurbations confirm both the view of the Royal Commission and the tendencies of the market. Dispersal on a grand scale now covers most of the lowlands of Britain.

At the other end of the spectrum, the Scott report, written shortly after that of the Royal Commission, was advocating the resuscitation of village and country life, not by an enforced dispersal of industry and unwilling town dwellers, but by improving living conditions and economic and social opportunities.[2] The Scott Committee was caught between a love of traditional rural life, coupled with a wish to protect agriculture, and a fear of urban intrusion. In this dilemma one dissenting member, the economist Professor Dennison, cut through to a recognition that agriculture and land were part of a modern industrial nation and must be treated on equal terms with the other parts, without special privileges. Today the force of Dennison's argument is much clearer, but at the same time the strong interests of the agricultural lobby, including the Ministry of Agriculture, Fisheries and Food and supported until recently by the Department of the Environment, have combined to industrialise and destroy much of what should have been conserved in rural England. In addition, the need to resuscitate village life, especially in the hill lands, has been forgotten, while the top end of the housing market has taken over many lowland villages, creating well protected enclaves and reducing opportunities for the less well off. In the light of market forces and social needs, this chapter considers where productive forces may lie in the future; what costs they may bring; and how current social and political influences are likely to increase tensions which will need reducing in new ways, including the use of land reform.

The process of planned decentralisation of factories during the war was continued and extended to houses and populations in the post-war years as a result of strong public support and political action in response to the need for reducing overcrowding in the cities. The costs of congestion were seen to be too high and it was thought that people ought to be given the opportunity to live and work in spacious new towns. Patrick Abercrombie's Greater London Plan stands as a grand design built firmly on the foundations of these beliefs, which had been expressed by Barlow, made possible by a new political will and legislation, and translated into reality by a vision which could see the metropolis in the context of the wider region. The plan opened up new choices for living outside the city, choices previously available only to the better off, but now open to a wider spectrum of the population by virtue of subsidised housing and newly located jobs.

Today, market forces continue the process of decentralisation for the better off, as planned movement slows down and the poor are left to the inner city or outer estates. Public attention remains focussed on the worst parts of the city, but it has now also turned to the countryside as the victim of industrialised and highly commercialised agriculture. Any future view of town and country seems bound to require a look both ways, in which the land can be seen as the platform for all life, with law and taxation evenly made and fairly distributed across the population.

The future balance of people across an urban countryside is a matter for conjecture. In agrarian economies, density is high in rural areas. In urbanising or developing countries, concentrations in cities grow at the expense of rural areas. In the advanced industrial countries, old cities lose populations to small towns and villages, albeit a fairly recent phenomenon. What is clear, however, is that while earlier rural populations were dependent upon agriculture, the new populations moving out of cities to once declining rural areas are dependent upon an urban economy, and even though the population levels of northern Europe are fairly static, the movement is likely to continue. Most new 'rural' dwellers adopt urban life-styles in the country, while farmers are 'urbanised' in the sense of using urban facilities.

Whatever the size of population, the economic and social conditions which determine the use of land continue to diversify, specialise, and develop. It is possible to see the process as one of perception, investment, development, and political encouragement or constraint. Earlier chapters have attempted to set out global conditions in which new perceptions are formed in the light of industrialisation, science, technology, political power, ecological influences, and social responses. No one can doubt that conditions for the future will imply new choices; amongst them, for the rich countries, will be the search for new life-styles outside the cities. This will be encouraged by the ecological influence and by a greater emphasis on the self-help or self-service dimensions in the light of growing productivity, telecommunications, and the increasing importance of the home for many workers. Although the towns and cities contain most of the population, people's travel and recreation cover much of the land, and a growing number live in close proximity to open country. The cities remain as centres of government, education, the arts and commerce; in other words, as centres of great importance. But to assume for them a continuing evolutionary role is also to accept a continuing urban influence outside, for productive forces are no longer as concentrated as they once were.

Productive Places

'Productive' has many meanings, but here the word is used to identify those places where the engines of the economy are found. Once these were mainly on the land and later in the mines and factories of an urbanising country. Today the locations are changing again, as service work and new skills replace the mass production workbench. These new workers are tied to neither land nor city factory, but seek out new places across the country, many of which are to do with the leisure and tourist industries, though others suggest the nurturing of more diverse possibilities.

In view of common but loose assumptions about production, industry, and services of all kinds, it is as well to be clear about both the nature of work and the reasons why it grows in particular places. The change from rural to urban locations and from agriculture to manufacturing is well enough known, but the changes from manufacture to service are less clear. In Chapter 4, the work of Jonathan Gershuny was discussed, and it is important to remember his distinction between service industries which contribute to manufacturing, those which are sold in the market as such (insurance, for example), those which are not marketed (of which education and health have grown large), and those which represent the final consumption of goods in the home.

As manufacturing has dispersed from the cities, so the services connected with it have also moved, although many high level services remain and new ones grow in the city. The traditional professional or financial sector also stays mainly in the city. These two are central to the production of wealth. The other two, welfare services and work in the home, are not considered productive in the same sense, and their locations follow patterns of population distribution.

The city has always been a place of dense employment, especially in trade, other services, and manufacturing. Whether it be for trade, commerce, or industry, the close proximity of people generates an interactive process in which the combined energies of mind, hand, and mechanical aid are far greater than the sum of the parts. The linkages among jobbers on the Bourse in Amsterdam, the manufacturers of jewellery in Birmingham, and the car and insurance companies in Le Mans, allow for easy accessibility of information and skills, creating productive markets of particular kinds. Every city has had its own successes and failures based on chance, design, and the impact of foreign or external influence. The literature on city growth is extensive, both historically and in contemporary research. From an economic or 'productive' standpoint, the success of a city depends upon what it can acquire and export. The export of goods and services brings in money to purchase other goods and services from outside. The particular combinations of commerce and industry in the so called pre-industrial cities were superseded by the age of Industrial Revolution in which coal, steam, factory, canal, and railway provided a mixture capable of more extensive production determined by the factors of markets for labour and consumption, new organisational and management capabilities, the availability of land and capital, and the costs of transport, power, and other services. All these gave rise to economies associated with concentration in cities, the so called external economies which accompanied economies of scale in units of production. The general environment of compact locations of skilled labour, the services of banks and the professions, and the ability to find land for expansion were all present.

In a competitive world of growing populations, it was inevitable that firms, markets, and products should expand and diversify. Thus scale and complexity increased, organisation became more complex, and so called diseconomies began to appear, both as costs of pollution and congestion and as rising rents and taxes on expensive plots of land. To escape these, and with the help firstly of railways and then of motor vehicles, electric power, and telecommunication, firms moved to green field sites at the peripheries of cities or along arterial roads. Other firms simply sprang into existence on these sites. In 1879 George Cadbury had moved his chocolate factory from an inner Birmingham canalside to green fields four miles out. In the 1930s the factories of London were 10 or 12 miles from the centre. Labour was still easily available, and new suburban services were provided. The new suburban developments attracted new investment, eventually leaving local authorities to deal with the growing costs of servicing an obsolescent inner environment which still has within it the nerve centre for providing essential services and skills to the now more widely distributed centres of production.

This dispersal continues today, and the evidence strongly supports the theory that lack of space in London and the old conurbations is the main problem as far as manufacture is concerned. The small towns and rural areas have gained the most: London and the conurbations have lost the most. The same trends are evident in North-West Europe and the USA. An example is seen in manufacturing employment, which in smallish UK county towns went up from 640,000 in 1959 to 825,000 in 1975, whereas in London it fell from 1,551,000 to 946,000 over the same period. The overall employment in manufacturing is now about equal between cities of

over 250,000 and smaller towns in rural areas. In the regions, East
Anglia was up by 70% over the same period, the North West down
by 25%.[3] The growth was south of a line from the Wash to the
Bristol Channel, but everywhere the so-called urban rural shift was
in evidence.

Today the size and congestion of large cities and conurbations
have reduced opportunities to expand on site, and green belts have
limited opportunities to move to the periphery. The research which
produced the figures quoted above also shows conclusively that it is
space on the ground and in buildings which is the critical factor. The
needs of modern machinery and transport require large land areas
and clear spaces, preferably at ground level. These are to be found
much more easily around small towns than in large cities. In a town
two miles in diameter, with a population of 15,000, only a very few
factories are constrained by land shortage. In Birmingham, 15-20
miles across and with a million people, 70% of factories are tightly
hemmed in. Growth is also stronger outside the older industrial
region. The reasons for this, in addition to land supply, are probably
to do with the levels of skill in both education and entrepreneurial
activity. Many newly skilled people live in the small towns, which
offer good living environments, and as local business connections
and land availability are easier in small towns, expansion is less of a
problem than in the large city.

Where towns are also associated with airports and motorways,
the conditions for growth are even greater, especially around Heathrow and the M4 west of London. Similar places occur throughout
Europe and North America, and, with associated services, provide
the heaviest concentrations of new style urbanised activity. These
include research establishments, often largely supported by government and military interest, as at Aldermaston and Harwell, and a
range of spin-off high-tech manufacturers and high level services,
where new knowledge and information play a big role. Proximity to
Heathrow is important not only for passengers, but for fast international servicing of high-technology systems. Staff are highly
skilled, and the necessary range of ordinary services — schools and
shops, for example — widens. Working populations lead the
demand for housing, recreation, and other land. In the UK the M4
corridor east and west of Reading is the centre of the new productive
Metropolis of London, leaving aside the City for the moment, and

smaller versions exist elsewhere in Britain, notably in the area north of Glasgow and Edinburgh, and to a lesser extent in South Lancashire. Cambridge is another advanced centre which is discussed later. In the USA the so-called Silicon Valley south of San Francisco is an earlier prototype of the new urban area. The infamous chip and the products which derive from space and other advanced research form one leading area of manufacture, but any consumer can see the extraordinary growth of new products in the shops. Some come from traditional industries, but many are quite new.

The old cities themselves must look to new roles as centres of production. The fact that they remain at the centre of the expanding regions is the best indication of their potential. Whatever the requirements of industry, research, and other services, the density of activity in city centres is still higher than anywhere else. Government, centres of learning, the arts, and entertainment remain, while tourism replaces manufacturing industry as a generator of services, albeit of a new kind. Although mass retailing moves out, specialised shops develop, while the traditional enjoyments of the market appear in conserved old areas such as Covent Garden in London and the Piece Hall in Halifax. Conservation itself produces a demand for specialised architectural and building skills, all part of the growing differentiation of functions in the advanced industrial countries.

The kinds of change which have occurred in industry are also occurring in the mass office developments which grew in the late 1950s and 60s. The procedure is not to move out lock, stock, and barrel, but rather to separate the parts so that routine tasks are moved into the suburbs and beyond, while high level functions remain near the centre. Thus, while overall employment falls, the concentration of skills remains. In the financial and trade centres, sensitivity of contact with world markets appears to require dense concentrations of human activity which can no more be replaced by telecommunications than can the church or the concert assembly. The market exchange shows no signs of going away, and the absence of a bourse in socialist countries does not mean that other forms of proximity, such as centralised bureaucracies, are not necessary for productive association.

The ties between the central city and its region, which together constitute the major locations for productive forces, are close, even though their area is expanding as a result of rapid communication.

The growing specialisation of the economy now demands a wider and more complex environment, and the demands are highest where the central places of global importance lie. The proximity of international airports to the centre is a good measure of its attractive power. The most productive places in the sense of activity at the leading edge of social and economic development are such world cities as Paris, New York, London, Tokyo, Moscow, and the growing capitals of developing countries. The resources are people and money in close proximity, and the demands are for ever better living, leisure, and working conditions.

The productivity of land is another consideration. Traditionally, we think of agriculture, but this industry is now closely associated with those of chemicals and energy, and will become one in which biotechnology plays a growing role. There are big questions hanging over agriculture as an extensive land use. Over-production, soil erosion, rising costs, falling incomes and over protection are factors of growing importance in the advanced industrial countries. In Europe and the USA too much money is paid out to farmers either to over-produce or, in the USA, not to produce at all. The enormous inputs of capital for fertilizers, energy, and equipment require ever larger scales of organisation, and while productivity per person employed may increase, productivity as an efficient and equitable use of valuable resources is going down: that is, the costs of such production outweigh other social and economic costs.[4]

The nature of agricultural productivity is ripe for re-assessment, not only for the reasons given, but also in relation to Third World activity where, for other reasons, agriculture is equally suspect as regards exploitation of cash crops for Western interests at the expense of a balanced home economy. But this is another, though related, story. As with modern industry, there is little doubt that production in the food industry will alter as a result of scientific research and development. Much of it has already largely dispensed with labour in the UK and USA, and both in Europe and the USA we continue to produce more while losing land to urban growth. In practice, really productive land is not as widespread as might appear from a flight over the countryside. Much apparently good agricultural land is cultivated only as a result of expensive subsidy (the Downs, for example), while other areas have much to do with gentrified landscapes and tax havens for investors. Alterations in subsidy and taxes would soon make clear where really efficient production was taking place.

Growing practices of intensive stock, poultry, and fish breeding also require less land, even if they also demand more resources of capital and revenue, but, as with manufacture, this process seems unlikely to stop unless a public movement rejects such treatment of animals. If it did, or if a movement towards more labour-intensive and traditional methods gathered enough strength, new issues would arise in relation to ownership, tax policies, development, and landscape. For the present, the point being made is that it is very unlikely that food production is going to require land to the extent that it has done. Of course, first-class soil and good climatic conditions, specialisation, and other factors will remain as vital considerations, but the ploughing up of thin soils on downlands is an absurdity. A more likely future pattern is an association of indust-rialised agriculture with the chemical and coal industries as part of the biotechnological future which is not too far away. Such an association is being explored by the European Commission.[5] In contrast, we are likely to see a growth of organic and small scale farming, with more small-holdings associated with other work.

The protection of agricultural land represents a social and polit-ical situation with deep cultural origins. The experience of war, the appeal to the emotions, the traditional connection between ruling powers and land ownership, all contribute to the maintenance of a veil which covers the real costs of modern industrial agriculture. Both globally and locally this veil is gone or growing thin, both for the labouring peoples of the Third World and for the prosperous leisured people of the rich countries. The facts are that truly productive agricultural places in the rich countries are shrinking in area, but becoming more intensive.

What we are witnessing is a growing demand on country areas by urban people. The economics of country land use will inevitably work in similar ways to those of urban areas. As the density of activity and demand goes up, rents and land values will increase, congestion will occur (as is now the case on the coasts and in national parks), and conflicts of interest will grow. The productivity of places will depend less on the amount of timber standing in the forest, or the quantity of gravel lying in the river valley, and more on the relation of these values to recreation, scientific needs, and other aspects of new activity and changing values. To what extent should the land support more people in fruitful employment, not traditionally as agricultural labourers and foresters, but as providers of services such as nature conservation, education, training and learning in the potentially rich environments everywhere, on both riverbank and hilltop? And with this as a start, what associated production could be developed?

Some production of a more traditional kind comes from efforts to develop local industries. In the UK, the Development Commission (established in 1909 to aid rural developments) has recently spread its wings by building over a thousand small factories, and it is also providing combined house/workshop buildings. The Commission works alongside the Council for Small Industries in Rural Areas (COSIRA), while Scotland has its strong Highlands and Islands Development Board, and both Scotland and Wales have their own Development Agencies. Some of these new rural industries are specialised in their own right, exporting or linked to bigger firms at home. At a more intense and sophisticated level, the small towns and villages of Cambridgeshire have become an integral part of a high-tech complex in which the electronic industry of the City, with the University, plays a major role. But whether high or low-tech, craft or leisure, the density of productive forces will increase as ease of communications and access to know-how combine with opportunities to live in pleasanter surroundings. The self-service economy portrayed by Gershuny and discussed in Chapter 4 is another part of the productive process which is growing fast. Here it is the home which counts, and as demands grow, the housing market is likely to extend its search for new kinds of environment outside town and city, a search in which land may play as large a part as the dwelling.

The example of Cambridge brings us back to the growing regions of East Anglia, its neighbour the East Midlands, and the other southern regions. The gains in manufacture are gains of firms which are still growing, not static or declining as in the cities. The flowering is strong and unlikely to die. On the contrary, historical evidence suggests that the present distribution of growth in small towns and once rural areas provides a pattern which will expand to create major areas of productivity in the next century. Even in the less prosperous regions the same pattern occurs. This is certainly true of lowland Britain, and growth is occurring in some of the hill lands.

So there will be a combination of agriculture, industry, recreation, and other extensive land uses, with a population which is neither rural nor urban in the old sense, but urban in the modern industrial sense, with a deep awareness and growing knowledge of ecological systems. It is the combination of urban growth and new values which will create the conditions for new approaches to live and work, conservation and design.

What of the currently less productive places? Like production, non-production is not easy to define. The gross domestic product excludes the most domestic activity of all, child rearing and house-work. If we add the do-it-yourself component (Gershuny's final production in the home argument), it is even higher. Neither are all the unemployed idle. Many work in the black economy (evading tax) or in the informal economy (exchanging services without exchanging money). It is as productive to mend a wall or repair a car as to build one. Many concentrations of this work are in the inner city and the old steel and mining towns and villages, although there are long and honourable traditions everywhere, especially in agriculture. In the USA one estimate made in the early 1970s put non-market activities at nearly half of GNP.[6] Lesser figures have been quoted for Italy and the UK. Even if all these are over-estimates, the amount of productive work is undoubtedly very large and has implications for the working of society which throws questions at conventional ways of measuring the nature and location of work and employment.

At the other end of the so called non-productive scale are those living on unearned income or pensions, all with money to spend and so creating a demand for goods and services: a retirement house, a garden, a boat, a video, or any other product with all its associated services. Indisputably, the ugliest concentrations of unproductive places are in the old industrial towns and cities, where unemployment in parts rises to 40% or 50% as a result of factory closures. There is nothing new about the phenomenon, but the only answers industrial society now offers are social security, a promised return to full employment, and further training. The first keeps the body alive, but does little for the soul; the second is at best a questionable assumption for the future; and the third, developing human potential, raises the question, 'Potential for what?' In the UK particularly, the massive expenditure on temporary work under the aegis of the Manpower Services Commission (MSC) is open to question, for without full employment it is only a temporary alleviation of alienation or boredom for a great many people. More recently, however, the MSC has encouraged genuine long term prospects in a range of imaginative ways. It is quite probable that a return to wider employment will be accompanied by shorter hours, more work-sharing and more leisure. In this situation jobs and homes are likely to be not only in the places which now hold an attraction, but also in those which need renewing and in others still to be developed.

Space and costs are crucial factors. It is one thing to live in a boxed flat while going out to work in office or factory, and quite another to do so without hope of leaving it for most of the day. There is no shed for a workshop, no land to dig, and not much space without or within the box to adapt for children's play, sport, and other necessities.

In these circumstances two requirements stand out. One is space in and attached to the home; the other is space nearby in which to be active. For millions there is at present no prospect of space in or attached to the home, and this fact provides a major reason for assuming that the demand for better housing will continue. There are some prospects for the use of nearby space, and many a redundant factory is now being converted to accommodate small workshops. On the new outer estates there is also land, generously provided as open space but now available for sport, food growing, and new workshops. All these situations rank small in wealth, but they are crucial for the unemployed, and they need developing. In the past, it was the perceived need to clear such places and rebuild which was the spur for planning and decentralisation. Today, it is the perceived need for employment which engages the efforts of local authorities and the Manpower Services Commission in establishing new small enterprises. If these stages are superseded by a combination of new social values which to some extent reject the protestant work ethic, embrace leisure more readily, are concerned about the natural environment, and look to self-service in the home, then new places productive of human wellbeing will have to be created, and they will not all be in the town. There is a case for relating the new places which are productive of wealth to new places which are productive of wellbeing, thus allowing more development into the country and bringing more space into the city.

The Costs of Development

If people and money are a necessary combination for getting something done, then land is the basis on which they do it, and development must be undertaken to fit the objective. The social capital which arises from past development, whether it be in skilled labour or city structure, is only too often a crumbling foundation on which to build anew, for social and material conditions are now different. Many people look for an environment which meets new needs and which, allowing for conservation, is neither *status quo* nor stagnation, but life renewed, often in another place.

There is a strong case for arguing that the major effort should be directed towards the places where people now live and work. At the same time, development implies new growth, new structure, and differentiation, in a social sense as well as in a biological sense. For people, new kinds of learning form the crux of successful development. Here we follow the implications of what has been said so far and apply them to questions of settlement. In doing this, some of the important questions of human development are deferred, but not forgotten.

The question of where to invest is not a simple one, nor is it necessarily one based on market conditions. Many a firm has developed because the wife preferred to live in a particular place. Whereas in the past the place was likely to be a town, mobility and the nature of work now widen the range of choices. Other conditions are also fluid: the cost of money, labour and land, the niceties of fashionable places, and the whims of local planners.

Whether it is more profitable (in the sense of both money and wellbeing) to build on green fields or rebuild on old land is the source of much dispute between developers, planners, and politicians. The economics of development is rarely clear cut, and very often the dispute is more about people's motives, hidden behind a list of figures, or an unequivocal stand for the retention of an old building or landscape. For present purposes, the intention is to throw a little light on the relative money costs of developing in town and countryside, not in an attempt to prove one or the other side, but as an illustration that choices are less constrained than present patterns might suggest.

From current market forces and planning applications, we know that there is a strong demand for development in, for example, Cotswold villages or the London green belt, where currently there are proposals to build a new town of so called 'villages' at Tillingham Hall. From research in the 1960s carried out when new towns and urban renewal were major items of discussion, it was shown that homes at the edges of towns were almost half as cheap as those in new towns 100 miles away. This was because new towns had to provide all services such as water and central shops, whereas those services already existed in the old towns. Houses built on cleared central sites were even cheaper than those at the edges, but once flats of five storeys or more were constructed, costs rose above those of the new town house.[7] Building high is expensive, and it was only feasible as a consequence of heavy subsidies. On the whole, it has proved to be an unnecessary and unwanted form of development in England. On the other hand, the 'social capital' of investment in services and buildings of all kinds makes it cheaper to build in an old settlement than to start a new town. Why, then, are new towns built, and why is pressure applied to build new 'villages' in green belts? Because it is not possible to provide an equivalent environment in the old city, and peripheral expansion in cities is frowned on.

The research mentioned above, and some recent work from the USA[8], demonstrated that the cost of services decreases as density goes up, but not at very high densities, where maintenance begins to add new burdens to cost. However, costs of land and services were small compared with those for house or flat construction. Today, land shortages and planning controls have pushed prices up in pressure areas such as the South East to levels which make it nearly impossible to provide cheap houses. Nevertheless, savings on services and land can be made if densities are raised, and so tight development is commonly advocated. To look at the market and its control in another way: if permission to build were easily available, land costs would fall, cheaper houses would be built and more decentralisation would take place. Some would argue that this would boost the construction industry and, consequently, the economy, but it would also raise service costs. There are also the costs of congestion, which have been well documented.[9] The constraints on industrial expansion have already been noted, and traffic is another obvious problem. Noise, lack of open space, and the servicing of an environment under pressure create further costs. In other words, there is often a good case, as Barlow advocated, for dispersing. Of course, it is still cheaper to provide water and electricity in dense urban development, but as social choice and the costs of congestion have shown, the country is prepared to stand the extra costs of lower densities. Other factors, such as energy for transport and heating, indicate that it is by no means conclusive that dense development is cheaper or more socially desirable.[10]

A classic document of the early part of the century which was influential in promoting suburban housing was *Nothing Gained by Overcrowding*, written by one of the founders of the town planning movement, Raymond Unwin.[11] Unwin showed by simple calculation that it was cheaper in land and road costs to build at low suburban densities than to construct the currently accepted terraces of town development. This was before the car was common and when most journeys to work were by foot, tram, or train. Agricultural land was cheap, the Council for the Preservation of Rural England did not exist, and the fears for land lay with the agricultural rather than the urban community.

Today, motor transport, telecommunication, and recreation loosen the bonds of existing centres, and the agricultural lobby is suspect. But there are other costs to consider. Schools, shops, hospitals, and other services can be supported only by fairly large populations, or so the theory goes. In practice, supermarket shopping has moved to the edges and the countryside in the USA, France, and elsewhere. Although it has been partially resisted in the UK, the pressures continue. Recently, fourteen applications for stores and hypermarkets near the M42 south of Birmingham were considered at two planning inquiries, but only one was approved. The speculation in land for potential uses around London's M25 is coming to boiling point, and the Tourist Boards have long been advocating more hotels near motorway junctions. Once established, new uses provide new employment, giving rise to demands for new services such as schools and hospitals. As we have seen, one result is less investment in the cities. Many new enterprises of all kinds are consequently being established by the market in rural areas.

The accumulation of all these developments cannot be ignored. The search for space, cheaper land, lower rates, and a good environment is not greatly constrained by the costs of transport, water, and

electric power. 'Nothing gained by overcrowding' is clearly a
message well taken by those with the capital to develop, for they
know the demand is there. It is those without the capital who have
problems.

The economic costs of dispersed developments are not an over-
riding problem for developers, as is obvious from the urban rural
drift of population and employment discussed in the previous
sections. But that the public has to stand some of these costs through
the provision of services is often inequitable and poses large questions about who pays and who benefits; these will be discussed later.
In the meantime, the nuclei of new habitats are there already,
although which will develop and which remain small it is very
difficult to tell. The economic costs are only one factor; planning
policy is another, and social and political pressures make a third, to
be considered later in this chapter. No one can deny the attempts of
planning to tip the balance in favour of existing urban areas. What is
doubtful is the effectiveness of the effort. After the war, urban
renewal was supported by heavy subsidies on land and public
housing, only to fail through social reaction against widespread
redevelopment. This was a period in which heavy costs were incurred
for the sake of public wellbeing by the replacement of appalling
slums, the provision of open space, and the reduction of traffic
congestion. There followed a phase of rehabilitation, with the
transfer of capital from new to improved housing, in itself an
arguable economic benefit, but fitting the mood of a people fed up
with bulldozers and demolitions.[12] In practice, a great deal of the
money was taken up by the better-off in the process of gentrification
and grants to owner occupiers.

Since the recession, public expenditure on housing has declined
steeply, although in this phase planning policy has put a new
emphasis on economic investment in our often obsolescent urban
areas. In practice, this policy has failed to stop a continued movement outwards, if necessary beyond the green belt, taking new
investment in services with it. While most of this has gone to small
towns, there has been a steady, if slow, addition to villages and areas
already containing scattered or ribbon development. The 'infilling'
here is cheap, for roads and services already exist. This pattern of
ribboning is centuries old and not by any means killed by planning.
From earlier days to the fast-growing new world cities, the linear

form has an attraction, one once formally adopted by planners in proposed 'linear' cities, but never quite achieved for other reasons such as land ownership, lack of momentum and capital, and the alternative merits of clustering. A modern but rather horrific example can be seen along the highway from Istanbul towards Ismalia: two and a half million people hemmed between the sea of Marmara and the inland hills in an eighty-kilometre-long ribbon. At the Bosphorous end, near the old city, some residential land has now been redeveloped five times since the war: a clear illustration of the force of rapid population growth on land values for the sale and rent of housing.

There is a broad relationship between population density, distance from a city centre, and land values. The further away from the centre, the lower the density and land value. While this obviously is the case, say, for Edinburgh and the Highlands, it is much less so for the lowlands of England and other largely urbanised areas. Some of the newer development at the edge of the city, for example, is denser than in areas nearer the centre, while land values in attractive market towns may be higher than in the city nearby. In poor inner city areas, values fall to very low levels as a result of high redevelopment costs, a poor environment, and, often, political opposition as well. Of course, commercial centres have the highest land values (and, in England, low populations), but with modern road transport, high land values are spread more evenly than they used to be. Everywhere local factors cause wide variations. An acre of inner city housing land might sell for a few thousand pounds; another in a small town for quarter of a million. Similarly, agricultural land at motorway intersections will fetch very high prices compared to similar land a few miles away.

It has long been argued that the profits to be had from the ownership of land, a God-given commodity, so to speak, should accrue to people as a whole, not just to the owner, particularly as those profits usually result from circumstances due more to social development as a whole than to the efforts of the owner. Since 1945 three attempts have been made to collect this betterment, as it is called. All have been made by Labour governments, and all have failed as a result of political change to a Conservative government. At root lies the conflict between personal motivation for gain and social tendencies towards fair rewards for community effort. In practice, there has been a slow trend in favour of public interest over private gain in the market economies, but little indication that radical change will occur. Far seeing local authorities have always been able to play the market for the benefit of the community, two notable examples being the advance public acquisition of land for development around Stockholm and the acquisition in the nineteenth century of outlying areas around Boston, USA, to form a city park system. Many authorities now own large areas within their boundaries.

Most European countries impose a tax on new development, and in Europe and the USA it is becoming more common for a developer to contribute towards the provision of such requirements as open spaces and community centres, the so called planning gain. In other words, individual contracts and agreements replace 'across the board' attempts to collect payments. It may well be that such individually assessed means of securing community benefit are better fitted to a mixed economy, a climate of negotiation, and a recognition of the growing variety and complexity of situations.

The argument about gain is complex, for it is in part based on recent economic analysis of the distribution of surplus value from goods and services arising from land exchange and development in a market economy. The owner, the developer, the planning or other controlling body, all contribute to a process of bargaining which eventually determines private and public benefits. In many cases this requires more than discussion of a plot or two. It may involve a much larger area including transport, other services, and the impacts of development on nearby users.[13]

The question of social costs which result from public policies is also difficult, but two studies well illustrate the problem: one for urban and one for remoter rural areas. The first comes from an exhaustive analysis of recent changes in the patterns of development in England and of the effects of planning policies, which see the containment of urban areas as important in the prevention of 'urban sprawl', the taking of agricultural land, and the spoiling of the countryside. Indeed, the study is called *The Containment of Urban England*.[14] The containment idea is an old one, but as part of postwar town and country planning it has its roots in a combination of three factors. The first is opposition to uncontrolled ribbon development and the scatter of houses, cafes, petrol stations, and other buildings. The second is the decline of agricultural fortunes and the need to reconstruct a healthy agriculture. The third is found in planning ideas about new towns, for which Letchworth and Welwyn Garden City provided living models. As a result of these factors, post-war policy emphasised support for agriculture, the prevention of scattered development, the creation of new towns, and the expansion of existing small towns. Green belts were part of the exercise. Three effects of all this were summarised in the analysis as follows.

Firstly, the monopoly control of land use by planning had succeeded in containing urban areas and raising their densities. Secondly, the suburbanisation of housing had been encouraged, because the decentralisation of work places, shopping, and other facilities had been discouraged. In other words, central work and services, with journeys from the suburbs, were favoured, in opposition to the market forces which, for example, seek to move shopping out of the large town centre, as in the USA. The third effect was to inflate land values and raise the cost of housing. Thus, only the better off could afford to buy in attractive places, creating, in the words of the authors, 'a new form of publicly sanctioned, publicly subsidised apartheid', in which the gainers were the wealthy and the losers the poor.

The social policy of containment fell unfairly, and the well-heeled were able to rest behind an approved veil of 'public interest' in the form of green belts and countryside protection. The more obvious social cost of heavy subsidies to lowland farmers, and an absence of concern by the Ministry of Agriculture, has been the loss of large parts of a cultural and scientific heritage. Because this is taking place before the eyes of those wealthier people who have benefited from planning policies, moves for a change now have considerably more political weight and, with growing pollution and the loss of wildlife, have gone rapidly up the political agenda.

The public costs of the prevention of pollution are heavy, but possible to face. The costs in loss of heritage are immeasurable, and the policies which encourage it make for despair. For example, the owners of unproductive wet lands or moorland have been able to obtain large capital sums for drainage or ploughing, or large amounts of money as compensation. This is in complete contrast to the case of the owners of urban areas who can be prevented from developing land and who are paid no compensation. This injustice is a social cost attributable to the powerful lobby of the National Farmers Union, the Ministry of Agriculture, the Country Land Owners Association, and the associated fertiliser, energy, food, and other industrial interests.

On the other hand, like the urban poor, the small hill farmer suffers. A recent publication makes clear the half-hearted attempts of government to help the remoter rural areas — 'the less favoured areas', in EEC parlance.[15] Government has favoured intensive capital investment for production; this encourages ranching and other large-scale operations, reduces employment and therefore population and services, and can lead to the destruction of the historic heritage: for example, through the neglect of stone walls. To this can be added the effects of second homes and expensively restored retirement homes, which result in the loss of cheap housing for local inhabitants. The problem is also present on mainland Europe, but the West German, French, and Italian governments interpret EEC policy differently, being more in favour of small farmers and community interests. The political weight of small farmers in these countries is still strong. In the UK it is weak and much less visible than the problem of the inner city, although deprivation is as severe for one family as the next. It is not simply a question of money availability as a whole, or even of EEC policy, although the NFU and many MPs and MEPs will say it is. It is a question of how the very large subsidies are distributed and how the directives from Brussels are interpreted.

The inner city poor and the small farmers may seem far apart in the problems which they face from the reduction of opportunities, but they are connected in the sense that land policies work against them both, however the interpretations may be couched. Both groups are, to some extent, left from past structures of agricultural and urban industrial employment; they are not productive in a contemporary sense; and their locations are starved of money for improvement.

It is doubtful whether the local economy will of itself provide relief for these groups. It is more likely that social costs will have to be met in one way or another. For farmers, it would certainly be possible to combine a restructured support system with the recreation economy, and so improve their situation. And there are always likely to be takers for small farms as a first step on the ladder. For inner city residents the problem is more acute, for skills are often non-existent or redundant, and the environment offers few prospects. Development here is likely to be measured more in training and positive support for self-help, aided by outside skills. These measures are due to be discussed in the following chapters.

The relationships between the economy, social need, and the use of land are not easy to establish, but it appears that current economic forces are not well matched by land planning policies, and that some social injustices arise in consequence. One key is the relationship of land to economic performance; others, the nature of control over land, the maintenance of healthy life, and the distribution of land wealth. Economic theory excludes an analysis of the role of land in production. This is not because land is not acknowledged as a central factor of production, but because it does not enter into the calculations made to assess economic performance. For example, investment in land and property, and its costs relative to alternative investments, are not assessed.

The Henry George argument has been referred to earlier and has been put forcefully by Fred Harrison in his book *The Power in the Land*. Its essence is that if the costs and availability of land were eased, new development would be generated, the construction industry would gather strength to meet undoubted demands, and this would lead to stimulus for further production. The reasons for high land prices are attributed to speculative land investment and the over support of land and property interests by the banks and other financial institutions, at the cost of investment elsewhere. Dealings in property provide a means of avoiding tax, as in exemptions from rates and capital transfer tax on agricultural land, quite apart from the subsidies added. Neither President Reagan nor Mrs Thatcher offer a challenge to land speculators and hence, in Harrison's view, risk not only the economy but also the validity of claims for market efficiency and its philosophy.

Territories and Rights

Given the wars and philosophies which have sprung from conflicts over territory and rights, it is not surprising that land use planning should be so controversial and so bound up with questions of

property, individual freedoms, and public control. Political economy, and economics itself, cannot escape the problems of private
property and the public interest, and, as we have seen, not all East
European socialist countries outlaw private property, while many in
the West increase control over it. It is also as well to remember that
property and enfranchisement have been closely related throughout
history, and that a property owning democracy must face new issues
about wealth, territorial rights, and social control.

The political philosophies of Bentham and the Mills accompanied the practical realisation that new laws were required to deal
with the urban problems of nineteenth century industrial Britain.
New concepts of public interest were linked to questions of sanitation, housing, public transport, open spaces, and all the rapidly
developing needs of a new society. For essential requirements,
powers of compulsory purchase were given to local authorities, and
during the late nineteenth and early twentieth centuries land reform
became a major political issue. The whole question of land ownership and its registration, land taxes, town planning controls, compensation, new towns, and the recouping of benefit for community
betterment was exhaustively discussed and written about. In all
areas except those of land registration and betterment, new principles of public control were accepted.[16]

A major step, accepted by all parties, was taken during the last
war, when legislation was passed to control all new development,
with no automatic right to compensation if it was refused. A
significant part of the law was the definition of development to
exclude such changes as agricultural drainage. The three post-war
Labour attempts to collect betterment all failed, and the development land tax, one used in common with many European countries,
was abolished in 1985.

The past century or more has undoubtedly seen a move away from
private to public interests in one sense, although this move has been
accompanied by a great increase in owner occupation of dwellings
and farms. It is pertinent to remember again Lord Milner's words
when the Liberal land movement was strong: 'There is no bulwark
to communism at all equal to that provided by a large number of
small property owners and especially small owners of land'. In this
situation, it could be argued that private interests have increased
rather than diminished. Another movement has been the use of

planning inquiries to discuss issues of national concern and so open up debates about airports, roads, and nuclear power stations which go far beyond questions of property and local public interest, merging with wider questions of human rights, morality, and the general direction of society. In this way, changes in land use have provided a forum for public discussion about social and economic issues, while at the same time planning is used by property owners to protect their interests through a combination of political authority and planning practice. The whole issue of public interest and private rights is thus confused and difficult to disentangle.

Patrick McAuslan has argued that there are three ideologies of planning law: the property interest, the public interest, and participation in democracy.[17] He points to the history of property relations and the practice of the courts, arguing that procedures are still very much in favour of property interests. The owners of land and property tend to be favoured in the long tradition of rights accorded to them, and undoubtedly the old procedures of inquiry into development plans were swamped by private interests.

But the public interest is equally suspect of bias when expressed in the bureaucratic terms of government and public authority. In the post-war period, it was too easy for planning authorities to forget the iniquities of the system as they affected the individual, and, in the name of public interest, the bulldozer cleared away too many homes with too little compensation, and too many small firms perished through insufficient compensation to maintain a future existence. The Franks Report of 1957 was set up to consider the working of such administrative procedures as the holding of an inquiry or hearing, in particular for the compulsory purchase of land. The outcome gave individuals access to the arguments of public authorities prior to Inquiries and, as such, was a blow for freedom, although it is also true that it helped property interests to regain some power. What Franks did, however, was to open up the question of participation, the third ideology, for it emphasised the public right to join in the arguments about matters of public planning.

Following Franks came the Skeffington Report on public participation, but it was noticeably a report about consultation rather than political participation.[18] However, there is no doubt that the climate for decision-taking has been radically changed, with the

replacement of old development plan inquiry procedures by the
broader (and less property related) examinations in public, which
have helped to widen the debate. More recently still, decisions over
the Channel Tunnel or the re-development of the London Docklands
have been taken without any public inquiry.

In practice, there are some other dimensions to the problem.
These are the private use of public interest; the question of planning
values held by professionals; the political control of territories; and
the influence of the European Community. An illustration is
provided by the general acceptance that it is in the public interest to
protect the countryside. Some of this protection is clearly national in
character and need: protection of the national parks, for example,
and of sites of special scientific interest, which are now in the public
eye. Past cases, such as that of the Cow Green Reservoir site in
Teesdale and the Dungeness nuclear power station, were the precur-
sors of the much wider current concern. Other cases are more
doubtfully of public interest. For example, a proposed power station
near Nottingham finished up on its site as a result not so much of
intrinsic merits as of private pressures.[19] But the debate was at least a
public issue. So have been the inquiries into the siting problem of the
London Airports, where the interests of residents around each
proposed site was clearly visible, and those with the most clout could
put up the strongest arguments. This raises questions about fairness,
questions which also arise when a public authority and all its
resources oppose small or disparate groups, as was the case with the
inquiry into the Sizewell nuclear power station.

There are also questions of development in green belts and in
countryside of landscape value. Here, private interest in the form of
local councils or individual participators can invoke the public
interest to protect home environments from intrusion by new
housing or other development. Of course, there is a public interest in
the protection of the countryside, but there is also a public interest in
promoting the economy and releasing enough land to keep down the
cost of housing. None of this is to suggest Machiavellian tendencies
on the part of special interests, but to show that distinctions between
private and public interest are far from clear, and that it is possible
for public arguments about green belts to be used for private
purposes of protecting house values and unspoiled views.

A more obvious category is that of outright political conflict such as occurred in many of the classic battles which were fought out in the post-war period. In these, the cities, often labour controlled, wanted overspill land in the surrounding Conservative shires to house their overcrowded populations. Manchester and Birmingham conducted long battles with Cheshire and Worcestershire cum-Warwickshire over proposals to re-house city dwellers. Here, the property and public interests took the shape of the better off and the less well-off sectors of society, but with green belt planning advocates and agricultural interests playing a large part in the argument. These local conflicts could be resolved only by national decisions in which the balance of judgement depended on an ability to meet a real problem of housing need one way or another, either by allowing territorial expansion by the big city, by new town programmes, or through the use of high flats and high population densities.

On the one hand planning depended upon a set of measurements: how many people and houses? On the other hand it depended on a set of values relating to green belts, agriculture, and countryside protection. Public interest was the dominant ideology, and it rested on calculations of slum clearance, the building of tall flats, and the inevitable need to house a growing population. As the latter need disappeared, the failure of redevelopment policies raised questions which undermined the legitimacy of much planning, while the use of improvement grants switched attention back to private owners and away from public housing.[20]

One other dimension of the problem needs mentioning, one which began in the USA and then moved to Europe. In the USA, the long tradition of private property rights and growing public concern about the environment gave birth to legislation in 1967 which required all government agencies to prepare environmental impact assessments to show the effect of major public proposals such as reservoirs and interstate highways. Proposals could be argued in court, and the public interest could be protected in the event of inadequate consideration of harmful effects.

The idea was taken up in several European countries and worked on by the EEC, with opposition from Whitehall, which claimed that the British planning system had no need of such safeguards. Whether right or wrong, the point is that directives coming from Brussels will change the context of British planning law, giving new opportunities for pressure groups to question proposals. Clashes over major

developments are likely to be seen in a wider context, with participation and evidence from further afield by experts called in from
other countries, as has been the case at the inquiries into nuclear
plant proposals at Sellafield and Sizewell. Other European influences will arise. In a recent case, an appeal was made to the European
Convention of Human Rights by a house owner who claimed a
breach of those rights. The house was adjacent to a runway at
Gatwick airport, and a motorway had been built nearby. Consistent
refusals to allow for a change of use led to the appeal. After
acceptance of the appeal by the Convention, the owner was offered a
sum of money by the UK government.

The principles of fairness and justice seem likely to be invoked
ever more frequently on matters to do with the environment,
whether these are concerned with houses, industry, nuclear power or
agriculture. This is perhaps especially true of agriculture, which is
not subject to planning controls and which in different ways across
Europe is a very sensitive issue. The all-pervasive nature of industrialisation and pollution transfers many questions from towns and
cities to the land at large, questions which require a new view of
property interests and people's rights.

Several questions arise from the consideration of territorial rights.
First, how can growing private home ownership be reconciled with
the public interest? Second, what procedures should be used, given
the problems about planning inquiries or their absence and the new
role of environmental impact assessments? And third, how can city
and shire conflicts of interest be resolved? To these can be added the
point about planning gain raised in the previous section. Together
with these immediate points, we should bear in mind the historical
trends of growing public interests; changing forms of government;
and the growth of negotiation and bargaining as processes of
reconciling differences.

The problem of private and public interests was faced in the
nineteenth century, when emerging modern local government and
the courts established the concept of public interest over the interests
of obstructive private land owners. Today, there are obstructive
home owners who readily object to almost anything. This problem
relates to the second: what are procedures for resolving conflicts? As
far as the home owner is concerned, the local inquiry is still a useful
means for resolving conflicts. But where bigger issues are raised, such

as those related to motorways, new towns, and nuclear power stations, the real problem lies, on the one hand, in the need to open out the debate, which can be an inordinately tedious business, and, on the other, in the wish to enforce strict rules to limit discussion, which can be seen as unfair and secretive. In the context of human rights, freedom of information, changing values, and struggles for power, it is the outcome of these issues which will eventually determine procedures. There is a clear need for open information as well as the application of rules and time limits.

If we now link these questions to city/shire conflicts and planning gain, it is possible to identify similar problems which are to do with fairness towards those locked in deprived old city areas and those looking for, and able to afford, green belt or wider pastures; and fairness between profits over the sale of land, or its development, and betterment for the community which has provided, say, the permission and the opportunity to tap into public services. The old city/country question is unlikely to be resolved without some strategic policy at regional level, and this is discussed in the next chapter.

Gain has its opposite in compensation. If a private owner suffers a new colliery on his doorstep, he should be adequately compensated. At present he is not, but the Channel Tunnel experience suggests a change in this situation. What we then begin to see are local inquiries and local bargaining on gain or compensation (offered publicly or through the market) within a strategic framework in which open information is discussed, particularly on the media. None of this is necessarily simpler than before, but it is more open and fair. Two groups in particular face changes in the near future.

One is the farming community, and the other consists of the residents of such publicly protected environments as the village and the green belt. The farming community is well aware of new public demands for the maintenance of attractive landscape, the conservation of wildlife, and the protection of special areas. Work by the Countryside Commission, the Farming and Wildlife Advisory Groups, and such authorities as Hampshire and Hertfordshire is changing ideas about public access and conservation and moving towards a greater variety of uses and more voluntary collaboration. The ubiquitous car already invades the village, and public use of and access to green belt land increases. Private environment is less sacrosanct. While it is possible to move to quieter parts of the country, these are becoming fewer. The territories are more public, and knowledge of the system of making decisions and appeals, as well as the use of expertise, is spreading. The conflicts which arise from this cannot all be dealt with by law and regulation, even though the courts will perhaps play a larger part than of late in contributing to public policy in many fields of planning and environment. Discussion, persuasion, and agreement must be used to resolve many of the issues, as is now happening. The idea of planning control over agriculture is less in tune with the times than the exercise of persuasion, whether it be by an authority or by the force of public opinion and the influence of the media.

No doubt central and local authorities will continue to attempt to act responsibly and efficiently in the public interest, but at present the attempts are confused as a result of fast changing social and economic circumstances. Central control and local determination are less simple than they were. The flow of funds from and into administrative territories is less straightforward, both through the workings of international finance and through the informal economy. If central government is not to become autocratic, and if local government is to maintain an accountable democratic role, new relationships which make clearer the rights of territorial communities will have to be hammered out, not only on the basis of provision of services such as education, essential as they may be, but also on the basis of local resources and new initiatives, backed by new law, and with taxes and expenditure geared not only to the traditions of macro-economics with the old sectors of capital and labour, but also to new ways in which spatial impacts on communities are better understood. In all this, agriculture will have to adapt to new kinds of social control, direction and, of course, help.

The ecological influence, from both global and local standpoints, is a growing factor in restraining economic exploitation. The trend from exploitation to conservation reduces conflict, while waste and scars can be repaired by new processes. There is a long way to go, but it becomes increasingly difficult to exploit and develop without fully accounting for the results. Planning inquiries, environmental impact analysis, and media interest expose any suspect culprit to view. To be sure, there are wily and secretive moves, but

Machiavellian techniques can be applied by ordinary groups of people as well as by princes.

Finally, there are values. Chapter 1 mentioned some of the post-materialist values of the advanced industrial countries, in which concepts of freedom and roots were important. It is not difficult to relate these to choices, rights, and territories, to decentralisation (one of the preferred freedoms), ecology, and conservation. All these matters are subjects of intense discussion, and even if not seen as post-materialist, represent new items on the political agenda. The ferment of interest is unlikely to subside in the light of such radical changes as the feminist movement and the ethical questions surrounding the development of biotechnology.

The complex of relationships between power and land is a new one. Old political philosophies assumed that land, property, and the right to govern were a natural order of things. Enfranchisement and socialism reacted to landed interests by dismantling them, and advocating public ownership of the new (industrial) means of production. But prosperity, consumerism, security, and the new science of ecology have all changed old political attitudes. In their place we have a structure in which wealth is widely distributed, although over a steep hierarchy, and perceptions of property do not necessarily mean the ownership of more than a small flat in the city, well furnished, and perhaps with a minor master's painting on the wall to replace the hearth, once so significant.

Nevertheless, land and houses are still important symbols of wealth and lifestyles, representing a growing proportion of fixed capital assets, and accommodating more and more varied activities than ever before. In the hierarchy, the pressures to extend these privileges to everyone provide a major motivation for self and social development which is not confined to traditional settlement patterns except by views established in another age. The territorial conflicts which thus arise will continue and, with market forces on the one hand and nature on the other, will demand new approaches to land, whether through law or procedures, design, or aesthetics writ large in terms of new feelings for life.

Land Reform

The case for land reform rests on six main arguments. Firstly, there is a mismatch between new economic structures and land policies which are based on past conditions. It is not easy to prove that the mismatch is positively harming the economy, but there is no doubt that while technological and economic factors are changing fast, land policy is not. There is a prima facie case for suggesting that changes in land policy are necessary.

Secondly, tight planning containment policies have led to very high land prices in favoured areas of new development, and generally raised house prices to levels prohibitive to the less well off. This situation in turn contributes to problems of stagnation in the inner city and also results in some over development in small towns. At the same time government is dismantling the old planning system in response to the need to adapt more effectively to the winds of change. However, the approach is piecemeal and without strategic thought about the future of our land and planning law.

Thirdly, heavily subsidised agriculture has increased land prices, thus harmfully encouraging investment from banks, pension funds, and other financial institutions. Although this situation is now changing, and there is concern over the future of farm land, no effective new policy has yet been evolved. The structure of farming in the UK may have to be considerably changed to meet the needs of an also changing European agricultural policy. In particular, the issue of small and large farms in relation to new economic forces and social preferences will have to be taken on board.

Arising from the second and third arguments are questions not only of difficulties for the economy but of unfairness in society. Social obligation is either misdirected or missing, and this is the fourth reason for land reform.

Fifthly, it is important to recognise the general failure of perception in relation to town and country, and a tendency to treat land questions unevenly and overlook the fact that in an urbanised society all land is there for fair, efficient, and life-sustaining purposes. The uneven treatment of urban and rural development and the illogicality of taxation policies call for a new look at philosophies of property rights and controls. In the UK we have a situation of strong land demands, limited supply, high prices, and basic questions as to whether the economy, conservation, or fair individual opportunities are being helped. At the same time there should be no question of letting the market rip. New methods of development and public control are required.

Finally, there is the need for some new vision from the design professions. Engineering, architecture, and landscape architecture are no different from economics or law when it comes to re-thinking the needs of a country. Traditional approaches are not enough, especially those deriving from private patronage with insufficient regard to the evolving public interest. New attitudes to land imply new requirements in its design.

Opposition to change comes from a number of sources. Although it is the least obvious in many ways, perhaps the most fundamental is national conservatism and slow adaptability to new realities. The myth of the yeoman farmer husbanding a beautiful landscape, and of the inevitable perpetuation of a bounteous nature made secure by farmers, ought now to be thoroughly blown, but it is not; instead it supports selfish protectionist policies without a public perception of the reality of an urban world, in which true conservation demands changes in the economics of land use and the values attached to conservation. We can identify this as cultural lag.

There are, of course, deeply held beliefs about the countryside which cannot be ignored, and these raise passionate objections to change like those made by poor John Clare at the time of the Parliamentary enclosures, and later by Wordsworth and Ruskin. In the face of industrialised forces with their disregard for atavistic feelings, beauty and solitude, the opposition is not only natural but necessary. The Green movement is a vital corrective, both intuitively and scientifically, as are attempts to replace wasteful industrial processes with more appropriate technologies. What cannot be gainsaid is the evolution of social development which includes the requirements of future populations and their use of modern medicine, education, cars, and television. The issue then is a choice between the selfish refusal to consider changes in the countryside, and the possibility of new ideas for its better use.

More obvious opposition comes from the powerful agricultural landowning lobby, itself strongly rooted in the old culture. The costs of support for this industry outweigh that of any other, and behind the projected 'good food' front lie the ranks of support industries in chemical fertilisers, pesticides, energy, biotechnology and others. With the growing weight of evidence against this specially protected group, it seems likely that changes will come in any case, either as a result of world market forces or as a reaction to the damage already done, or as a response to the inequitable support of rich farmers at the expense of poor farmers. Here again the beliefs can be respected, but some are to do with a rural era long past, and its associated values, many of which are no longer appropriate to a new society. At the same time, taxpayers' money is being used in ways which are neither in the public interest nor in the best interests of farmers themselves.

A third group of resisters lies in the ranks of some town and country planners, albeit supported by the 'public interest' side of agriculture, and by new territorial magnates with private interests in opposing change. Planners are nearly all employed by local authorities to serve local interests, but their own ideology of countryside protection comes from an age of sporadic development between the wars which threatened to spoil the appearance of large areas of land. It was natural that public opinion should legitimise new planning controls, but in doing so it hardened old perceptions of town and country as separated entities, rather than as one land to be used in the best interests of the nation as a whole. In doing this, planners and the public have contributed to the problems of inner cities by a strict application of green belt policies. The private use of public policy to maintain the *status quo* adds to resistance in this sector.

The cities themselves, having provided the major force behind the dispersal of urban populations across the land, would not apparently take to further loss of population enthusiastically. They now have a justified self-interest in concentrating attention on their own plight and attempting to secure more investment. At the same time, if there were to be more freedom to develop outside, this would stimulate the market, the construction industry, and the economy, and allow more change to take place within the city on the principle which allowed planned decentralisation to occur after the war, in conjunction with slum clearance and redevelopment. That the latter development often turned out to be a failure was in part due to an attempt to keep too many people in the old places, and to encourage the process by paying too much (with government subsidy) for land

and high flats. Thus, even if they are not actual protagonists of land reform (as they were 100 years ago), the cities might ponder the advantages of a deal which would combine land reform with lower city land values and more aid for city services.

The final group of interests can be found in the financial institutions and rich people who invest in land, for profit or pleasure or, as Henry George suggested, as a long term hedge against all kinds of future possibilities which might increase values. The opposition from these sources is not always easily identifiable, but it is very real. These are powerful lobbies, motivated as much by their strong mixture of public, private, and cultural interests as by active opposition on their own behalf. They can always appeal to the public through another front, thereby appearing neutral and of general benefit. The onus is thus on others to take up arms against them. Some would argue that the present system of town and country planning, public inquiries, and voluntary change in farming and conservation practices are providing, or will provide, adequate means for change. If so, why has Mrs Thatcher's Government established enterprise zones and urban development corporations, approved a Channel Tunnel regardless of public discussion, and attempted to force through changes in the Metropolitan green belt to allow for new housing? If this is all to do with market forces, it is also to do with individual enterprise and life-styles.

The present economic situation and the piecemeal government reform of planning law are leading towards a confused situation in which the post-war foundations of land policy are fast eroding. Almost certainly the old laws and regulations need radical re-structuring. However, what the government is doing is amending planning law at the same time as trying to deal with the control of local government expenditure, the grant and rates base, and its own macro-economy policy. For example, the Local Government, Planning and Land Act 1980 is a messy mixture of aspects of rating, grants, capital expenditure of local authorities, and planning provisions for setting up urban corporations and enterprise zones. A new bill is now being proposed for continuing this kind of approach which is at best an *ad hoc* response to rapid change, and at worst a confused attempt to introduce new strategies for development and its control.

At the same time, the future of agriculture is under question,

becoming vulnerable to public opinion and political action through
its destruction of wildlife and our historical heritage. Short term
changes in world markets — especially from the USA grain pro-
ducers — or in the European community agricultural policy seem
likely, but do not solve the central problem of refuting the rural
myth of agriculture as steward and protector of the land. At the
centre of interest in maintaining the *status quo* in the UK are the still
strong landed aristocracy, royal landowners, and the hosts of the
NFU and the Country Landowners Association (CLA).

The case against current policies of agricultural support has been
put strongly enough in economic terms.[21] Undoubtedly, the biggest
beneficiaries of public subsidy are the largest owners amongst the
groups just listed. As support is cut, certain steps follow. Initially,
incomes and land prices fall, encouraging different ideas for investment and change of use. The wildlife parks were one early example
of such change as a result of heavy tax burdens and other costs. The
leisure and tourist industries are growing and are heavy investors in
land. Another change could be the intensification of some agricultural production — as in the pig and poultry industries — and the
return of grasslands now wrongly used for corn. Equally, the concern
over meat production costs in terms of land, energy, health, and
Third World malnutrition might force different changes in land use.
The taxation system would determine whether woodland might be
encouraged in association with leisure activity. A third area would
be in building development: large scale planned 'villages' which
would only benefit a few owners (unless market transactions were
replaced by some form of national scheme in which profits would be
more widely spread), as well as more scattered small scale development.

The EEC is currently discussing new strategies for agriculture.
Naturally, in the light of French and Italian interests, there is a heavy
emphasis on the small family farm as a way of life not to be
discarded. But there is also a view for integrating agriculture more
closely into the general economy, through links either with tourism
and recreation or with small scale industry. A more positive policy
than the one which now operates through such agencies as the
Tourist Boards, the Development Commission, or the Council for
Small Industries in Rural Areas (COSIRA), might find favour with
present landed interests for a number of reasons. Firstly, it would

bring in some capital from land sales. Secondly, it would provide possibilities for part-time labour, either to replace machinery (which research suggests would lead to an improvement in current production), or in relation to the growth of organic farming practices. Thirdly, it would provide some new employment and population. Eventually, such development could bring with it new services. But perhaps, most importantly, it would give opportunities for new work and life-styles outside urban boundaries.

This new life would be more closely integrated with farming than either present commuter village life or tourist activity. The reduction in subsidies to large farms would also provide opportunities for diverting more to small farmers and increasing provision for the creation of smaller units from large estates. This should not be envisaged as a general attempt to break up big units or as a regression from advanced practices. Rather, it would result from a restructuring of the industry so that, as in other industries, opportunities to start on the ladder would be created as a result of land use and tax policies. High-tech farms would remain as industrialised landscapes in areas best suited to food production by soil, or in proximity to chemical complexes. The possibilities of such bio-technical developments in Europe have been explored by the Community. But let us not pretend that they are to do with old-style landscapes and farm practices. Like industry, they would be rated, and indeed, rates for agricultural land would be one way to help restructuring for the general benefit, working against large gentrified holdings and in favour of smaller intensively worked units.

A consequence of such changes would be genuine demands for land by those who wished to work on it, rather than speculative investment by financial institutions. The economic basis would be sounder and more equitable. Land values would be related to density of employment and land use, and, while still high in a small country, they would help to decrease values in the over congested cities, thus allowing for more open space where it is needed.

Attitudes are changing, but need to change faster. Since the last war it has been a cardinal principle of town and country planning that all development should be contained within towns and villages. The isolated house is abhorred, unless it is a farm. Even on farms, planners have striven to prevent the erection of another house or two for fear of a return to the 1930s' ribboning or scatter. The reasons given for this policy are either landscape protection or the costs of services such as sewerage, electricity, and school buses. At the same time, planners and others have deplored the de-population of rural areas and the closure of schools, shops, and local services. Given that the economics of location change for countryside, as well as for city and town development, why cannot we accept the demand for what might be called 'non-contained', or more picturesquely, 'home-land' settlement? To be sure, there will still have to be planning, but it should start without prejudice and with a consideration of some of the new situations already discussed in this chapter. There would also be a need for new procedures of control and management over land in order to prevent ugly and unneighbourly intrusions.

The previous section referred to public inquiries, planning gain, and compensation. To changing practice can be added the experience of forty years of post-war planning, countryside access, and management agreements, not only in national parks and the Forestry Commission lands, but also, more recently, in the urban fringes. A major problem in planning has been that although conditions attached to planning permission can be imposed, it is not always easy to enforce them; consider, for example, a chalk extracting company which goes bankrupt and leaves a scar on the landscape.

In Chapter 1 reference was made to the work of Jürgen Habermas and his thesis of social development from a recent stage of traditional conventions of law and order to a post-conventional contractual legal orientation, with a universal ethical principle orientation. In the discussion about gain, the contractual argument is also raised, and if we add to these ideas notions of decentralisation and government of new kinds, it is possible to envisage new procedures for handling conflicts previously dealt with through planning inquiries.

Three categories of issue may serve to illustrate a new situation: those relating to single large owners, those relating to a large number of owners, and those which affect whole cities or regions. Under the present post-war laws governing national parks and the countryside, agreements can be made with owners to establish access for walking and other recreation. It would be possible to combine such agreements with planning permissions in order to secure not only 'gain' but also such matters as maintenance and, if uses became obsolete, reclamation. The traditions of leasehold estates provide historic examples of control through contract.

More recently, the 'Span' developments in London and elsewhere did the same for smaller new housing developments where open space and paintwork had to be maintained for the benefit of all. Another example is the ironstone restoration in Northamptonshire, where agreed financial contributions from public and private sources enabled restoration to take place immediately following extraction. A very recent example is the establishment in Shetland of a community fund from oil revenues in order to compensate areas which are disturbed. It is the principle of a contractual obligation which counts.

For larger areas with many owners, it is obvious that local authority policies would be required, and the new government proposals for simplified planning zones are a step in the right direction. These would allow for such policies as industrial or housing development. Their success would depend not only on the legal basis for agreement, but also on prior public discussion; in other words, on genuine community activity and commitment through democratic local government.

For the third category we can look at current arguments about the availability of housing land in cities and green belts. Here a game is played out by developers and planners on the land chessboard, but without sufficient common knowledge of the rules which govern the complex motivations of landowners, potential house owners, developers, and those with responsibilities for the public interest. These last include, of course, the public; and on the nature of the real issues the public is badly informed by experts, politicians, and the media. In particular the dynamics and flows of transactions are not well researched, and the secrecy of transactions can lead to deception and outrage, as was shown by the arguments in Cabinet and Parliament over the future of Westland Helicopters and British Leyland. Unless government is seen to be open and fair, it will lose credibility or become dictatorial in its attempts at imposition. Of course, *realpolitik* and Machiavelli will always be around, but the public players are becoming more aware.

The hard questions of compensation and fair taxation (including rates), are all tied up with this problem. A special difficulty is the imbalance between inner and outer city, between building land and agricultural land, leading to over development and, in the case of subsidised and non-rated gentrified agriculture, to under development. These problems need taking together in relation either to rates or to local income tax, a situation discussed in the Layfield Report on Local Government Finance, and now under government review again.[22] The basic requirements of an economic and constitutional framework which were considered by Layfield were accountability, fairness between individuals and between areas, consumption and investment, efficiency, stability, flexibility, and comprehensibility.

No firm conclusions came of Layfield's considerations. The Report argues that the system which has developed is confused by conflicting objectives. It is often regressive. Its purpose and its sense of fairness are often difficult to determine. It does not reach a single conclusion but opts for either central or local government as taking the main responsibility. Two dissenting voices lay more emphasis on a half-way house and a causation running from political aims and policies to financial mechanisms.

Obsolete political attempts to relate problems of population distribution, needs, and equitable taxation policies through the rate support grant system (which the government auditors have effectively damned), would give way to simpler measures of re-distribution.[23] Some such centralised re-distributions are necessary, but more importantly decentralisation of power and resources in political ways is the best way of developing local capabilities. This question is discussed later, but the essence is to change from macro-economic and expenditure patterns to a balance of regionally based determinations. Post-war regional policy, like the rate support grant, has been centrally determined via regional administration. A better future would lie in constitutional and administrative decentralisation.

An important part of post-war new town and housing policy was the subsidy in support of public housing. This has virtually gone, but we cannot expect to have the positive encouragement of new countryside development without a new look at help for the less well off. There are limits to owner occupation as a solution. Council or new town housing early style is not an answer. Instead, a device for providing publicly supported purchase or rental, within the fabric of private or housing association development, would avoid the stigma of 'estates'. The policy is commonplace in the United States and could certainly be used here.

Another aid to the less well off could come from using long experience in Europe to find ways in which co-operative housing is financed and encouraged. These should include land purchase and enable both inner city and country authorities to help the less well off. Trusts are a growing way of running various industrial and housing ventures. These too, given new policy and taxation law, could help to achieve the balance of private and publicly aided development in the process of decentralisation, combined with the regeneration of old areas.

The extent of population movement is uncertain, but if the economy and social preference indicate the need there is no reason why the over concentration of cities should not continue to provide a reservoir of demand. As the nation became 'urbanised' in the mid-nineteenth century, so it can now spread its urban population back on to the land. A clear political choice about the relative roles of town and country land, without the prejudice of old perceptions or vested interests, is now required.

Such a policy could appear as an unpopular 'destruction of the countryside' policy, unless properly presented in relation to principles of social justice and a fair distribution not only of wealth but also of a decent environment. The former requires new and more sophisticated relationships between centre and region in the context of devolved powers, and better financial procedures within the overall context of a mixed economy and social market. The latter requires a change from simple planning control procedures to a more sophisticated process of management in order to develop a new environment appropriate to the age. The whole process is not only in need of new thought, but involves a wide range of interacting factors. At present a sense of direction and necessary strategy could be hammered out at a political level, but a broader view of the system as a whole is required.

Many changes are, in one sense, taking place already in the true British fashion of slow compromise. The problem is that in the process social stress is growing, as perceived inequalities of opportunities, income, and environment increase. A bold political programme is required, which does not compromise too willingly, but which recognises relationships between people and their work, the use of money and the use of land. At present new programmes such as those of the Liberal and SDP parties largely ignore the land question, except in terms of conservation, and do not recognise its force for economic and social development of a new kind. Land may not seem to be at the centre of the problems of economic and social obligations in England, but it certainly is for our earth as a whole, and the question of a new harmony of economics, ecology, and life opportunities will assert itself as a broad human need, to be worked out in detail for each region of the globe.

Beyond all this, the vision of a new country could be portrayed for a nation sorely in need of new opportunities. The traditional love of nature and the wider understanding of conservation and ecology, the common democracy of interest in our land and the need to break with the past, which is already finding expression in new concepts of work and wellbeing: these are the cornerstones of a new structure. Civic and scenic heritage must be respected, but at the same time new lands for all life can be designed if people wish to open their eyes and consider the realities. The job may not be easy, but it is possible.

As with so many other specialisations today, some fundamental re-assessment of purpose is required in the design professions. A recognition of the context in which new development takes place today will require a shift of attitudes comparable to that which took place in the eighteenth century during the landscape movement. It would appear that the public interest will demand some wider vision of new structures and landscapes in the context of economic change, ecological necessity, and public participation. In their turn, the individuals who make up the public must widen their view beyond their own little plots or large farms to the need for dealing with land in a more socially responsible way. We can no longer afford property owning attitudes which ignore future realities.

PART 3
A FAIRER COUNTRY

Chapter 6

System

The process of changing a complex society is full of hazards: political, economic, and personal. The approaches vary according to national cultures, political philosophies and other deeply rooted habits and values, and, as was suggested in Part 1, nations must adapt in the light of their own issues and characteristics.

The uncertainty and speed of events demand not only quick individual responses, but also coherent institutional views across the board, whether at home or internationally. This requires some systematic approach and objective view, if horizons are to be seen and approached. Past centuries in the western world have relied for progress on science, technology, new liberties, and rational discussion. The development of knowledge has been ever more specialised, but in the past decade or two those who are most aware, whether in the growing economies of South East Asia, on the boards of multinational companies, in developing research or academic disciplines, or as individuals, have realised the need for new interdisciplinary and participatory skills of management, planning, and communication in the anticipation of events which are uncertain and not therefore forecastable. In this process, scenarios, brainstorming, lateral thinking, gaming, and futures studies all play their part.

Such books as *Small is Beautiful* evoke a response because they are in harmony with the need to escape from the trenches of the past. The ability to take in the central aspects of wide change, and to consider everyday actions accordingly, is not yet common; but it is growing and, if we are to survive and prosper, this new way of looking at the world will have to spread fairly quickly. What follows is firstly an attempt to look at the kind of system which is emerging and the need to devise new models; and

161

secondly an application of this to England's past, present, and future.

Towards New Models

We should not be afraid of models and systems, even though they often appear to be related to the space race or biotechnology, rather than to human wellbeing. Our own brains are prime modellers of ideas, observations, and actions, and only their better use is likely to get us out of our present mess. This is easier said than done, but a glance at history shows how constructs have changed the social system.

The achievement of the Greeks was their ability to escape from the primitive mental world of magic into one of new philosophical and scientific thought. Only hard conceptual thinking allowed the foundations of western civilisation to be newly laid and treasured long enough for the Renaissance to flourish. The Renaissance itself asserted new visions, soon to be joined to the world of modern science (a system of beliefs in itself), via the observations and discoveries of Copernicus, Galileo, Newton, and their followers.

The powerful effects of this changed system of thought were combined with the Reformation of Christian thought and action, which allowed for economic development freed from old constraints. The enlightenment added rational belief to science, and a wide acceptance in the ultimate values of material progress, values which still provide the basis for the modern world. But worlds constructed by man can collapse under the impact of new observation and thought, as they did under the influence of Galileo and Darwin, so creating a new system for subsequent action. A nuclear, technological, and biological age now provides the new basis for thought in the advanced industrial countries, while old religions and other cultural differences cause conflicts across the world.

The characteristics of such changes are not uniform in either components or pace of development. Nevertheless they can be assembled into a framework which accommodates them one way or another. All the great changes listed above have come about through the eventual common recognition and acceptance of the values of new ideas. The ideas must be sufficiently robust to withstand siege, undermining and assault, as those mentioned above have done.

During the process great conflicts inevitably ensue and can prove fatal. The challenge of today is to avoid the ultimate conflict. One of the more recent aspects of social evolution has been an understanding of the dynamics of open systems. In an era of the ascendancy of science, the laws of the physical world system provided a dynamic understanding of motion, gravity, heat and light. But this achievement itself can now be seen as a less open system than that which encompasses social evolution as well. The dynamic of modern society is largely one of economic growth, but for some the moral imperatives of religion or the new moral imperatives of life provide alternative visions.

Successful open systems exhibit a capacity for balanced change, as does the natural world, though even here the shocks of volcano and cyclone greatly disturb the system. Social evolution has now reached a critical point in its demands on the natural world, and some balance must be found, if civilisation is to develop. Open systems need open minds; closed minds are closed systems, unable to cope with change, and they lie at the root of the problems of rapid adaptability, so that social learning is not matched to technological advance. This is the crucial issue.

The biological basis of humanity contains genetic factors which relate to social evolution: for example, the defence of life and security, the acquisition and holding of territory, and the ethical side of man as a social animal. Speech, along with social and technological development, created a set of world communities with very different characteristics. In the rush of West European industrialisation, the conflicts between value systems were and are often extreme, old beliefs having to be reconciled with the desire for higher material standards of living. War, as is now the case in the Middle East, often results. The addition of population growth, more wealth, and the demands on resources and space create today's insecure conditions, while biotechnology conjures up visions of contorted beings in such fearsome landscapes as those conceived by Hieronymous Bosch.

The process of system change can be seen as one of social adaptability to a continually changing environment. The motor and its controls must be newly sketched out, sometimes in small adaptive ways, but occasionally on the scale of the work of Newton, Rousseau, Darwin, and Marx. New perceptions are the first stage in such major shifts of thought, whether they be perceptions of religion, of science, or of society. Following these comes a broad and long stage of learning and its diffusion through word and message, once slow, now fast. Theoretical explanation and a predictive capability were the strengths of the physical sciences, once linked to the power of God, then to understanding of the natural laws. No such laws were found by Rousseau or Marx, but what they did was to lay the basis for new attempts at social order. Acceptance of such work is one base for revolution or for slower evolution, and in the adaptive process law and regulation are changed in accordance with social demands. Salutary shocks are part of the experience which leads to change: flood, war, pollution, or some other destructive force.

Past eras of change have spanned centuries of knowledge and learning, with sufficient diffusion to achieve wide support. The speed of modern events is very much greater, and the time-span for learning and adaptability much shorter. It is a few minutes, or even seconds, to midnight, and it is dark. No great vision appears, but shafts of light are thrown at our consciousness, and their number is increasing. They will not come from established positions within the old structure, but from scattered phenomena and people, until new leaders can model the pattern and secure a political following.

As many have pointed out, the picture will not necessarily emerge from pursuing existing specialist fields of knowledge. It is more likely to assume a form, perhaps impressionistic, perhaps scientific like ecology or biochemistry, but in any case one which can allow specialist fields to merge and so develop anew. The cross-fertilisation of science with the social arts will be necessary if any harmony is to be achieved.

This is in no way to suggest some deterministic outcome for society, but to show that a greater awareness of possible outcomes is necessary. It is for this reason that the soft technologies of scenario building, gaming and future studies have emerged, together with more sophisticated monitoring of change both in the environment and in money supply. These join the more exploratory far-fetched theories of science fiction and the other explorations of fiction to provide new insights and arguments for increasing perceptions.

At the end of Chapter 1 a summary of the major factors in current social evolution was attempted. The first factor is the accelerating speed of events; the second, the emergence of new values in regard to life as a whole, in the nature of politics and views of justice, and in the philosophies and beliefs underlying science and economics. Third is the continued march of science and technology on a road which may change its direction but is unlikely to be closed. Fourth is the need to reconcile high level economic activity with a domestic economy; fifth, the conflicts of central and local power; and sixth, the importance of systems thinking and effective adaptation to fast change.

These are broad matters open to much argument, but they contain some of the crucial issues and choices which societies must make. In England justice and freedoms are high on the agenda, as are economics and questions of decentralisation. The political environment has changed radically from one of consensus to extremes and fragmentation. Society is now in rough rapids and a fast changing landscape.

Diagram 1, *The Changing Demands on Environment*, illustrates the major social, economic, and physical components which make demands on the environment and suggests differences between the old and new order of things. If we agree about the development of democratic freedoms; if we want cars and telephones, as well as a life in some harmony with nature, then changes are necessary. The diagram shows at the top the present demands which are made on the environment. Population numbers are obviously crucial, but levels of wealth, consumption, and technology — transport, for example — are the factors which continue to increase the demand.

The top right-hand box represents the natural world.

The boxes opposite the Old Economic and Social Order represent the situation in which we now live. Left is the growing industrial world with, until recently, apparently endless space for expansion. The central box represents the cities and manufactures of the Industrial Revolution. The right-hand box represents a world of economic thought in which resources of land and air were, until recently, seen as limitless or freely exploitable; such 'free' goods were implicit in economic theory. At the bottom, The Emerging New Order suggests that growing wealth and the demands of an educated society will require participation in reconciling demands with the capital resources of the planet. These will have to be accommodated within a recognition of an urban society where the limits to

Diagram 1

THE CHANGING DEMANDS ON ENVIRONMENT

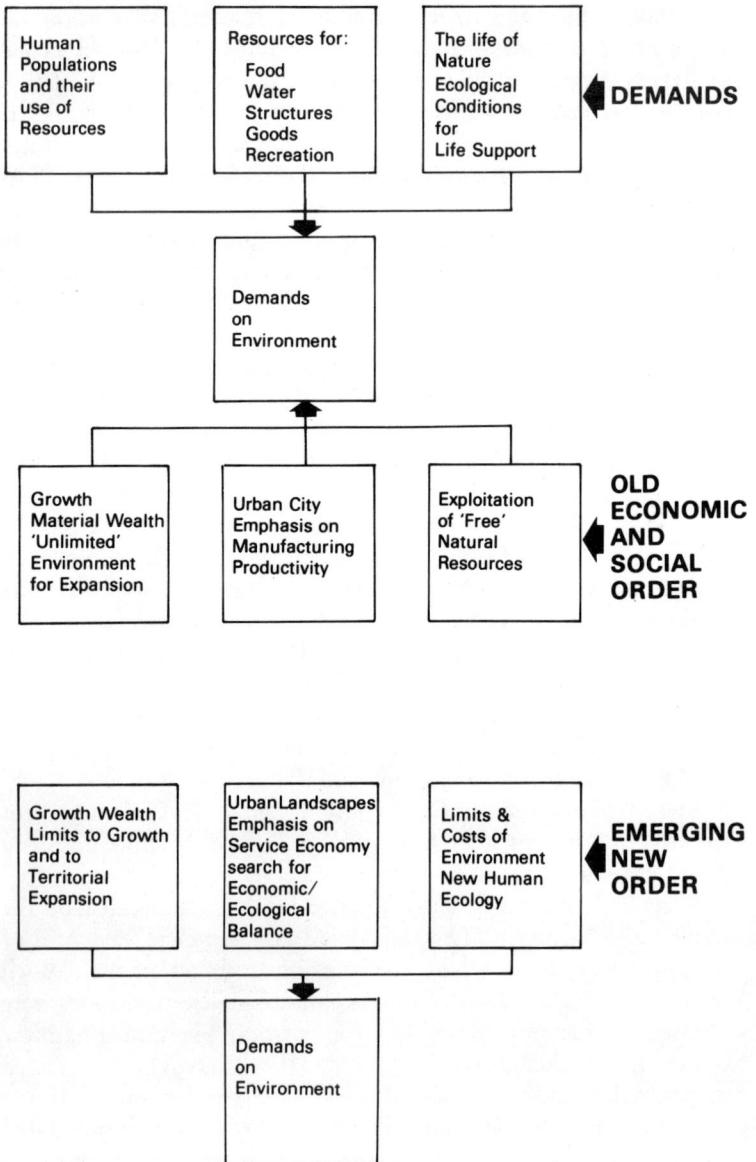

Human Populations and their use of Resources	Resources for: Food Water Structures Goods Recreation	The life of Nature Ecological Conditions for Life Support	**◄ DEMANDS**

Demands on Environment

Growth Material Wealth 'Unlimited' Environment for Expansion	Urban City Emphasis on Manufacturing Productivity	Exploitation of 'Free' Natural Resources	**OLD ECONOMIC AND SOCIAL ORDER**

Growth Wealth Limits to Growth and to Territorial Expansion	UrbanLandscapes Emphasis on Service Economy search for Economic/ Ecological Balance	Limits & Costs of Environment New Human Ecology	**◄ EMERGING NEW ORDER**

Demands on Environment

possession, acquisition, and growth (Fred Hirsch's 'Social Limits'), will relate to the demands for life in new ways. The central box suggests that urbanisation and the economy will need reconceptualising as they move into the age of services and information. Urbanisation as a world phenomenon will have to be designed and managed in tune with nature: the human ecology of the right-hand box.

For many, all this is self-evident. For others, a clear distinction between old and new orders may seem irrelevant or unnecessary. Those who favour the *status quo* will resist any change. Others, especially in England, will take a pragmatic and empirical step-by-step approach, of a kind which one American planner has suitably

Diagram 2

NINETEENTH CENTURY ENGLAND
IN URBAN TRANSITION

Environment

● Perceptions of an
  unlimited world

● Outset of global
  industrialisation

Land & Economy

● Age of science & technology
  applied to manufacturing innovation
  & products

● New structures of organisation &
  management for industrial production

● South north
  shift

● Learning to
  control impacts
  on environment

Social & Political

● From old values, landed
  wealth & privilege to
  scientific rationality,
  new wealth, and
  representative
  democracy

● Iron laws
  of the
  market

● Central local
  power shift

● Political reform &
  utilitarian philosophies

● Growing civil service &
  provision of public
  services

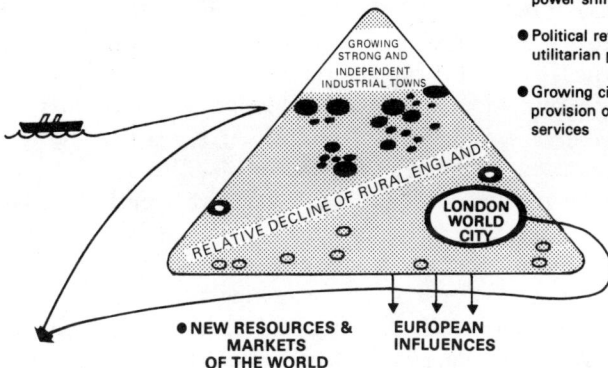

GROWING
STRONG AND
INDEPENDENT
INDUSTRIAL TOWNS

RELATIVE DECLINE OF RURAL ENGLAND

LONDON
WORLD
CITY

● NEW RESOURCES &
MARKETS
OF THE WORLD

EUROPEAN
INFLUENCES

termed 'disjointed incrementalism'. Well, if we are disjointed incrementalists, so be it. It is unlikely that Elizabeth I, Newton, or Darwin would have seen it like that. Steps must nevertheless be taken and the prospects ahead seen with some clarity. The changes implied by the choice of prospect will require strategy and tactics which include altering the machinery of government and law to fit the aims. Of course this is difficult.

The context in which the country has developed its environment, economy, society, and government is illustrated in Diagram 2. The triangle represents England in the late nineteenth century, amidst the growth of industrial urbanisation. Industrial power is moving to the North in a period of rapid population growth, utilisation of coal, and the application of science and technology to innovative manufactured products. New structures of government are coming into place, having moved from *laissez-faire* to the socially orientated political philosophy of utilitarianism. The wealth created from industry has superseded land wealth as the main source of revenue, while local taxes (mostly rates) allow for public expenditure on such utilities as water, sewerage, and street-lighting. Colonial expansion and investment grows, and sea trade prospers.

During the twentieth century the gradual increase in central government organisation and expenditure on education, housing and other services strengthened the dependency of local government on the state, until central grants exceeded 60% of local government expenditure in the early 1970s. In their development, government departments emerged as reflections of sectors of the economy or services; agriculture and housing are clear examples. So economic and financial statistics were collected to inform these special departments. Gross product and expenditure, imports, taxes, and wages provided the figures for national economists and treasurers to assess economic performance and prepare budgets. The period saw a large self-reinforcing development of centralised bureaucracies, while urban populations continued to grow.

Diagram 3 represents today's situation. Urban influences have spread across the English landscape, and the power of the old industrial cities is relatively less, whilst new, once rural, regions grow prosperous. The economy is increasingly concerned with the application of innovative scientific and technological processes, with the use of computer and telecommunications, and with the

Diagram 3

TWENTIETH CENTURY ENGLAND IN POST-URBAN TRANSITION

Environment
- Perceptions of limits
- Transnational global pollution
- Threats to life

Land & Economy
- Age of science & technology applied to services innovation & process
- Interlocking networks of organisation from global or local scales

Social & Political
- Conflict between dominant old order economic growth & nationalism & emerging new international order
- Adapting to conflict through participatory social exchange

- North, south shift
- Learning to conserve life & environment

- Learning to reconcile demands of wealth with fair distribution of resources & appropriate technology

ACCELERATING SPEED OF EVENTS

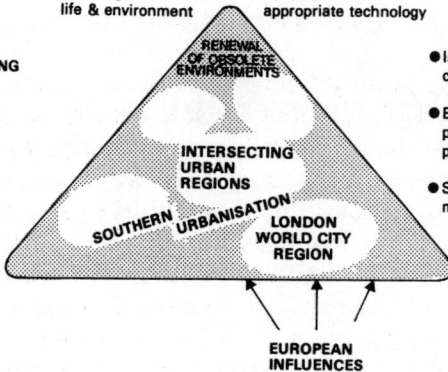

- Issues of international, central & local power
- Emergence of new political philosophies & political geography
- Search for a social market

RENEWAL OF OBSOLETE ENVIRONMENTS

INTERSECTING URBAN REGIONS

SOUTHERN URBANISATION

LONDON WORLD CITY REGION

EUROPEAN INFLUENCES

power of information. The scale of the economy removes control from localities to the distant headquarters of transnational and financial institutions unconcerned about local impacts. Central government has regained much power from the cities, and an obsolete local tax system (rates) has run into difficulties, both in the application of fair treatment to old and new areas alike and as a primary means of supporting local services. Greater centralisation exercises stronger control over departmental spending programmes, leaving a small caucus surrounding the Prime Minister and Chancellor of the Exchequer to determine priorities and amounts. It is the combination of autocratic power and unfair distribution of tax revenues which raises new issues and gives rise to searches for a better system of government.

The failure of the present model is the failure to delegate, to offer responsibility more widely down the line, to invest new capital wisely, and to treat populations equitably. The old forms, including trade unions which have neglected the wider view and concentrated on wages, do not fit the new life of a Britain compelled to rely more and more on its own resources and native wit. Central power will always remain. The question is: how will it be exercised under the influence of the mobilisation of democratic power at other levels? If autocratic and élitist rule is rejected, then forms which offer independence must be accepted, and as knowledge grows and becomes ever more accessible under the impact of telematics (computerised telecommunications), diffusion is likely to be wide.

The goals in the face of all this are truth, justice, fairness, moderation, and social accountability. To match issues and needs requires faster effective learning, which includes changes in the social culture, involving class and attitudes to industry. To resolve conflicts requires the development of new soft technologies, of management and of organisation, using the growth of psychological knowledge, new communications, and public awareness in order to develop the means. Of course, the root conflict over means and ends remains, but in the game of rapid learning it is to be hoped that ethical man will prevail over aggressive man from within his own nature and from his awareness of nature as a system of life.

Old Forms and New Life

The Charles Addams cartoon shows several caterpillars watching a butterfly attempting its first flight. Says one to another, 'you will never get me up in one of those things.'

Human institutions have so far failed to learn the lesson of changing life and form and are not yet in tune with nature's law, but the time will have to come. In looking for change it is the process of responding to the pressures of events which provides the evidence for possible future states. Thus pressures at the top of the international agenda are the threats of nuclear and trade wars within a rapacious and inequitable global system of nations, and the looming presence of ecological disaster. In facing these, people are conscious of the inheritance of aggression, acquisitiveness, injustice, and social responsibility.

The evidence of need for change is growing fast. The nuclear issue represents a madness in mankind (less womankind), which relates to an obsession with technology and acquisition. Through the military and national states it is linked to industry, finance, and trade wars, and to narrow theories of economics rooted, as religion has been and still is, in a past world.

The emerging responses of international movements provide the life which can create new forms of institution. The constraints are nationalism and such old sins as greed and envy. In all this the concepts and practices of economic growth are not at present contributing enough to world stability, while science could be pursued with a greater sense of purpose in the same direction. The working out of change, however, is a task for such individuals and groups as those who first opened up new horizons for science, economic growth, and social processes.

The shifting paradigm contains central zones of friction between the parts, especially between cultural values, wealth and poverty, economic development and environment. Within these zones new ideas and social activity strive to make clear the need for oil between the wheels. These impulses may come from individual change-agents linked to new international institutions (as in Oxfam and other non-governmental agencies), or from local activists at work in the yeast of a new form.

Nuclear threat is a problem for the great powers spurred by fear, unrest, and the patent waste of resources. The conflicts within economics, trade, and the environment present a different challenge. Common observation, reinforced by scientific evidence, has made it obvious to economic theorists and practitioners that systems based on old measures of capital and labour, with their assumption that the resources of the planet are free to be exploited by humanity, are no longer valid. From John Locke to Karl Marx the idea was held that the earth's resources were infinite and could be used accordingly by private individuals as well as by communities. This is no longer an acceptable premise, for one of its results has been to exclude consideration of the natural world from economic theory, which concentrates on money and labour. The concepts of the mode of production itself, together with theories of labour, consumerism, capitalism, and socialism do not accommodate any measures of the most important capital of all: our biosphere. In economic parlance there is no such thing as a free lunch, but until economists draw this lesson into their own theories and practices, the discipline will be destructive of human wellbeing.

The headlong rush of economic wealth and progress is already being retarded by a recognition that the free goods of nature are no longer 'free', and by the moral indignation aroused as a result of destruction and waste in an economy whose accounting takes little heed of the earth's capital, on which it depends, or of the effects of economic practices on the poor nations of the world.

One way or another political economic philosophies will have to face up to new ways of dealing with these realities. As populations and demands grow, so lands and their resources become relatively more scarce and valuable, and so costs rise. At present many of these costs fall on the poorer nations, who pay heavily in loans and face the necessity of growing cash crops for the rich nations; as has been said, the Third World has become the market garden for the rich. But the rich cannot escape from other aspects of the problem nearer home, as conflicts over the siting of a third London airport show. Here, too, there are limits to the exploitation of environment, albeit at the opposite end of the scale to that of the poor countries. The two are linked through the operation of the political beliefs and economies of industrial society, and it is industrial society which must change.

The starting point is life itself. To accept *Homo sapiens* as a biotic factor in the wider ecological system brings us face to face with one of the basic issues of our world. It makes us stand outside and see ourselves as a part, rather than the centre, of the system. This is something that the West had to do once before, when the astronomers put earth in its proper place in the solar system. The East has known better. In one western country at least the problem has been faced. In the Lower House of Parliament in the Netherlands, on the 11th December 1979, the then Minister of Public Health and Environmental Protection, Dr Ginjaar, rejected the anthropocentric approach of the Health Council. He advocated that policy must be moved towards the desired quality of environment to protect the health both of man and of plants and animals by maintaining ecological balance.[1]

In less formal terms this approach is growing within the scientific community and the population at large. It goes well beyond earlier recognition of the need to protect national parks and areas of scientific interest. At root it demands firstly a replacement of spendthrift and destructive industrial practrices which produce pollution (such as acid rain) on continental scales; secondly, their replacement by alternative technologies; and thirdly, some limitation on consumption of space and resources by the rich so that more is made available for the less well off and for life as a whole.

The change is already under way, but it will need to accelerate if there is to be much hope of success. The examples of the Netherlands, the Greens, and alternative economics are with us while traditional economics is moving away from concepts such as the gross national product, with its absurd inclusion of such 'products' as the costs of preventing pollution and its equally absurd exclusion of the value of domestic labour. Growing numbers of reputable economists are challenging the conventional wisdom, and for two years 'The Other Economic Summit' (TOES) in London has been discussing alternatives to the present international banking system with the aim of preventing the exploitation of Third World Countries and improving approaches to the problems of environment. It has also discussed the displacement of labour, the need for a social wage, new concepts of work, and new practices to replace the present chaotic systems of tax and security.

Economics is a means, not an end, and the critical problem is to re-define the political and social ends to include a recognition of values outside the market, particularly of less material needs which have been lost in the race for material consumption and the pace of technological development. Somehow new relationships must be forged between various levels of economic and human activity.

It is unrealistic to assume that large scale industrial development is going to be stopped, but on the other hand such industry is employing less labour, and if high productivity can meet much of the demand for goods, then people can engage in other pursuits, some on a more domestic scale. These may be of a conventional kind, including small and medium sized firms, but much will be new work at home and in local communities. So we shall have an economy of large scale high productivity firms with skilled labour in low numbers; and smaller firms and individual enterprises with skilled and semi-skilled labour in large numbers.

It need not be assumed that this dual economy will divide the rich from the poor. Rather it can be assumed that social obligations will determine reasonable maximum and minimum rewards within an inevitable hierarchy. What is more important is that the wealthy will not be allowed to exploit either the poor or the environment. This carries two implications. The first is that power, both political and in the form of resources, will need to be shared more fairly and be decentralised; the second that we shall have to learn to live with a requirement to match economic development with environmental conservation.

Pursuing the question of economics and environment first, we see that the long held disregard of the effects of development on the quality of our environment — the so-called 'economic externalities' — is now changing to a fuller recognition that this view of development is no longer tenable in the advanced industrial countries, and that these countries have a responsibility towards those still developing. This is a responsibility to assist in the creation of non-polluting industrial and urban development and also to conserve the vital natural resources of soil, water, plants, and animals.

Such policies as those based on 'the polluter pays' principle, as well as the policy of environmental impact assessment, are a start for the advanced countries. Together with conventions such as those of the United Nations, they enable the Mediterranean countries to conserve sea life. Many bilateral and multilateral agreements elsewhere, such as those relating to the Rhine and Danube, exert a similar influence. But the gap between industrial practice and the maintenance of a quality environment will take some decades to bridge. Production processes for cars and power stations are good examples: they vary across countries and must be slowly reconciled. Again, in the USA environmental groups and environmentally conscious States are profoundly affecting the pattern of coal mining and hence the nature of employment and the social structure. The interconnected character of industry makes the whole process slow and highly resistant to change.

The other problem within the economy is political, both internationally and internally, with the need to decentralise power from too much national control. It is the corporate state — the common interests of national governments, the military, and big business — which is the major reason for the continuation of the old economic system, and which above all is resulting in high unemployment, both in the growing Third World cities and in those which are declining in the West. More seriously, the centralising process makes a mockery of true democracy, especially in the UK, which is one of the most centralised in the so-called free world.[2]

Europe offers a test bed for the new order. Various nations of the Community continue to pursue political union as a goal, with the UK strongly opposed and insisting on a step-by-step approach to practical daily problems. Inherent philosophical differences are also political realities, but the secret for success lies in the ability to reconcile traditionally different ways of thought and genuine differences in culture, resources, and expectations. Fairness in trading practices is a crucial part of the British case for moving forward, and, if conceded, can bring a change of attitude to union, for there is nothing like money to keep people from raising a fuss.

This still leaves the problem of environment, which becomes ever more difficult in relation to the use of space for new development. For several millennia people have turned the natural landscapes into cultural ones, at first on the basis of small populations and later as an expression of the rapid growth of urbanisation. While population growth in the West has now slowed down, development continues across the continent as a result of wealth and technology. Future landscapes will continue to change.

Nineteenth and twentieth century urbanisation has created a pattern of cities spreading out into their surrounding countryside, towns, and villages; of green belts and country parks for recreation; of prairie cornlands on the sunnier, better lands; of major industrial plants with growing automation and less labour; and of connecting networks of roads, utilities, and air waves full of information. The present view of the landscape is a chrysalis from which we need to break out in the face of the natural demands of wildlife and human life. There is a need for a sustaining environment for all, a need to take the opportunity now presented with the development of new information systems not dependent upon over congested urban areas, and of food-producing industries no longer dependent upon extensive land surfaces owned by the few. Above all, the motivations for a great variety of life-styles should be leading us more quickly to the deliberation of new land policies.

The age of the relatively self-supporting city is now replaced by one of new and complicated relationships in political and financial control and power. During the past fifteen years UK central government has exercised increasing control over local authorities. Road programmes, housing grants, restrictions on capital expenditure, and now on rate levels, have one by one increased the power of the centre. The reasons presented are clear enough. The national economy has come under growing strain, and the levels of grant to local authorities were over 60% of their expenditure, allowing for easy spending on necessary but not always wealth producing, services. Local authority expenditure being approximately 25% of all public spending, it was necessary to cut back, in the interest of national economy, or so the argument has gone.

With such cuts in expenditure and rate funds comes an erosion of power and discretion in local government and in other public agencies. This is exacerbated by privatisation or the selling off of profitable ventures to private interests. Thus we have the situation of an advanced democratic state eroding local democratic activity and relying on the market to provide the answers. At the same time unemployment is tolerated, and the less well off are supported by the use of oil and other revenues and taxes.

The Audit Commission has criticised central government's handling of the £9 billion in grants to English local authorities as ineffective and unfair, and in particular it points to the problem of achieving proper advance planning by local authorities in the light of rapidly changing central targets. The Commission blames the system for adding £1 billion to the local rates bill between 1981 and 1984.[3]

Those who argue that local spending must be controlled in the interests of the economy at large can be countered by the evidence of the USA experience, which makes no attempt to relate local authority expenditure levels to total public expenditure. Apart from the particular nature of the USA economy, it might also be deduced that state (or regional) funding and controls exert the requisite influence on economic affairs. Here and in Europe there is much to learn. More seriously, the continuing centrality of financial control, combined with the lack of accountability, is a sure road to the end of local democracy.

Whereas government must govern, in England, rather than in Wales or Scotland, it is not sensitive to regional and local needs. That the north begins at Watford is no joke: it seems to be what the village of Whitehall thinks.[4] It is deplorably the case that central government has a very poor perception of other regions. (Perhaps this accounted for the problems of Richard III when he came south, for he was by all accounts a good northerner). All major West-European governments, and indeed East-European countries also, have a level of regional government, as does Scotland. Except for the Conservatives, all the major UK political parties have proposals for some form of regional level of government. The argument is essentially a simple one: sensitivity to local needs, the ability to devote resources with some knowledge of local conditions, and the opportunity for learning and development which is implicit in the idea of democracy. It is a pity that the Mother of Parliaments cannot learn from the Mother of Democracy and the fifty United States, but without the dogma of the market.

The lower levels of government which exist in Europe are based on the historic power of urban and rural areas. All countries have undergone major structural changes in an attempt to fit the realities of a new world to the administration of government. The point to be grasped, however, is that administrative boundaries are not easily related to the workings of modern society, and what is needed is a clearer understanding of the relationships between geographic and administrative areas on the one hand, and of the dynamic of social and economic change on the other. New mechanisms can then be developed.[5]

At present, even a first class local government system is impotent in the face of the impact of the decisions of a transnational company to close a factory. The community affected has no redress in this situation, and new social structures and processes have not been developed to reduce friction. Redundancy pay and social security do not necessarily lead to new self-development, even if the environment is made easier for entrepreneurs.

Grass-roots political pressures at local and regional levels will demand the right to exercise choices of development, services, and life-styles. In no other way is it possible to see market development in tune with democracy. The linkages between large and small activities could be established through well articulated networks and new relationships, and the obligations of European and national bodies to provide funds and social mechanisms for deprived regions and localities will be a major incentive for coming to grips with financial problems in ways which reflect European as well as national priorities.

This is already partly the case with methods of determining the distribution of some of the Community's regional and social development funds. Both priorities and better methods for the effective use of funds within integrated social, economic, and environmental programmes are already there, with Naples and Belfast acting as major testing beds. The mutual learning is at present slow, but can gather speed, and a reformation of ideas and practices in Western Europe may be closer than we think, although no doubt difficult decades lie ahead. If the era of European war has gone, then the demands of nationalism are less important, while the new demands of technology and government in a common environment require a working out of new concepts for living together.

Democracy in Europe extends upwards to the European Parliament, but also downwards to parts of cities, where elected members join other representatives of the people to discuss political issues. This wider grass-root activity provides nurseries for experience in political action, and is joined by independent pressure groups such as Friends of the Earth, of which there are growing numbers, both public and private. Democracy has become a very different animal, the system of taxation and redistribution more complex, and much of the decision-making very far removed from democratic or parliamentary control.

The task of understanding the processes of international change and of meeting the threats to life and wellbeing is clearly enormous. National ideologies and competitiveness will continue to bring conflict. But an understanding of the jungle will build up if the holocaust is avoided, and new ideas and tools can be forged to provide growth where there is now disintegration. The system is not necessarily bad: it is what we make it. At the end of this book some of these issues are discussed again; but for the moment some of the practical questions in England will be discussed.

Chapter 7

Latticed Landscapes

Forming Urban Structures

The creation of forms comes about both through social and economic change, which is difficult to understand and control, and through conscious policies which aim to shape the direction of this change. The interaction between controlled and uncontrolled change lies at the heart of the problem of fitting life to structure and adapting structure to social evolution.

Today, after a long period of intrinsic belief in progress through science, technology, and material growth, humanity has reached a point which compels reflection about purpose and examination of the road taken so far. A major reason for this is the crumbling of the natural world in the face of technology, population, and economic growth, and military conflict. In this situation land occupies a central place as the habitat and support of man and all other life forms. The urbanising forces of the last two hundred years, after centuries of agricultural economy, have embedded in our perceptions a view of rural and urban life as two separate things. This view of the world is no longer tenable. It is time to use our knowledge to reform the urban landscape.

The relationship between intrinsic development of form and conscious design can be seen in two periods of urbanisation, which may be conveniently described as present urban and post-urban. Present urban includes the old cities which grew at their peripheries, and in which town planning sought to create order in layout and design. Design traditions were drawn from the past works of kings and princes.[1] The process of urban expansion, whether by grand design or otherwise, was questioned in the nineteenth century, when ideas of utopian settlement, green belts, and new towns were put forward; but it was not until the 1940s in Britain that this urban stage became accepted. As a result, the peripheral expansion of large cities was halted, green belts established, and new or small towns expanded beyond the green belts. This city regional planning in the UK was accompanied by countryside protection, the promotion of national parks as places of recreation, and the preservation of natural beauty.

It must be emphasised that this is a British picture. It occurs elsewhere, but in Paris, for example, the green belt and new town stage was replaced by adding six 'new cities' to the periphery, a solution more in tune with French urban traditions. Pressures beyond are nevertheless strong, leading to the expansion of small towns.

All these obvious urban pressures are accompanied by the less obtrusive but extensive demands for such things as golf courses or pony paddocks. Together they push up land values in the countryside and encourage speculation in agricultural land. At the same time, these forces are to some extent contained within a designed form which arose to meet the needs of the earlier part of the century. Although overall population growth is more or less static, social and economic structures, (the growing number of single person households, for example) as well as technological changes and global influences are dynamic, thus giving rise to new forms not yet consciously related to overall land use. It is the design of new relationships which is now needed to fulfil the requirements of the late urban stage.

While new settlement patterns are required, it is also true that at every period old areas are liable to be renewed to meet unforeseen demands. The concentric rings of urbanisation leave obsolescent hearts which must eventually succumb to renewal, although historic parts may be conserved. So it was with early clearances, and so it continues today in the inner city and new industrial wastelands. The various landscapes are related to each other in continuous cycles of use and re-use. Naturally, the larger the urban area, the more important becomes the process of recycling that area for new effective use.

To work within this process is to plan and manage over wide areas, seeing the board as a whole before executing each move. Town planning and its successor, town and country planning, are appropriate for parts of the changing game, but a wider and more strategic process of management and planning is now required. It is admitted that the perception of need for any major shift in the present process of land use changes, and its accommodation is not always easy to see. It is rather like those pictorial illusions in which a face may be that of an old or young woman, or two faces appear as a vase. There are alternative views; but as was argued in Chapters 3 and 5, there is now a case for bringing land perceptions and reforms up to a point where they will match economic and social changes.

The formation of new urban structures depends on investing capital and materials in building and open spaces; on the flexibility of movement within the constraints of social and economic choices and limits; and on the vision and innovative capacity of many people. Money capital, the materials of land, minerals and water, and urban structures are in constantly changing relationships. But land is fixed in quantity, is in increasing demand, and therefore growing scarcer and needing better conservation and management. The same can be said for our heritage of historic settlements. At the same time new development and the casting away of old structures must go on, and we have yet to develop new mechanisms to cope with the stress resulting from the loss of work or old community.

The capital invested in urban structures is enormous. The tangible assets of people in the UK in 1975 were (and still are) held mainly in housing, which represented 42% of a total of £482 billion. Other buildings and works comprised 27%, with plant, vehicles, and agricultural land making up the total.[2] Financial assets are small compared with these, but of growing importance in guiding new investment. Movement in these figures represents, for example, the flow of people, housing, and industry from cities to small towns, and investment in favoured commercial property and agricultural land by the financial institutions. The movement will not stop. The 42% in housing (£206 billion), was held in a housing stock of about 20 million. Even at a 1% replacement level (which assumes that houses must last 100 years) we need to build 200,000 homes each year.

Like industrial growth, most of the new housing is in growing smaller towns, and it is in this scatter of settlements that economic activity and employment are highest, generating their own momentum. The old economies of urban concentrations still operate for many services in those towns, although there is now the greater flexibility offered by modern communication. But the costs of congestion, obvious in large cities, also operate here, forcing people and activities outwards. Unless this happens, pressures on the historic core grow and conservation becomes very difficult.

The constraints, choices, limits, and visions are well illustrated by the reforming programme of the post-war Labour Government, in which planning was part of the creed, whether for economics or for the shape of London and its new towns. The political will required to carry out the London programme matched that needed for many of the great urban schemes of history, structuring the metropolis in novel ways.

Another classic case in England occurred in Cambridge, where the rapid growth of new industry (notably some electronic), and traffic, threatened the historic centre. In 1950 a planning report presented to the County Council recommended a policy restricting growth in the City and in the villages around it.[3] In 1948 the City had a population of about 86,000 and the surrounding district about 17,600. A future overall limit of 120,000 to 125,000 was set, and industrial expansion discouraged. However, concern over the loss of research and development opportunities, linking industry and university, led to the setting up of a science park in 1974, marking recognition of the need to change, and high-tech development has since flourished.

Today the City has been contained at 100,000, but the area around it is under heavy pressure. While the original villages have grown little, there are now 74,000 people in the area of Cambridge District, linked to the City for employment and services. In spite of policies of 'no growth', there has been a growth of 40% in such areas between 1971 and 1981.[4] Lewis Silkin, father of the 1947 Town and Country Planning Act, might smile ruefully if he could see the situation. He once said that going into Cambridge at the end of the war, and seeing the ribbon development along its roads, made him decide not to give planning powers to the smaller towns and cities of England, such as Cambridge, because they were not capable of dealing with unplanned growth such as ribbon development. Instead he would let the counties control the situation, and he gave them the planning powers. But growth continues and is not necessarily stopped by planning control. It is not only employment, but life-styles which attract people to move to certain places.

Growth is closely related to the provision of services, and the village settlement policy in Cambridge has concentrated on the larger 'key' villages for both. However, as demands continue, questions arise about this policy. The dynamic process as a whole is to do with the attraction of Cambridge, and has led to restrictions on City expansion, to the consequent pressures of village expansion, and to the problem of the costs of services in scattered development. The Cambridge planners acknowledge the argument that new technology is making some smaller and cheaper service units more viable, and so there are questions about the need for concentrations in key villages.

This is an important issue, for if smaller villages can be allowed to grow, this would not only suit many preferences, but would help maintain other services as well. Until now the assumed economies of scale in education or such utilities as sewerage systems have pointed strongly the other way. The key village concept has long provided a rationale for both economy of investment and control of development. Yet even where it was applied with great severity, as in the old colliery villages of County Durham, communities refused to die and sought to develop. Old and new communities both hold strongly to local identities, and the argument about local issues and wider realities is still central to the future of urban form.[5]

Large cities contain half the population of the UK, but in almost all there is decline, whereas in the small towns and rural areas nearly all are on the increase. So the balance of population between the two, now roughly equal, is moving outwards. This presents two parts of the cycle of use and re-use, new and old. Obsolescent cities cause people to leave, but the land in these cities must be used effectively and the fabric renewed. Free choice in the market results in the movement out of old areas. The links and flexibility of approach within this cycle, and the capacity for adjustment, provide for movement in the structural disposition of the quantities.

Several factors need considering. One is the process of population and economic movement. A second is the distance factor: what relationships exist between settlements? A third is the planning factor, not only town planning, but the carrots and sticks of economic regulation. Rates are a fourth.

The first factor was the subject of the central part of this book.

Even if population is static, there are still strong forces at work to change its distribution, and in a small land the movements are apparent almost everywhere. Many of the costs of connection and services have already been met, as with the motorway system and electricity grid. The installation of cable systems will be another crucial factor, and high densities of population are not essential. One of our most spacious new cities, Milton Keynes, is a pioneer in cable investment. It is obvious that once investment takes place there will be influences for new development. Nevertheless cities and their hinterlands are no longer as self-contained as they were; it is the system of cities which conditions the movement.

Distance has also been discussed. It is now more a question of time than of miles. How long to get to the airport, the city centre, or the nearest market town? In 1945 the measure was about 30 miles, or one hour's travel. This was the basis for the location of Abercrombie's London new towns. In the 1980s one hour on a motorway represents over twice the distance. Draw a sixty-mile circle around major centres, and most of England is covered. But we are not talking only of travel. New indigenous activity is growing everywhere. The problem is to find new sites and deal with the inertia of old locations. Planning policy, our third factor, has two parts. Town Planning seeks containment and the renewal of urban settlements, but at the same time must follow and guide market preferences. Today there is a buyer's market, and most local authorities are looking for work, jobs, and rates. Land is allocated accordingly, except in special areas such as national parks, green belts, and some closely protected environments where local influences seek to keep development away.

The attempt to force renewal through containment by green belts is not proving successful, for people and jobs simply move across to the ring of towns beyond, and there are no regional authorities in England which can control this process. The lack of private investment in the worst hit areas which are left behind requires a growth of public spending for social and economic reasons and for the prevention of waste. The links also lie in the financial system of investment and subsidies, and the complex process of public expenditure and macro-economic policy. Regional policy has long recognised the need for a carrot-and-stick set of regulators, although it is of limited use in a mixed economy, and even a centrally controlled economy can by no means force development into desired shapes and forms.

The strength of the old industrial cities lay in their local productive power and ability to sustain services through the raising of rates. Their present weakness is in falling production and too great a reliance on central grants to pay for services. The smaller growing towns, and the shires, are more self-sufficient, but still heavily dependent on central grants. It is in the nature of things that the more prosperous areas gain in many ways. They attract new growth, have less unemployment, smaller amounts of obsolescent housing and industrial stock, and they do not have to support heavy central services such as public transport. The redistribution of wealth can be exercised from the centre direct to every authority (as it is in England), but it can also be exercised in part from regions (as in Scotland), so redressing imbalances which can be seen and measured more clearly close at hand. Neither can careful planning from the centre replace more sensitive and responsive local control, as the experience of France has shown.[6] At the same time, the influence of the European Community provides a corrective with its ability to direct funds and regulate national governments.

Most of the tax yield in the UK comes from income, with smaller amounts from VAT, corporation tax, excise duties and rates (of which well over half are commercial). The lower the household income, the higher the percentage paid in rates, although rebates are paid to the lowest groups. A switch to local income tax would increase local independence and is a feasible option.[7] It would, however, reflect the prosperity of particular localities and could increase disparities. Neither the Layfield Committee of Enquiry into Local Government Finance, nor Mrs Thatcher's dislike of the rating system has yet resulted in an acceptable proposal, but it is obvious that local independence can only be gained through local access to revenues. In principle an increase in such revenues, together with regional government to secure detailed redistributions, would seem necessary to meet Layfield's requirements of accountability, fairness, efficiency, and flexibility.

This requires a voluntary shift in political power away from the centre, equivalent to the shift which took place through economic forces in the heyday of industrial urbanisation. The abolition of the Greater London Council and the Metropolitan County Councils of

England is no answer to local democracy and ignores the regional dimension. But whatever the organisation, we are still a long way from a genuine development of democratic processes for local government. And local government exhibits the same tendencies to over control in what has been called the *Local State*.[8] Here the philosophy and structure of representative government and bureaucratic values is equally inhibiting for the development of grass-roots activity.

Recognition of the problem has led a few local authorities to devolve power and money to smaller parts of the city. Amsterdam, for example, is actively experimenting with the creation of decentralised units, a development in participatory democracy which has reduced the overall numbers of bureaucrats and costs of services. The linkage of such top down actions to the growth of community initiatives requires but a small step to establish new forms of democracy which tend to a participatory rather than a classical representative model.

A new partnership could cross not only administrative boundaries but also public and private sectors. The close association of industry with a locality has now been lost in part, for in the case of multinational firms, decisions affecting communities are likely to be taken on another continent. Some wide economic and social means must be found to cushion the impact of closures on whole communities. The problem with local government is its relative lack of functional independence compared with the past; functional in the sense that it contains within its boundaries both the productive units and the people who run them; that it raises rates to pay for most of its services; and that it is responsible for those services.

The scale of economic production and technical development has taken industry, electricity, water supply, and other units of the local authority into private and public bodies at national and international scale. The old form of local government does not easily fit the new society. Neither does reorganisation get to the roots of a problem which lies in the international economy on one hand and in new local activity on the other. At the grass-roots there is life of new kinds, with communities requiring help in building and development.

The invention of new forms of government would seem to be a crucial part of any new system, for the association of different levels within a global as well as a domestic economic dimension is part of the process now being experienced. In the sense of social development the emergence of modern local government, with enfranchisement and representative democracy, was the means of directing the affairs of national and local governments in which the economic system had not yet reached its present international scale. Many forces now suggest that formal political structures need changing.

At the international level we must expect to see new controls or put up with a phoney democracy which gives only a partial say in public affairs. At lower levels, there is a case for regional authorities to allow a more sensitive use of resources. In large cities, decentralisation of power to lower levels is a requisite of a participatory democracy.[9] This may all appear too complex, but that is what society has become. The growth of new parts has meant that the links between political units and independent agencies have been developing strongly over the past decades. It is obviously essential that a regional water authority, for example, should relate closely to a planning authority in strategies for new development or the replacement of old services.

Development corporations for new towns and the old docklands as well as agencies for depressed areas are other bodies independent of local authorities, but have to work closely with them. The need for so many non-elected bodies is often questioned, but as reflections of a more complex society, with highly differentiated functions, it seems difficult to avoid them. What is missing is political accountability. Again, as with international activity, new forms and controls must emerge or democracy will be devalued. Some of the problems of identifying the links between the growing numbers of agencies are already well researched, and their political implications have also been made clear.[10] These are crucial problems for the control of our future. If the unaccountable forces of industrialisation prevail over democracy, the exploitation of land will continue, and the poor will suffer a growing erosion of the quality of their environment, as well as of their lives.

Why the continuous bid for new lands? In part it is the search for a quality of life and an environment which is not easily found in the old cities. In part the sheer economic problem of land shortage and an obsolescent city infrastructure. What is missing is the ability to grow anew and regenerate successfully at the same time, as in a healthy forest, where the process is self-regulating. But the scarcer land becomes, the more obvious is the need for such a regeneration process. This understanding of the cycle and its balance is central to the ability to reduce waste and to make the most of old and new together.

In the nineteenth century nature herself informed the philan-thropists in their search for a better environment. There was a call for space and gardens and food; but at the same time new lands had to be found because there was little space and no legal means of renewing the old. When the means came in the following century, renewal was often crude, frequently relied upon imported cultures (as with flats from continental traditions), was made expensive by land prices and construction costs, and brought little of nature to the city.

At the same time, the system of urban industrialisation was to all appearances likely to persist, with continuing employment in docks, factories and offices, daily commuting to work, and, after 1945, a new welfare state to look after unemployment, retirement, and health. The collapse of much of this system is in itself a call for radical responses in the use of labour, money, and land. New skills and money for investment are focussed mainly in new places, and the cycle of renewal is not being made effective. Not only are the poorest areas getting worse, but many of the newer, including the new towns, are becoming poor. We are living on our capital. The effort required to invest in these areas is not being made by central government, and local government has less to spend.

Connections are not being made, in particular those between job creation, social welfare, and urban renewal. Yet enormous sums of money are being spent. These billions of pounds go in contradictory ways. The young are encouraged to develop new skills, but the jobs are not there, and initiatives to work part-time are partly removed by the trap which reduces security benefits in consequence. The bureaucracies which administer the schemes are expensively central-ised, and there are large productivity gaps in the performance of the social services, as Gershuny and Miles have pointed out. The provision of necessary services in a centralised situation runs counter to the logical need to use the resources with detailed knowledge of local communities, which already bear a large part of the burden themselves. Roger Hadley and Stephen Hatch make clear the extent of present dependence on the informal and voluntary sectors and argue the case, with examples, for moving towards greater decentralisation. Apart from economy, it is obvious that personal and social development is greater where local involvement is fostered.[11]

Scarce capital could be used to provide buildings and equipment, while expensive labour can be greatly augmented by voluntary and part-time help. Training programmes could be geared to such developments, as they could to other local needs. For example, the renewal of houses, play areas, and old factory space is an obvious task. More difficult is the creation of spaces for new activity, whether city farm, garden, or work room in the house. But given the means, human potential at grass-roots would force cracks in the institutional concrete fabric holding it down, and would develop a filtering process for movement to spacious suburbs.

Politically, the process requires three sets of actions. First, the strategic connection of the resources just mentioned with national guidelines to lower authorities. Second, political units with the power to distribute resources fairly over geographic areas which cover regions (not just parts of them) and to enable small areas to function with some independence. Third, a fairer distribution between new and old lands, rich farming and marginal farming, new territories and inner cities. The top levels of government, business, and finance may find the lower levels tedious and difficult. The lower levels no doubt find the upper inaccessible and unhelpful. But both vertically through the hierarchy and horizontally across the urban landscape connections must improve, if cracks are not to grow wider.

Earlier in this book reference was made to the long-wave economic movements first identified by Kondratieff. According to his theory, the next upturn in the economy will not come until the mid 1990s. At the outset of this book the belief was also expressed that rapid adaptation would be crucial for survival and that things would change more quickly than in the past. It was also conjectured that, like economic long waves, there were equivalent waves of social reform and decline. After nearly two decades of relative depression and one of harsh market influences, encouraged by monetarist policies, we may soon be due for a change. If this were so, how would we expect forming urban structures to accommodate the lattice of varying landscapes? Like a good film, the movement will need structure and plot, sensitivity and aesthetic, as well as conflict.

The actors and the sets exist but must be used creatively. Whilst we would be foolish to attempt the creation of a neat design, we would be equally foolish to ignore the possibilities of managing our lives and land more effectively. What are the main tasks which could be attempted as part of a scheme for adaptation?

Diagram 4 illustrates the nature of our forming urban structures. Centre left is the old city with its suburbs, and next to it the later green belt with new and expanding towns beyond. This is what most people see as the present urban area. To the right of the diagram is the area which is now expanding fast and has been here labelled 'Post-urban form'. Most people see this as country life, but a country life which enjoys all the fruits of industrial society.

Below is the cycle and re-cycle of work, households, and the search for better environment. As the balance shifts away from the old city, so political power is likely to decentralise, as has been seen recently with the growing control by the Alliance over the old Tory shires. There will no longer be the same attitudes to old landed interests. It

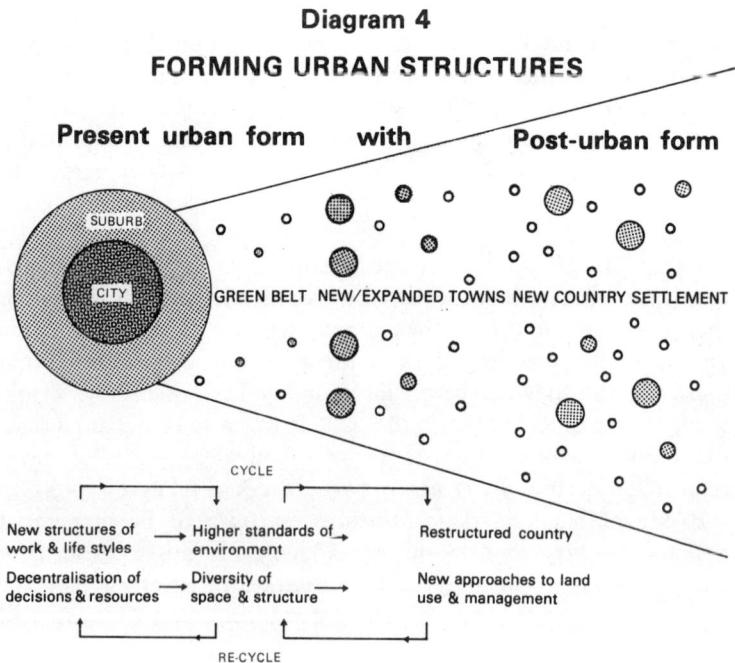

Diagram 4

FORMING URBAN STRUCTURES

Present urban form   with   Post-urban form

SUBURB

CITY

GREEN BELT NEW/EXPANDED TOWNS NEW COUNTRY SETTLEMENT

CYCLE

| New structures of work & life styles | → | Higher standards of environment | → | Restructured country |

| Decentralisation of decisions & resources | → | Diversity of space & structure | → | New approaches to land use & management |

RE-CYCLE

is to be expected that new perceptions of the nature of the use of land will emerge, with ecology playing an important role, and with a recognition that modern urbanisation requires new kinds of activity.

The concern of the 1960s and 1970s with government organisations to fit expanding urban patterns could give way to greater attention to the linkages and mechanisms which relate the parts, using the rapid exchange of computerised and televised information throughout society in a search for new relationships and views of the whole system. Some would see this as no more than an explicit recognition of the present tendency, the outcome of current market and government activity. Others might suggest a more positive need to shape urban society anew; this would require, amongst all the actors, a clearer recognition of their interdependence.

The earlier discussion on land reform rested on six main arguments: the mismatch between new economic structures and land policies based on past conditions; urban containment with its resulting effects on land prices, together with the current dismantling of the old planning system; equivalent problems as a result of agricultural subsidies and change; the absence of clear policies relating to social obligations to those who did not benefit from these situations; the failure to perceive the place of all land in an urban society; and finally, the need for vision in the re-design of the fabric.

Given the over-valuation of much old city land, the generous reservoirs of land in our inter-war suburbs, the misuse or gentrification of some agricultural land, and the need to develop more effective mixed use and conservation policies in rural areas, it is possible to prepare the ground for new urban structures. This would not be undertaken in the same way as the chunky post-war new town and urban redevelopment programmes. It would be finer grained across the new urban landscape, less comprehensively engaged in clearance or large programmes and more sensitively geared to local needs within strategic guidelines from the centre.

In the obsolescent cities an accelerated process of rehabilitation and the creation of more attractive landscapes woven into the townscape would eventually provide places worth living in. In the suburbs communities which are work places as well as dormitories could evolve as a result of less rigid zoning and more sophisticated ways of controlling nuisance. In agriculture the working out of a policy for the better development of capital resources of land would require some genuine design and management programmes inspired by the now too infrequent examples of the Countryside Commission.

Only a sustained public and private partnership without the drag of old ideologies is likely to achieve these changes. The way to regenerate life in outworn areas is a lesson still to be learned by governments of the so-called advanced industrial countries, and it must run parallel to new life outside them. Only public recognition of the fact that the processes of regeneration and new growth are linked, wherever they are, will bring governments to act fairly towards all the varied urban landscapes at different stages of fortune. Encouragement and restraint must go hand in hand with a system of expenditure and control which avoids lurches and jerks, allowing the cogs in the machine to engage smoothly in the running system. The parts cannot work well on their own; but the nature of each and the way it works will be different. Hence some overall design must guide the movements in complementary ways, leaving individuals to move in freedom over an ever changing pattern.

Local democracy and grass-root initiatives will demand something more than the present planning system. In city and country, the ownership of land will be an important factor in the ability to develop or conserve, and it is unlikely that the multitude of individual families will be satisfied with running only their own homes. They will also want land for extended work and leisure activities of higher quality than exists in either the ravaged industrial areas or the lifeless agricultural landscapes.

Town and country planning is not the answer. Quite new instruments, including management and planning across society, will have to be devised within a participatory democratic process if we are to learn to handle the scale and complexity of an uncertain future. Conflicts there will be, but negotiation can go further than bureaucratic diktat. Environmental education, which has been in existence for only a decade or so, will bring up a generation whose ideas about our environment will be very different from those accepted today. The long battle between property rights and the public interest can be expected to show some movement towards greater communal involvement in design and development. On the large scale of airports and motorways, governments at national and regional level will have to take a strategic view and arbitrate between many interests. At local levels, communities worthy of the name will learn to govern, as villagers once governed the use of their common land.

New perceptions of the global environment are slowly permeating every section of society, including the sphere of political economy. The changes which are likely to emerge as a result are probably as significant as those which gave rise to the modern world. In this process it is the rediscovery of nature which binds people together and which provides the foundation for an organic rather than a mechanical system.

Developing Places

The settled places of the urban landscape have always shown great contrasts of wealth, opportunity, and quality of environment. As we move into a new era of change, the contrasts appear greater as a result of unemployment, poor housing, and the concentration of ethnic minorities in some city areas; at the same time, many of the better off move to small towns and villages.

Nowhere is the need for public recognition and action greater than in those areas of unemployment and threatened livelihood, whether they be in the old industrial inner city, the post-war council estate or the remoter rural areas. Whatever the energetic and prosperous can achieve for themselves, public aid is essential for the poor and often alienated sectors of society in these areas, and the opportunity is here. Telecommunication, home learning, community schools, co-operatives and other innovations and ventures provide a technological and social environment which is being developed anew, where centralised services can be complemented by and shared with local initiative, and where participatory democracy can be fostered to construct new communities.

The pattern is emerging, but overall vision and central policy is lacking, although initiatives at the grass-roots are growing. Perhaps the major failure is the absence of a thrust for social development (rather than social services), entailing both the requirement to decentralise funds and the responsibility which this would bring. Yet within the cities anyone with an interest can discover a host of developing activities and enthusiastic people, mostly working on unsecured shoe-string budgets, often in temporary premises, and certainly without even the initial financial and organisational support which complements traditional services effectively.

It may be that the process is uncertain and temporary, but how far the formal economy can re-engage the unemployed is equally uncertain, and many have decided that it is not worth while waiting. Hundreds of community ventures in work and housing, in local enterprises of new kinds, and in the personal initiatives encouraged by Manpower Services schemes are creating a new environment of work, leisure, and self-organisation. Such movements are linked to the formal structures of industry and local government.

Risks and casualties are high, and there is criticism of this pioneer and exploratory work, but all these initiatives can be seen as part of a new mood. They fill a gap left by the cutting of local authority public expenditure and are also straws in the wind in the move toward new forms of public and private association and enterprise, in which grass-roots activity is seen to be more rewarding than passive receipt of government services.

It is not just a question of cash. The restructuring of work is a necessary adjustment to new industrial practices and a conscious choice about preferred life-styles. The situation is fully discussed by Charles Handy in his book *The Future of Work, A Guide to a Changing Society*.[12] The self-service economy is the means for linking these two changes, and nowhere is it more necessary than in areas of high unemployment. But here, as in the inner cities, new government initiatives are also essential.

It is a sad reflection that UK government concern with the inner cities sprang from a fear that the country would experience the riots and problems of the USA in the 1960s. Home Office and Department of the Environment studies were initiated, and reports about inner cities published. The concept of multiple deprivation was officially recognised: a mixture of homelessness or bad housing, unemployment, the position of ethnic minorities, overcrowded schools and more.[13]

In 1977 Peter Shore, Secretary of State for the Environment, diverted public expenditure to specified deprived areas, to introduce the inner city programme, operated by programme and project authorities in a partnership between central and local government. However the riots of 1981 showed how far the measures had failed to redress the problems of inner cities. The subsequent inquiry and report by Lord Scarman led him to write:

> I conclude that much could be done to achieve a better coordinated and direct attack on inner city problems, and I recommend action to achieve it. One of the objects of such an approach must be to ensure that the resources which the Government judges the nation is able to devote to the inner city are effectively spent.
>
> The approach to inner city problems also appears to have been deficient in two other important aspects. First, local communities should be more fully involved in planning, in the provision of local services, and in the management and financing of specific projects. I should like to see, for example, greater consultation than exists at present between local authorities and community groups about the allocation of resources to projects under the Urban Programme. I have been impressed by the quality of the evidence I have received from community groups in Brixton and elsewhere, and by the enthusiasm evident, for example, among tenants' groups and ethnic minority leaders during the visits I paid to housing estates in Brixton and to community groups in Handsworth. Inner city areas are not human deserts: they possess a wealth of voluntary effort and goodwill. It would be wise to put this capital to good use.
>
> A second deficiency appears to lie in the extent to which the private sector — banks, building societies and other business companies — is involved in the process of inner regeneration. The private sector is not, in my view, an alternative to adequate public sector involvement; both are needed. I have, however, noted with interest the evidence contained in a paper submitted to me on behalf of the Railton Road Youth Community Centre which describes the work of The Local Initiative Support Corporation (an offshoot of the Ford Foundation) in developing community programmes in decaying central city neighbourhoods in the United States of America. It may be that here, as in other respects, American experience has valuable insights to offer.[14]

The second point was taken up by the then Secretary of State for the Environment, Michael Heseltine, with the bringing together of a financial institutions group (FIG) in Merseyside and the setting up of a task force for improvements. A particular effort was made with one of the worst council estates in Knowsley District, near Liverpool: Cantrill Farm, now named Stockbridge Village. Here £8 million from the private sector was matched with government funds to upgrade housing and its environment. Much has been done but, as always with improvement, those residents least able to meet new costs are being squeezed out. Physical help must go hand in hand with social and economic help if deprived communities are to become able to help themselves.

With regard to Lord Scarman's plea for better co-ordination, the Birmingham City Planning Department has initiated a series of local inner area studies, identifying the problems in education, employment, housing, crime, and many other concerns involving other departments and community interests. Government urban aid money has been channelled in an organised and regular way, which has influenced major spending programmes and created awareness of the importance of making connections between all these activities.

These initiatives are indicative of what must eventually become widely recognised and acted upon; mutually supporting interests with capital, guidance and other help from government and private sources, and joint effort from within the community. There is no reason why such areas should not develop many opportunities for new work and leisure, bringing some social cohesion and control into the worst hit areas. But aid must be consistent, and real skills allowed to develop. The old idea of delivering services from the centre to a relatively passive population is being replaced by a combination of these central services (schools and social welfare are examples) with non-governmental associations representing a wide range of interests.

The task of creating communities is large. For example, the Birmingham core area contained 270,000 people in 1984, half of whom were in the worst 2½% of officially designated deprived areas in England and Wales. But the problem is not confined to the old city core. Chelmsley Wood, built in the 1960s and 70s on the east side of the city, contains 50,000 people in what is in effect a council estate the size of a new town, and it has severe problems of unemployment. Kirby, east of Liverpool, is the same size and of similar age. Today 25% of all its dwellings have been demolished, and unemployment approaches 40%. Factories on the local industrial estate stand empty, large numbers of residents survive on social security, and there is little money circulating to support shops or other services. Transport to central facilities from these estates is expensive, be it to hospitals, central shopping, or entertainment. The Knowsley Borough Council is assisting local co-operatives and volunteers, encouraging what local firms there are to spend locally, so as to increase the flow of money, and tackling education and training. Together with other areas they receive help from the European Community.

Estates such as these occur in every major city. There are a million inadequate post-war flats, in addition to the six million pre-1914 terraces, in the inner cities. To treat such areas as recipients of the equivalent of poor law aid, rather than to see them as places for personal and social development is a disgraceful reflection on government. In spite of the efforts, there is still an enormous need for changed central perceptions and greater resources. If the Department of Social Security could become a more positive Department of Social Development, a start might be made with the billions at its disposal, in an attempt to move from paternalistic to collaborative attitudes.

The problems of unemployment, poverty, the decline of housing stock, and all the other attributes of deprived areas, will not go away without some radical changes in thinking and action. It is not simply a question of replacing one government by another, for the international money institutions will prevent lavish public expenditure. Far more important will be modest increases in expenditure, a determination to link central and community, public and private efforts more closely, and a development of such approaches as that of Birmingham (which itself began an experiment with decentralised government in 1984, following earlier initiatives in nearby Walsall).

Much could be done quickly, in tune with the general speed of events. To avoid more riots, they ought to be done quickly. The social mobilisation of political skills and a growing knowledge of the system can enable that change to take place. Only vision and political will are absent. Guidelines from central government would build on what has been achieved, encouraging participatory work in the inner cities with the carrot of modest increases of expenditure. Local authorities could be required to set up decentralised offices with powers of decision to spend at community levels. Private sector interests from local banks and building societies, voluntary groups and management expertise (seconded from firms or offered by retired managers), would join in the process.

Easy communication between cities and links across Europe could provide both internal strength and formal connections with higher level organisations. It could be positive people rather than paternalistic provision from the centre which would activate the change. But the problem does not stop at the inner cities or outer estates, however large, for in the flux of population movement and the housing market, neighbouring suburbs are subject to pressure as well. In Birmingham, after the war, 30,000 houses were demolished in the area surrounding the city centre. Many were mid-nineteenth century court houses, the kind of slum which no longer exists in Britain. Since about 1970, when the reaction to wholesale clearance grew strong, a similar number of houses have been or will be rehabilitated. These are mostly pre-1914 terraces, of which there are over 80,000. Already the next batch of 30-40,000 has been identified.

These areas reach half way to the city boundaries and are fringed by inter-war suburbs, some already in decline, with poor maintenance and defaulted mortgages. The problem is similar in every major industrial city. At least in the suburbs and post-war estates there is some space, be it in gardens or in green swathes. In the inner city there is little. Cars must park in the streets; there is no room for trees; back yards must do instead of gardens. These very conditions ensure that further demolition is likely for the areas at the bottom of the housing market. Those displaced will have to go somewhere, and they will be moving into other parts of the city.

As they do, the better off will also move, and those nearer the top of the market may hop over the green belt and choose the small towns beyond. There is also some return movement. Encouraged by local authorities, private builders have built houses for sale within the inner city, successfully raising standards and attracting buyers, but unless the wider environment is improved fast, investment will fall off and new areas become blighted. Housing Associations have catered extensively for private rentals, and improvement grants have led to some gentrification, for the inner city is well located for work in the centre, and journeys are cheap. There are also psychological attractions for those whose parents or grandparents once lived in the earlier city, and the pull of such roots has been noted in Glasgow, The Hague, and other places. These various attractions will undoubtedly stabilise and improve many areas, but if the inner city redevelops and central business or leisure areas continue to grow, places further out may well decline in turn, unless we can find better means of prevention, and learn to relate social, economic, and physical change to local and government initiatives.

While the city may be in decline, it is not going to die. At some point it will have moved to a relatively stable situation, but it will be a different place from today's, with a smaller population, less economic power, and a better general environment. As an example, the traumatic shocks suffered by Liverpool continue, but in the process much else is happening. The Docklands Development Corporation is making capital out of a potentially magnificent site which includes the outstanding docks built by Jessie Hartley in 1845. The 1984 Garden Festival has left some well-designed open space behind. The Tate has recently announced a £9 million scheme to house modern art. New small open spaces and pedestrian streets have been established in the centre.

The City is moving towards a new role after three hundred years of port and commercial prosperity. That it had to suffer riots and massive misery in the process reflects badly on its own and central government. Political antagonism has overridden good government, adding greatly to the economic problems of decline. Grass-roots initiatives in the 1960s, like the Shelter Neighbourhood Action Project (SNAP), and the Education Priority Area programme all aided by a Liberal Council full of good intentions, have all failed to put Liverpool back on its feet, and the City has been forced by a new series of riots and subsequent central government initiatives to accept imposed organisation and developments in an attempt to help it forward.

Clearly, some lessons are being learned, but attempts are still crude, often disconnected, riddled with political and professional jealousies, and without a real understanding of the city as a living system. The management of this complex and uncertain environment has yet to move from a stage of response which simply reacts to the worst, to one of anticipation, prevention, and creative partnership between communities, government, private industry, and finance. Of course conflict will continue over resources and priorities, but the worst evils of the old industrial city have now gone. New levels of security, understanding, and ability ought to allow for more creative development and design.

While attention is still focussed on the old cores of our cities, the suburbs are also undergoing change. Some are being affected by movement from the poorer areas, but a good deal more is happening as the suburb begins to alter its role. Populations in the suburbs are in decline as a result of smaller households. Every outer Borough in London lost population between 1971 and 1981, in total over 200,000 people. It may be possible to reverse this trend, but it is very unlikely that in the filtering through from inner to middle to outer suburbs enough space will be found to stop overall decline for some time.

Nor is the problem helped at present by the characteristics of much suburban semi-detached housing, built for small families with their two and a half or three bedrooms, and thus too small for easy subdivision. Yet much of the demand is coming from the growing number of single people, old, young, separated or divorced. The big old Victorian house is well suited to their needs, but the small semi is less easily adapted. However, it is possible: the gardens are there to build into, and so there is space. There may well be a tendency for higher densities to appear, for at the same time quite a lot of open space is being sold for new houses, or for work places, in order to replenish local coffers in hard times, or provide a large sum for the local tennis club.

New work places are going to be as important to the suburbs as to the inner city. Long held policies of trying to keep factories and supermarkets away from residential areas are now breaking down, and there is as much journeying to work between suburbs as to and from the centre, quite apart from all the school, recreational and personal visits made possible by the car. This circuitous activity is reinforced by green belts, and in the case of London by the M25 orbital motorway.

The changing nature of employment, with more people working at home for larger concerns, is also likely to place new demands on the suburban home. Rank Xerox is one of the firms capitalising on communications technology and the personal motivation available from people able to work freely within their own home areas, creating networks of small outliers associated with the firm. The scheme is not confined to computer work, but is available to a wide range of other information skills, and the location of all this outlying activity is irrelevant to headquarters. Independence is encouraged, but belonging to a firm is important to many, and links can be maintained. Rank Xerox are also exploring designs for adapting homes now being developed in Milton Keynes new town as well as in old city houses. Work has also gone into neighbourhood office and social centre development.

This kind of development keys in well with J. Gershuny's self-service economy thesis which was discussed in Chapter 4, and it has other implications. Journeys to work could fall, community bonds develop, the space available in low density suburbs could be used more effectively, the decline of cities slowed down, and their economies strengthened in new ways. Planning ideas about segregated residential and work places are having to change, and here again national guidelines are necessary, complemented by local initiatives. As with the inner areas, suburban communities will need to organise new democratic processes to determine the future of their areas, but in the case of the newer suburbs central funding should be unnecessary. There might be some good reasons for using the fringes of the city for new kinds of development which require spacious settings for small research and production units, with a little new housing as well. Green belts are overdue for re-examination, but not for exploitation.

The effect of green belts is to prevent city growth at the edges where it is cheapest and easiest, but the laws of land economics ensure that agricultural values are raised here by the hope of development, however strict the policies. Farming can be less secure for this reason, and also suffers trespass. The so-called fringe areas are not easy to deal with. Green belts are simple solutions to a complex problem. They suit many, especially those who live in or on the edge of them, but as Peter Hall has convincingly shown, they also work against the less well off by raising land prices and therefore house values.[15] They throw pressures onto attractive small towns and, where crossed by motorways, create new pressures difficult to resist. In any case, planning policies allow for institutional and recreational uses, and these are becoming larger. Research shows the extent to which change is taking place.[16]

Examples of concrete development appear in the green belt between Birmingham and Coventry, where the National Exhibition Centre, an expanded Airport, and a recently approved high-technology site have been seen as necessary for the economic regeneration of a newly depressed region.

Any decline in support of agriculture, or in the rating of agricultural land, would encourage faster change. Realistically, the green belt is becoming an urban parkland where high standards of design can be imposed, where use is intensifying, and where selected landscapes need special protection. One benefit which can accrue is a landscape less damaged by tree felling, insecticides, soil compaction and poor drainage in those areas where heavy agricultural equipment has already caused problems. A richer wildlife would be a result, and the city itself would be better off in consequence.

Within the West Midlands conurbation there is a nature conservation strategy which sees major open areas linked by canals or disused railways with smaller sites as stepping stones. Operation Greensight in Liverpool is active in the central area itself, establishing better conditions for wildlife and closely involving schools and environmental education. Operation Groundwork, based in Manchester since 1983 (now the Groundwork Foundation) is concerned with the improvement of the environment in the scarred industrial landscapes of the North West: scarred, but full of industrial history and potential attraction. The linkages from centre to green belt (a very moth-eaten belt in South Lancashire), are the physical manifestation of a rising awareness of the value of wildlife and its place within the city, not to mention its place in the country. The green belt has a crucial role as the main reservoir of space, but its use cannot be seen as a simple measure for city containment. It is an integral part of the urban fabric.

Thus the green belt is a place for recreation and wildlife; it has strong economic attractions; it presents problems for those seeking cheap housing; and it is changing its land use from productive agriculture to the landscapes of institutions or recreation. Special protection, selective development, and more sophisticated management are all called for, but, unlike the city authority, green belts normally comprise several local authorities, and co-ordinated policies are not so easy. Regional strategic planning may well be the best answer, in association with other major functions.

In attempting to allow peripheral expansion and new villages in London's Green Belt, Mrs Thatcher's Government had to retreat before a conservation onslaught. The proposals leaned heavily towards the market, the conflict was inevitable and the resistance right. But more thoughtful changes to green belt policy are due, and in particular, where economic forces prevail, they should be accompanied by new investment in woodlands, hedgerows, nature conservation, public access and multiple use, reflecting the special nature of these largest urban parklands. This is a problem whose solution will not be effectively designed and implemented without a strategic view of some kind.

What of the smaller towns and villages beyond? What is likely to happen to the towns is illustrated by what has been described already in the case of Cambridge. They are under strong pressures and risk both their historic centres and their pleasant open nature. As populations mount, land values increase, open spaces are developed, densities and congestion grow, and the problems of the big city, in embryonic form, are only too easy to see. When populations reach sixty or seventy thousand, the feel of a small town begins to disappear, yet it was their very smallness that provided the space and the attraction to industry and residents in the first place.

The alternatives are to hope for a reversal of city decline or to develop the many even smaller towns and villages. But even if the city stabilises, much of the momentum for growth will remain in the middle-sized towns, and the preferences of their inhabitants are more likely to be for a smaller place than for the city. There are already continual small developments, but, as was suggested earlier, these could be more positively encouraged to provide choice and maintain services. The reversal of early drift from country to town and city is not only happening but is a process desired by people. Whatever resources are pumped into the city, new work and leisure opportunities are growing in the country, and agriculture does not need to hold all the acres it has.

The barriers to such change can be restated briefly: policies for agricultural and countryside protection, the cost of services, and the opposition of existing residents, including farmers. An alliance against rural development in prosperous areas contrasts strongly with attempts to attract it to more remote places. Villages are villages, whether north or south; is it necessary to treat one set as centres for investment, and another as protected dormitories? Of course, market pressures require different forms of public intervention, but not to the extent of losing sight of those common attributes of the village which require certain levels of population and services in order to function well.

An interesting commentary on village life and planning policies has been made on the Devon village of Hatherleigh, once a small market town, now a key settlement in the County. After falling in population throughout the century from nearly 1300 to just 900 people, it is now again on the increase, peopled by those of working age as well as the retired. Over 100 immigrants have come from all over Britain, and the number of people in farming has risen. Problems in sewerage and health services have occurred but are not seen as insuperable if providers can move away from a preoccupation with supposed large-scale efficiency. In Cornwall, which has increased its population by 25% in 20 years, research suggests that the increase is due, not to the retired, but to those who have moved home to take up different work in a more congenial environment.[17]

Villages, those real yet mythical images of an idealised pastoral existence, are embedded in the literature of the country, always, as Raymond Williams has shown, existing as a memory or perspective which can be traced back century after century in an endless evocation of idealised being.[18] The sentiment, as well as the sentimentality, is powerful and cannot be discounted. As has been noted for the villages of Cambridge, which are by no means the most beautiful, they continue to exert a strong attraction.

Practically every plan for a rural area has a village conservation policy, but at the same time recognises that schools and services require centres of population, so that key villages are identified as those for investment and modest population growth. Between the specially conserved and the key village, are the host of hamlets, detached pieces of suburbia or mixtures of many kinds which make up the villages of most rural areas. Some grow, while others, as a result of strict control over new building, decline; for households are getting smaller, so that if the number of houses remains the same, the population goes down and services diminish accordingly. The control operates not only through planning for the conservation of architecture and landscape quality, but also through political pressure from within the village to prevent newcomers from changing a well protected territory. It is not only a lack of services but also similar political pressure to prevent the installation of new services, such as sewerage works, which curbs the growth of new houses.

It is obvious to anyone with an eye to see that villages in lowland England have less and less to do with farming, more and more to do with new life-styles, retirement, or commuting. In this context, how should they be considered? One category can be isolated, the compact old village in its landscape, displaying all the charm of traditional church, manor, and cottage. Like fine architecture, such creations demand special protection. But these, while numerous, are in a minority. What of the rest?

Questions of the demand for and the cost of services are less easily settled. Within commuting distance of towns and cities demand is strong, but in remoter rural areas it is often weak. In both cases key villages are selected for expansion, on the grounds that services can then be provided more economically. This is true in the public arena of providing schools or mains sewerage. In a private sense of own car transport, or the use of septic tanks instead of mains sewers, it can be argued that the choice of going to a small village should be allowed, especially in an age when more people may wish to acquire a few acres of land as well. In practice, quite a lot of such development does go on, in spite of the policies; it can be afforded privately. Nor should local territorial opposition be allowed to abuse public policies of restriction for private purposes.

The dispersal from city to small town and village is almost certain to continue, and the opportunity to live and work in the country could be widened without loss of landscape or agriculture. The main proviso would relate to sensitivity in design, for it is landscape which is the dominant feature, and it is the open land which provides the harmony of nature. To 'preserve' village character while the prairies grow around them is a nonsense. If rural conservation and design are improved, more buildings can be put in unobtrusively, and new communities can develop, of a kind more closely fitting the needs of an urban society in which land plays a new role, with life support of a new kind, economic, ecological and social.

In this respect there are problems common to villages, inner cities and other relatively deprived areas of settlement. The scale of cities, their organisation, and the application of technical and social services has created a situation which works against the small unit. Part of any solution must lie with the decentralisation of responsibilities and the acceptance of a wish to live, work, and share in the affairs of small communities.

The identification of place, its *genius loci*, and the creating of life and work, are central to human development and become ever more relevant in the face of large-scale international technology and economics. The appropriate design of our urban landscapes requires a combination of re-thinking at the centre and creative development in all the parts. As the chapter on perceptions attempted to show, there is no need to stay with old views of town and country. The new urban environment is all-pervasive. The view of country areas held by urbanites is of course different from that of traditional country dwellers. For many of the former, land is seen as solace, recreation, or sheer escape from the city; for more traditional dwellers, as the harsh reality of, and involvement with, nature. For many industrial farmers, it is different again: an open factory for producing food and profit. These categories are inadequate as a basis for approaching land problems today, but they illustrate attitudes and the need to resolve conflicting values.

As the simple dichotomy of town and country breaks down under the influence of new social mobility, communications, and relationships; as life in relation to nature takes on new meanings; and as locations for settlement change, we can expect a wider understanding of inter-relationships. In this nothing is more important than agriculture, but although it is far and away the largest user of land, it accounts for only 2.2% of the UK gross national product and can no longer be defended at all costs on the grounds of war or other strategic needs. It has slowly begun to accommodate ideas of wildlife conservation, of tourism and recreation (which comprise 3.5% of UK GNP), of shared uses, of its industrial nature, and of public concern about its responsibilities.

There is nothing so harmonising in urban life as nature. On the farm, along the motorway, or in the town, trees, crops, grass, water, and land form can do more than all the developers put together. Inevitably the same kind of planning thought must be given to rural land as has been given to city planning. This is bound to mean a re-examination of its base, its support and its control. If public money is to be spent to support agriculture (and estimates vary from £8000 to £13000 per farmer every year), then control and accountability are inevitable.

Once again it must be asserted that this should not be only a centralised operation. It is precisely because Brussels and Whitehall are so involved that much of the crude work of destruction has occurred. Localities can evolve their own more sensitive patterns on the basis of mutual understanding and discussion, but within frameworks of guidance from higher levels. As with social developments in the inner city, so social development will have to take place in the country as more and more ex-urbanites live nearby and claim part of their heritage.

Already such changes as the horseyfication of Surrey and other pastures, or the threatened ribbon development of piggeries elsewhere (and the preparation of the first ever local plan to control pig farming!), throw up new questions about the association of urban life with agricultural land, about markets and their control, about design, social disparities, and land use. When combined with considerations of pollution and other urban effects, they underline the need for both overview and local discussion. Twenty-first century Britain replaces nineteenth-century Manchester as the focus of the new urbanism. Then the cities wrested power from the territorial magnates, with Parliamentary reform and free trade, but also with a terrible toll on the industrial worker. Now wealth and power are more widespread and must be reflected in new views of rural territory and its values.

There is no tidy solution, but there is a need for equity of treatment, which implies national action, and a local working out through and below the structures of local government. Ministries of agriculture and social security must become ministries of resource conservation and social development, in deed as well as in name, with strategies in tune with the needs of the next century. If part of their action were to push decisions down to levels appropriate to the scale of the problem, better democracy would result.

A re-structuring of government also requires a re-structuring of the ways in which macro (national) economic policies are prepared, so that more independence can be granted to local development. Other centralised activity, such as our banking system, also needs to be dispersed. Again, the professions could help to accelerate the process of citizen involvement by providing better information about research and development. Things are already happening, but they could go faster.

As society views the problems of humanity and the globe, it is possible to sense the undercurrents of change in attitude and expectation. It is difficult to believe that the old rigidities can remain although it is acknowledged that conflicts will occur as they break down. The shell can release new life as well as develop itself.

And the common perceptions made possible through telecommunication provide a starting point for discussion in every locality.

The present climate of political extremism and unrest is evidence of deeper changes. As throughout history, such unrest must be worked out in the power structure, before any new consensus can emerge. And because the global pattern is more obviously connected, many of the home changes will emerge as results of unexpected happenings elsewhere. As President Nyerere of Tanzania said recently: 'Must we let our people starve in order to pay our debts?'

So the UK will be carried on a tide of events whose timing is very uncertain, but where new undercurrents are felt and partly understood. All who are concerned must see that the adaptation of our values and institutions is inevitable. For the Third World, the place of land and agriculture in social and economic development is obvious. For the fast urbanising countries, the problems of cities will be of equal importance, but the old industrial nations will have to search for quite new answers, and a fairer use of land must provide some of the answers.

Chapter 8

Four Imperatives

In a rapid course amid the torrent of events, it is difficult, if not impossible, to reflect upon the wisdom of present actions. Without quick action troubles may be upon us before we can prepare to meet them. On the other hand, if the ship is leaking, it is prudent to search for a haven, to repair and reflect, before rushing off again.

The United Kingdom has been caught in this torrent without adequate recognition of its own strengths and weaknesses, with too insular a view of the world and with slow responses. The post-war decline of power and wealth was no doubt difficult to anticipate, but when the shock came in the 1970s, Mrs Thatcher's Government eventually responded as it did in 1979, until growing differences of view, both within and outside Downing Street and Parliament, resulted in growing extremes not only in politics, but in wealth distribution and social division.

The impacts of these forces gave rise to a new political party, the SDP, which, as an Alliance with the Liberals, is already shifting the balance of power. Some have had time to reflect, seeing horizons which go further than adversative politics or insular prospects. Whether the nation can recover its balance effectively remains to be seen, but there would seem to be four imperatives if some success is to be achieved.

First is awareness of what we are, where we have come from, and where we want to go. If a new role is to be found, some common understanding of our cultural heritage is required. Secondly, new ways of politics and tackling problems must be found. The old skills in government and management are no more use than old skills on the shop floor. Quicker learning for the anticipation of future events is imperative, with a wide appreciation of the changing nature of the physical world (and thus its economic and social structure) reflected

209

in the proper use of resources, whether of land or other public goods. Third is the need for a better appreciation of the physical world. This is the ecological imperative. Fourthly, the causes of freedom and justice, which are coming back into wide public discussion, must now be seen anew and in relation to international factors.

Why is it that land is not seen as a political issue, except in so far as the Green policies of the major parties are there to acknowledge public concern over wildlife, scenery, or more selfishly the protection of private territories in the name of public interest? The reasons argued in earlier chapters are to do with layers of historical attitudes, a failure of economic theory and practice, failure to develop new perceptions, consequential self-deception and lack of ethical principle. In short, they are to do not only with the culture of this country, but also with some of the recent economic philosophies of western civilisation. Notwithstanding all this, and given the importance of private property and profit, (now entering the communist world more strongly as a recognised human need), it is time to reconsider the place of land in our structure of beliefs.

History shows a slow emergence of the view of land as a 'public good', to use the economic jargon, or as something to be held for 'the public interest', to use a term much favoured by planners. The new argument about private and public interests has naturally tended to revolve around present structures of ownership, law and rights. However, if we are moving into a new world, then, as with economic production or telecommunication, new structures will emerge and it is these that we must try to anticipate.

Discovering Culture and Role

Philosophers over the ages have attempted to deal with ultimate realities, and science has played its part in the same search. Today, the growth of self-knowledge through the early psychological novel, existentialism, and personal and social psychology in this century has brought many individuals to some understanding of their being and motivation. Modern studies of regional and national characteristics are now growing in number, and in the light of such earlier explorers of knowledge and culture as Vico and Montesquieu, are attempting to build new knowledge with relevance to a future world where mutual understanding will have become ever more important.[1]

In Chapter 2 some of the characteristics of English life were mentioned, and in any attempt to bridge present gulfs and find a more harmonious future, it is surely important to understand the strengths and weaknesses, not only of the constituent parts of the United Kingdom, but of their regions as well. Outsiders are probably better than we are at analysing such things, and reference has been made to the views of Barzini, Dahrendorf and Weiner on Britain, and to the work of Hofstede on the characteristics of many nations.

In a recent and perceptive article, L. A. Siedentop points out that because representative government in Britain developed long before the great late eighteenth century age of liberal doctrine, it was caught by historical circumstances which perpetuated old attitudes to class, rather than fully exploring the ideas of individual freedom taken up in the revolutions of North America and France[2]. Thankfully, things are changing, but there are other problems. One which Siedentop also identifies is the British reluctance to deal with general ideas. The strength of scientific and empirical traditions is complemented by a weakness in accommodating concepts and structuralist thought. To read Edmund Leach on Levi-Strauss reveals the weight of cultural baggage and the mind-sets of centuries of thought in different old nations. A related problem comes from our lack of commitment to industry and the failure of government and ruling élites to accord it the status it receives in other nations.

Earlier reference to a new book by J. C. D. Clarke reinforces some of these historical problems, in particular the maintenance of an *ancien régime* in England until the repeal of the Test and Corporation Acts between 1828 and 1830. Weiner has said the same thing in different ways. Attitudes to class, land, hunting, shooting and fishing remain. Only now are we beginning to move. This is not to divide class too sharply. Fishing licence costs produce one of the most contentious issues for any water authority, and the lobby is strong. Having lost his acres, his forests and his commons, the Englishman is jealous of an ancient right.

Strong individualism brings hope. There is not only some change in attitude through such initiatives as Industry Year 1986, but also a correct identification by Mrs Thatcher's Government of the need to release entrepreneurial skills. Recent research suggests that the nation may have human resources of a more promising kind than those found elsewhere. The work has been done for the United

Kingdom National Economic Development Office by Taylor
Nelson Monitor, and discusses national populations according to
three categories. To quote the *Guardian* report:

> Taylor Nelson describes three stages of human development: the
> agricultural era, producing 'sustenance-driven values'; the industrial
> era, with 'outer directed values' and the post industrial era of 'inner
> directed values'.
>
> Those still remaining in category one are not simply the unemployed
> and the poor. They are people motivated by security, for whom survival
> means clinging to an existing lifestyle. They tend, for instance, to watch
> sport *en masse* instead of taking part, and their borders between work
> and leisure are sharp. Category one people have, of course, already had
> it.
>
> Category two people are motivated by esteem and status. They are
> materialists, orthodoxly ambitious, traditional, and pro-authority.
> Taylor Nelson concedes that category two might defeat the trend in the
> medium term, in which case Britain will be in a worse economic mess,
> because we will have no hope of beating more natural category twos like
> the Japanese.
>
> But, says Taylor Nelson, category three are the more likely winners in
> which case we are quids in, long term. The New People don't care about
> the world's opinion of them. They don't much care if they are
> unemployed or employed, since the terms have little relevance to their
> individual enterprise outlook in which work is play.
>
> Their criteria for success are within themselves, but they have broad
> horizons, a good understanding of world issues, and a high tolerance of
> other people's positions. For category three, education is education; for
> category two education is training.
>
> The New People range well beyond the do-gooders. Taylor Nelson
> includes among them those Silicon Valley style entrepreneurs who care
> more for the excitements of discovery and the competitive flux of
> change than for money, and who become millionaires by accident.
>
> Thus a category one might decide to eat less because food prices go up,
> a category two might do so to retain the accepted shape in a corporate
> suit, but a category three would do so just to feel better.
>
> Taylor Nelson's surveys show that category three people have ad-
> vanced so fast in Britain that they already represent 36 per cent of the
> population.[3]

The discussion of category one and two people is somewhat dismissive. Many of them contribute a great deal to the nation through

attachment to old values; but the point of need for rapid change is taken.

The international league table shows Holland at the top, with 47% in category three. Denmark and Britain have 36%, West Germany 26%, the United States of America 19% and Japan 10%. What we are witnessing is a conflict between old and new attitudes which goes very deep into the national psyche, but the outcome of which will determine our future. The slow muddling through so characteristic of the nation may get us there, but it is doubtful. The speed of events is already creating new issues at an alarming rate: the disillusioned jobless, the exasperated black minorities, and other neglected people. Like the bitter conflicts arising from our industrial past, these new conflicts will bring another heritage of wounds difficult to heal.

It is up to us all to open out the discussion and it is a relief that many in the Church and elsewhere are now doing so. But it is not enough to re-engage in the old debate on social obligation. A more positive attempt to introduce ideas and concepts into traditional ways of thought will be necessary. If there really are large numbers of New People, then the messages should be coming from the media. Some are, of course, but it is also salutary to read Julian Barnes' reminder of Flaubert's view that 'The whole dream of democracy is to raise the proletariat to the level of stupidity attained by the bourgeoisie.' Tocqueville's tyranny of the majority is not so easy an animal to budge. If new worlds demand new philosophies, however, then the role of the rich countries relative to the globe, to the poor, and to each other, will presumably have to be re-defined, although each region and nation will provide its own way of becoming different.

There can be little doubt that this country must raise the status of industry, must improve its management and learn to apply scientific and technological skills to industrial development. There is a first-class role for the UK to play in high-tech work as well as through such bodies as the Intermediate Technology Development Group (following the work of Fritz Schumacher), for the Third World and at home. On the social front it is high time that we moved from concepts of poor law and dole to those of positive community development. Until this is done, dignity will continue to be violated.

The association with Europe reminds us that nationalism is, on the whole, a recent phenomenon; that two of the oldest nations are France and England, and that we are witnessing a new community of nations which could mark quite a new stage in the exploration and modification of western behaviour. The role which the United Kingdom can play in this wider process is complex but unique. The links with the United States of America and the Commonwealth surely offer imaginative opportunities for making progress, both in Europe and in the inner city. But racism and flag-wagging will hinder progress. Unfortunately, the current wave of monetarist and privatised thinking, although a corrective to over bureaucratic welfare, adds further fuel to the fires of conflict. It is here that politics takes over.

The Politics of Problems

The clearest indication of a change in British attitudes is the rise of the Alliance, with plural politics replacing the old two-party system. The arguments for the old system are strong and may have been appropriate for the past. It is now questionable whether they apply to the future. Even if the Alliance fails, it is likely that new political structures and approaches to issues will have to replace the old, if the difficulties of transformation to a new world are to be overcome.

In approaching our problems, deeper thinking and lateral thinking are necessary new requirements for a nation not yet fond of concepts and with a history to some extent isolated from modern European movements. If we could more effectively key in to other cultures, the exploration and negotiation which have been, after all, part of our history, can be given prominence over adversarial politics and class conflict. Fast learning is crucial to all our institutions, and many still rely on old approaches, whether of reliance on technology and science in their isolated development, or of falsely based trend forecasts for economic growth or the demands for services and other needs. Industry has learned that these methods are inadequate in themselves. A wider ranging approach to uncertain futures requires think-tanks, alternative scenarios, gaming, and the freer kind of operational research first developed during the last war.

The new information society changes human relationships, as did the industrial factory society after millennia of agrarian and commercial living. All are now learning to communicate in new ways, from primary school children to prime ministers. Because the connections between the two and across space are now novel, but nevertheless real, much else follows. One of the earlier laws of cybernetics (the science of communication and control) was that of requisite variety. In essence, this explains how the variety of a system relates to the variety of controls within it. In a very loose way, the growth of international activity, combined with the desire for local control of our lives, requires far more sophisticated ways and means of relating these effectively. 'Think global, act local' is a basis for a changing social and political philosophy, but the more detailed implications for every institution present enormous challenges.

When we weigh the apparatus of modern industrial planning, scientific measures of environment, computers, data banks and their use, against the variety of human existence, it is clear that the flows of information require new structures of thought and social relationships, as in such innovations as the Open University. The new intelligence systems have extraordinary power, whether it be in industry, in government or in the community, but, as Nora and Minc have warned in their Report to the President of France, the problem is to ensure that we are not over conditioned by machines, that individual freedoms are safeguarded, and that we do not create a new deprived class.

The structuring of new approaches to problems has been slower in our government than in some countries. Given the complexities of modern government, and the need to respond to events quickly, it is essential to take up the new techniques quickly, for unless society can match internal politics and management to the rate and change of external events, the torrent will carry us from one crisis to the next.

The rise of a participatory democracy, what Karl Deutch has called *Social Mobilisation and Political Development*, and the views of Jürgen Habermas, which discuss a progression from conventions of law and order to post-conventional contractual legal-cum-ethical orientations, suggest that the ways in which issues are resolved in the future will be far removed from those of the past, relying more on debate, social contract and principles of natural law.

Up to a point, of course, nations are caught in their present systems of conflict-resolution or economic theory, and governments attempt to apply the rod or to control the uncontrollable. At home, local authorities are over controlled as a result of a rigid adherence to central macro-economic policies and traditions of expensively bureaucratised or rigidly unionised services. We are now witnessing an over correction of recent trends at the expense of jobs. At the same time the structure of work is changing and new grass-roots activity is growing, but it is starved of funds when it comes to local development. However, the connections between global and local politics, legal powers, financial resources and human development could be made far more effective.

In return for any new local freedoms, however, local communities will have to recognise that in a shrinking world claims on territories and other resources must be shared more readily, with a willingness to work out new associations and social mechanisms to complement paid services. The organisation for such development will require various levels of authority, agency or voluntary organisation, working within a well understood system of government which will depend on shared, open and highly effective systems of information and methods of negotiation. The new information technology of computer and television provides one part of the necessary equipment, but the structures of political control will have to be more diverse than we have been used to. Regional and provincial levels of government are one requirement. Local and community structures are another. Independent powers and resources would be essential to both. Scotland points the way to regions; Amsterdam to communities below the city level.

It is not the number of levels which matter so much as the mechanisms for relating the levels, both vertically and horizontally. In a world of growing complexity new kinds of communication, management and control become essential, as they did at the outset of the Industrial Revolution, with its innovative procedures for running railways or the government. It is commonplace to say that change can only take place at the margins, step by step. Whilst this is true in one sense, in another it is false and destructive of any attempts to secure radical change. In the past riots, if not revolutions, were the responses to the need for radical change, and the same is true today. External events now create an imperative to adapt without such responses.

There are many needs which could be met in the context of international events and political philosophies: for example, the freedom of information and citizen rights now being demanded from many sides. Those who doubt the need for changes of this kind would probably have doubted the need for synchronising clocks and timetables in a new national railway system. But old methods are inadequate for a fast changing world, as current political movements suggest.

More difficult than following the dictates of technology is the following of dictates on ethics or morality. And yet, do not the problems of starvation and pollution cry out for new human concepts of natural law? Have not the Greens, the Greenham Common Women, the conservationists and media stars laid the foundations for these concepts? The big clash of acquisitive material consumerism with the laws of nature has still to come, or there may be instead a process of attrition. In the Third World land ownership has provided the spark and the clash in many countries. In the rich countries land is at present a sleeping partner in the political struggle, although fought over tooth and nail. It may not be so for long, providing as it does the basis for nature and a decent life.

Humane Ecology

The land will support us only if we have natural sunlight and air to live by. The courting of nuclear war or ecological disaster will, if taken over the edge to catastrophe, render all other efforts to maintain life relatively futile. So, on the over-riding imperative of nature in harmony — of human and other life together — rests the imperative of securing a fair and balanced use of land for the people of the globe.

A Malthusian view of population and food may no longer be an appropriate way of looking at the balance of life, but something equivalent is evidently true. If starvation does not hold down the population, then floods or war may do so. If the optimistic technological fixers are right, and there are no limits to growth, with the sea and space still freely available for exploitation, then we head towards a global community of continuously over-reaching quests, with man likely to suffer the fate of Icarus or, to give a more recent example, of *Challenger*.

Returning to earth, so to speak, we are faced with the everyday realities of human endeavour, justice, and an environment fit to live in. Endeavour, justice, and environment can be read as the biological needs of work and play, social harmony and deep affinities with nature. A great deal is going to depend on whether the old values of the western world continue their dominance, in conjunction with the military mind and its industrial complex. There could be sea changes. But even if there are not, the rising tide of Asian economic strength, combined with philosophies different from those of the West, is going to force Europe to look to a much more efficient use of its resources and to new ways of meeting rising aspirations.

It is perhaps significant that the desire for life nearer to nature has emerged most strongly in the United States. In 1970 Charles Reich wrote a best-seller, *The Greening of America*. In it he drew together many of the new ideas within the consciousness of human life. The greening was a growth covering all aspects of life. We still wait to see how this new consciousness develops in the face of old-style economic growth and military aggression.[4]

What has been witnessed in the USA during and since the 1970s has been a dispersal of population to the smaller towns and villages, and between 1978 and 1982 the number of small so called hobby farms below fifty acres has risen by about 12% to 116,000, while the large farms (over two million) have declined in number. In Oregon, the State to which settlers took the trail rather than going to California, then as now a leader in ecological concerns, the increase in small farms is about 14%, while medium sized farms have increased by 8.5% and larger farms have decreased in number. In Oregon's Willamette Valley south of Portland, a hundred mile stretch in which the State is attempting to protect commercial farming, most farms (65%) are under fifty acres. Although these have been, until recently, encouraged by poor control and the tax laws applying to farms, the desire is there, and seems likely to spread.[5]

It is worth noting that in Italy 86% of holdings are under 10 hectares (24.7 acres), in Germany 50% and in France 33%. The United Kingdom has 24%, but with 33% of large holdings (over 120 acres, not large by British standards), is well ahead of all other Community member states.

With the traditions in Europe, pressures to maintain family farms are likely to lead to 'social wage' support, and if this comes, the United Kingdom will also qualify. But it is not only pressure of this kind which applies; there is the equally fundamental need to be more productive over the whole land, not just in the present urban areas. Unless this can be done, economic and social problems will continue.

Having advocated the use of scenarios and future studies as the best way of moving into an uncertain future, let us consider four possibilities for land, which we can call status quo, trend growth, decline, and social development. Status quo implies the following: a continued perception of land as being largely outside mainstream economic thought; old notions of rights relating to private property on the one hand (including such feudal attitudes as trespass), and public interest on the other (for example, the securing of some access to open land in national parks); and powers of compulsory acquisition with the elimination of automatic development rights. The scenario would also assume a market in land which continued to allow the better off to take it over at the expense of the less well off, and to treat this private territory as something to be protected (via town and country planning) from development. New demands by the wealthy on a limited land area would raise prices near the main centres, the inner city would remain deprived, and farming would continue to be relatively better supported. This scene could be extended, but perhaps the point is clear.

The trend growth scenario assumes that we shall one day resume economic growth of a kind which will fit the equation of population + wealth + new technology = more land for building development. Broadly speaking, the status quo scenario will also apply, but there will be far more development. Present ideas of urbanisation will lead to new 'villages' (read new 'towns'), such as Tillingham Hall; new industrial estates will assume the name of industrial or science 'park', and there will be more supermarkets, golf courses, leisure and conference centres, and no doubt other things. As agriculture is re-assessed, the land problem will ease, for strict controls over changes of use will no longer apply. At the same time more attention will be given to wildlife and countryside conservation. On the other hand, land as a 'positional good', to use the term of Fred Hirsch, will become more desirable and more expensive. Conflicts over its use will grow, and so will the polarisation of rich and poor over space. This is a perfectly feasible scenario, but it leaves questions about the less well off and the likely changes in social values relating to a materialist society, Third World issues or wider ecological concerns.

The third scenario is decline. In *Europe 2000*, Peter Hall describes a scenario at the end of the book, having edited the work of two hundred experts from ten countries covering topics from international affairs and the economy to the family, class and the environment.[6] In it he contrasts a new and prosperous small country community sharing work and services and living at high standards, with a demoralised inner city population of terrorism which has caused many to flee. He covers other ways of life, but it is the declining city which is painted in such sorry colours. There might be land in abundance for the well off, although the bandits would probably re-appear, but decent land in the city would be eroded. The job of renewal and re-cycling would be too expensive to undertake. If our society fails to develop its economy and continues to put up with extreme social and political divisions, then this scenario will include not only a declining city, but also a declining agriculture, a fall in public services, and a country that has lost its heart.

The fourth scenario assumes root changes in social values, combined with new perceptions of land in the post-industrial world. This brings in the post-urban country discussed in Chapter 7. It rests on assumptions about a changing economic base in which work disperses from the old patterns of settlement, is more home-centred, and is combined with the growth, not so much of leisure, as of activity which relates toil, craft, and a social exchange informal economy. This will of course combine with the opportunities and marketed wealth of a high-technology society. One basic assumption is that a greater dependence on our own land area will be needed, to develop not only resources of minerals, water, wind and sun but human and wildlife resources also. These are likely to relate to new perceptions of the needs of world populations and the use of land, so aiding the transition towards a more balanced home ecology. It is of course easy to decry this view in the face of an acquisitive and self-indulgent society. However, James Robertson points out that what he calls SHE values (Sane, Humane, Ecological) may well gather strength.[7]

The timing and direction of world events will do much to determine the particular outcome that we may face. Scenarios are not discreet, and elements from all of them or quite new ones, may appear. At the same time step by step changes are taking place, and each will help to determine the future. The value of scenarios, if developed, which these are not, is to increase awareness of the possible consequences of decisions, and so to move purposefully towards a future in which some contingency thinking has prepared the way for everyday action. In a world set on industrialisation everywhere, and given the acquisitive and self-indulgent nature of people, it is easy to be apathetic or dismissive. This way, perhaps, lies ultimate disaster. It is the endeavour combined with salutary shock which may lead to a more hopeful future. Nowhere does the shock come home so quickly as the one made by war or outraged nature, of which starvation, alienation, pollution and waste are all parts.

Towards Fairness

When John Rawls published *A Theory of Justice* in 1972, the oil crisis was just round the corner, and environmental concerns were beginning to loom large. At a time of relative peace and prosperity in the West, notwithstanding war in the East, the attempt to consider justice anew in relation to a rich democracy was the stepping-stone to a fuller examination of certain moral issues which had been out of the general debate about progress in the West. In looking back to the Utilitarians, to Kant and to Aristotle, it helped to expose new issues and formulate new approaches. These could be taken with arguments elsewhere about the bomb or within the Greens, for example. Kant, in old age, wrote a treatise on *Perpetual Peace*. He was a believer in democracy, and sensed some of the feelings and scientific attitudes now emerging in the idea of man as an ethical animal. His formulation of the *categorical imperative* is fundamental to arguments of justice.

These comments on justice, democracy, peace and philosophy are made only to highlight the growth of moral concern in the West. Rawls' principle of justice as fairness has been taken up by David Owen, presently leader of the SDP, and there can be little doubt that in the coming debates over the future of this country, the old cry for justice will re-emerge in relation to the new sufferers of injustice. Already, juries have shown this concern, as in the case of Clive Ponting, and the law is looking to new questions of rights for citizens. Ideas are fermenting, and action will follow.

In all this, concentration has naturally turned to questions of unemployment and new work, inner city deprivation and the rights of minorities, especially blacks. But in trying to work out solutions for sectors, the whole view is not seen; it is as if a battle were commenced without strategic thought.

This book has attempted to view land in the wider context, and however unsatisfactory the outcome, the fact remains that unless we can re-define and re-design our ideas, laws, and practices about land, problems of the economy, and social wellbeing will be isolated in the search for solutions. The whole is greater than the sum of the parts; so let us at least make sure that we take on board each part and hope that the whole will indicate ways forward.

Throughout the book reference has been made to historical and cultural questions, to the relationship between city and countryside for an urban population, and to the ways in which private wealth and territories clash with public interests. In the end, only the productive capacity of people and their resources of land and capital, fairly treated, can provide the money, the work, and a land worthy of past traditions. The eternal conflict over who earns and who pays, over surplus profit or public ownership, over taxes and compensation, continues. But as has been discussed, if a fair distribution of opportunity to work and to pay is to be sought, fundamental changes in attitudes and structures of administration will be required.

In regard to land, a number of aspects have been dealt with. These include the balance between regions (regional policy); the balance of government support (rate support grants) to cities and shires; and the absence of equity between 'development' and agriculture and forestry in relation to rates, subsidies, tax relief and planning controls. The resultant lack of fairness in terms of land prices and house prices, for those locked in the inner city or deprived of work opportunities, is obvious, and the argument that the forces of the market must dictate the situation has the same ring as the arguments which prevented ready food from going to the starving Irish in 1845.

The highly pressurized London region could be relieved if decentralisation became a policy not only for government (to alter the way in which sectoral economic policy and expenditure now works against the other regions), but also, to give just two examples, for banking and transport, in particular air transport. Ours is a small country. Manchester, Leeds and Birmingham would be better off with a stronger local emphasis, so following the example of every

other major region of Europe. Central government would nevertheless have the responsibility of ensuring that taxation and subsidy
policies guaranteed public help for the deprived.

Taxation itself is tied to old ideas which could do with a shake.
Mrs Thatcher recognises the problem of an outmoded rates structure. The same could be said of income tax. In the broad picture, the
changing structure of work, the decline of an easily collected pay-as-
you-earn (PAYE) policy, the dispersal of activity across the land,
and the demands for a participatory and decentralised democracy,
shift the perspective from a paternalistic welfare, city based society,
to something new. In particular, we need to see security and positive
social development as joint aims, with tax policies adapted to them.

The so called tax revolt which arose as a result of 'proposition 13'
in California, to cut property taxes (rates), was followed by others in
the United States. It did not institute or sustain large cuts, but it did
open the eyes of citizens to the ways in which their money was spent,
and to choices of methods for collecting tax. This awareness of tax
policy is likely to grow elsewhere, and with such questions as
education and environment will probably become part of the
political debate. The adding of local income tax to property taxes
could foster local initiative, choice, responsibility and accountability. It might also, by the sheer proximity of work practices to
government, cope better with the black economy.

Simplicity, ease of collection, progressiveness and effectiveness
are some of the principles behind good tax policies. Income tax was
originally accepted for these reasons, but the scale of modern
taxation suggests that it might now be more effective to allow some
to be collected locally, and new local taxes to be devised. To avoid a
polarisation of rich and poor places, a regional level of government
would allow for redistribution. This level, according to Layfield,
would be appropriate for the collection of local income tax. It might
also take over commercial rating, leaving domestic rates to be
collected at the lower level.

The complexity of all this is fully acknowledged. But the central
points remain. Democracy implies local power and responsibility;
the nature of democracy is changing; and so also is the spatial
distribution of wealth creating activity. New attitudes to work and
security accompany these changes, and while new structures of
taxation policy will no doubt be slow to evolve, in the end they must

respond to a new society as they did in the nineteenth century. The alternative of a centralised non-democratic process and an expensive dole queue cannot easily be countenanced.

From John Locke to John Rawls a central view of land has been the private right to treat it as an expendable market commodity. This was understandable in the seventeenth century, with the world still unexplored. In the twentieth it is indefensible. John Rawls did not include the environment when discussing public goods. Perhaps after the oil crisis he might have done so, but it is doubtful. The Lockean attitudes remain, and as there is now no more Indian land, well, there is the sky. It is incumbent on all nations, however large, to give more thought to their land as the real basis of social justice.

This is an age to which, if they survive, people will look back as we now look back to the other great turning points in social evolution. In such periods there are no solutions for the future, only a confused set of largely unconnected or conflicting ideas and actions about today and tomorrow. It is acknowledged that, however arguments are presented, they are no more than arguments: stages in the changing view of nature and the attempt to understand it. But if the eternal values of natural law and justice hold good, then the priorities of rights, freedoms and fraternity will continue to assert themselves, and the seers, in particular Blake, Wordsworth and Ruskin at home, will be justified in their attempts to assert such values as childhood, green lands or work; in Ruskin's own words: *Unto This Last*.

The rights of private property are, in the end, less important than the right to enjoy a family, a home, and a place of work. A selfish society may encourage private rights and territorial attitudes, but these are no more appropriate today than they were before the Industrial Revolution. On the other hand, individual enterprise and good neighbourliness can be encouraged. It operated in the old country, but then as a relationship between squire and worker in a class-structured age. The later socialist brotherhood achieved the welfare state, only to find that it, too, was overtaken by events.

Today signs of the values of neighbourliness are reappearing, as cows and cars, shop people and customers, make space and time for each other. More problematically, land and house owners are, naturally, reluctant to accept change which affects their view, and rather as the peasant in an eighteenth century landscape painting was given little personal value by the aristocratic owner, today's owner gives little value to the needs of modern urban life once they intrude on his surroundings.

In the city, the problem is less. The bustle of urban life leads to the expectation of a changing scene, and it is always possible, for some, to go down to the country. In a landscape which must now accommodate a post-industrial society, similar changing scenes are on the near horizon. Rather than fight the old trench warfare, would it not be better to re-think the strategy and tactics? If enough people were able to extend their personal values to an active commitment to rebuild communities from within, and to recognise the needs of declining and expanding areas of the country, progress could be made.

The force which holds together a great deal of what is worthwhile in the city or country is nature itself, from window box to mountain top. The best places to live are those which enable people not only to cultivate their gardens, but to climb a mountain as well. The other force lies in the biological basis of human society. Conflict there will be, but fair play is something which is also understood naturally. In a crowded country this means the acceptance of physical change, provided that we can achieve the principle that no individual should suffer the cost of public decision without fair compensation. Let us hope that the global village will provide enough example to enable each villager to share a common inheritance of nature.

Notes and References

Chapter 1

1. The story of the limits to growth, its assumptions and implications, is now a large one. The original work came in a Report for the Club of Rome by Donella and Dennis Meadows, Jorgen Randers and William Behrens III, *The Limits to Growth*, Earth Island Ltd., London, 1972. It has been followed by refinement, critique, and a large literature of new studies, amongst which two of the most thorough are *The Global 2000 Report to the President*, Allen Lane & Penguin, 1982, addressed to the President of the USA; and the 1980s' *World Conservation Strategy* of the International Union of Conservation of Nature and National Resources (IUCN), the UN Environment Programme (UNEP), and the World Wildlife Fund (WWF). A summary book, published by Robert Allen, is *How to Save the World*, Kogan Page, 1980.

2. Jürgen Habermas, whose work has only recently become available in England, provides an interesting guide to social action in historical sequence; from the pre-conventional levels of obedience, to present conventions of law and order to a post-conventional contractual legal orientation, with a universal ethical principle orientation. The concept can be found in Habermas, Jürgen: *Communication and the Evolution of Society*, translated by Thomas McArthy, Beacon Press, 1979.

3. The concept of an informational agora has been advanced in a Report to the President of France, by Simon Nora and Alain Minc, *The Computerisation of Society*, Paris, 1978, MIT 1980. The context is one of a plural society requiring free access to information and reaching agreement by compromise involving ever larger communities and long-range views.

4. One of the earliest books on the post-industrial society was by Daniel Bell, *The Coming of Post-Industrial Society: A Venture in Social Forecasting*, Heinemann, 1974. Forecasting is a misleading term, having given way to a less deterministic way of thinking about the future. A world view can be found in the publication by the Organisation for Economic Co-operation and Development, *Facing the Future. Mastering the Probable and Managing the Unpredictable*, Paris, 1979. In this, changing values are given attention with a reference to Ronald Inglehaart, whose book, *The Silent Revolution*, Princeton UP, 1977, is a study of changing values in Europe and the USA, with emphasis on the search for new meanings to life. It includes reference to the concept of the social mobilisation of political skills, which come from Karl W. Deutch, *Social Mobilisation and Political Development*, American Political Science Review 552, June 1961.

5. Harrison, Fred, *The Power in the Land. An Inquiry into Unemployment, the Profit Crisis and Land Speculation*, Shepheard-Walwyn, 1983.

6. In his recent book, *English Society 1688-1832*, CUP, 1986, J.C.D. Clarke suggests that the old Corporation and Test Acts following the Revolution of 1688, by excluding non-Anglicans from public office, held back reforms which eventually came with the repeal of the Acts between 1828 and 1830 and the Reform Bill. Seen in this light, the great changes in political philosophy and practice assume a new significance which has implications for the way in which we now see other historical inheritances such as attitudes to land.

7. The printed page and specialism encourage linear ways of thinking. Arthur Koestler discussed his concept of bisociation, a broader process of thought, in *The Act of Creation*, Hutchinson, 1964. More popular studies come from Edward de Bono, *The Use of Lateral Thinking*, Compton Printing Ltd., London, 1967; and Tony Buzan, *Use Your Head*, BBC Publication. A recent research publication is by Gilhooly, K.J., *Thinking. Directed, Undirected and Creative*, Academic Press, 1982.

8. Kuhn, Thomas, *The Structure of Scientific Revolutions*, University of Chicago, 1962, and from a different perspective see Barnes, Barry, *T.S. Kuhn and Social Science*, Macmillan, 1982. Ilya Prigogine has moved from science to social science in an attempt to cross frontiers. See Prigogine, Ilya, with Sohieve, W. and Allen, P., *Self Organisation and Dissipative Structures. Applications in the Physical and Social Sciences*, Austin UP., 1982.

9. Brandt, Willy, *North-South. A Programme for Survival*, Report of the Independent Commission on International Development Issues, Pan, 1980.

10. Higgins, Ronald, *The Seventh Enemy*, Hodder and Stoughton, 1978. Velikovsky, Immanuel, *Mankind in Amnesia*, Abacus, 1983.

Chapter 2

1. Barzini, Luigi, *The Europeans*, Penguin Books, 1984.

2. Hofstede, Geert, *Cultures Consequences. International Differences in Work-Related Values*, Abridged Edition, Sage Publications, 1984.

3. For a European account of industrial and political change see E.J. Hobsbawn, *The Age of Revolution, 1789-1848*, Weidenfeld and Nicolson, 1962. The Thesis of the Protestant Ethic can be found in Max Weber's *The Protestant Ethic and The Spirit of Capitalism*, written at the turn of the century and published by Unwin University Books, London, 1930, and R.H. Tawney's *Religion and The Rise of Capitalism*, Pelican, 1937. The Open University now provides a unique service through its published course units and television broadcasts. Thus familiarisation with a wide range of knowledge is very much easier than it used to be, especially for those not within academic institutions. In the area under discussion, for example, Course A 309, *Conflict and Stability in the Development of Modern Europe* is invaluable, while for the UK Course D 202, *Urban Change and Conflict* serves an equal purpose.

4. The Commission of the European Communities in Brussels has published a

wide range of studies on the economy and related matters. Three interesting publications are: *The challenges ahead. A plan for Europe,* 1979; *The Old World and the new technologies,* 1981; and the report of the *FAST programme* on the influences of bio-technology, information, and the transformation of work and employment, 1982. It is perhaps in the field of research and development that practical progress is greatest, with such developments as CERN.

An example of practical co-operation is the European Strategic Programme for Research and Development in Information Technology, (ESPRIT).

5. See reference 4, chapter 1.

6. From an article by Sir Adrian Cadbury in *Personal Management*, April 1982.

7. Rosenblatt, J., *Tourism as a component of International Trade,* in *The Measurement of Tourism*, British Tourist Authority, 1974.

8. The FAST report, quoted in 4 above, refers to local economies and new initiatives (including the Campaign for Real Ale in Britain, and its stimulus to the growth of small breweries!). A study of participation in 21 European towns can be found in a report prepared for the Council of Europe by Brian Goodey, *Towards a Participatory Culture in the Built Environment*, Strasbourg, 1981.

9. Jacobs, Jane, *The Economy of Cities*, Jonathan Cape, 1969. There is an interesting argument to the effect that Adam Smith, in laying the foundations of modern economics, did so in the then belief (held by most educated Europeans) that man was born into a garden about 5000 BC, and Smith had to invent the sequence of production assumed in the *Wealth of Nations*.

10. For an account of European regions and their changing populations and urban structure, see Peter Hall and Dennis Hay, *Growth Centres in the European Urban System*, Heinemann Educational Books, 1980. And for world cities see Peter Hall, *The World Cities*, Weidenfeld and Nicolson, 1977.

11. Commission of the European Communities, *The Regions of Europe*, Second Periodic Report on the Social and Economic Situation and Development of the Regions of the Community, 1984.

12. Williams, Raymond, *The Country and the City*, Chatto and Windus, 1973. In *Mythologies*, Roland Barthes has a piece on *The Blue Guide* which contrasts the Guide's unreal doggerel of landscape appreciation with travel as an aid to understanding the realities of everyday life. English translation, Jonathan Cape, 1972.

13. Pevsner, Nikolaus, *The Englishness of English Art*, Architectural Press, 1955.

14. See Reference 6, Chapter 1.

15. Quoted in Offer, Avner, *Property and Politics 1870-1914,* Cambridge UP, 1981, p. 380. Offer discusses the wide complex of land, law and political movements. The history is taken further in Douglas, Roy, *Land, People and Politics: A History of the Land Question in the UK 1878-1952,* Alison and Busby, London, 1976.

16. Weiner, Martin J. *English Culture and the Decline of the Industrial Spirit 1850-1980*, CUP, 1981.

17. Dahrendorf, Ralf, *On Britain*, BBC, 1982.

18. Regional Studies Association, *Report of an Inquiry into Regional Problems in the United Kingdom*, Geo Books, Norwich, 1983.

19. As part of the surge of concern over environment and resources came *A Blueprint for Survival*, Penguin, 1972, by the Editors of *The Ecologist*. The authors argue from ecological principles for the decentralisation of cities and political institutions. Decentralisation is part of Liberal philosophy and is taken up by the Social Democratic Party.

20. Tawney, R.H., see note 3 above. The discussion comes in a section on *The Land Question* in Chapter 3.

21. Simpson, A.W.B., *An Introduction to the History of Land Law*, OUP, 1961.

22. Hirsch, Fred, *Social Limits to Growth*, Routledge and Kegan Paul, 1977.

Chapter 3

1. The concept of the S curve derives from mathematical formulations of change in the physical world, but it has been usefully applied to many fields, notably by the economic historian W. W. Rostow in *The Process of Economic Growth*, OUP, 1960. Today's vision of collapse and catastrophe can also be applied as a reverse concept.

2. Hoskins, W. G., *The Making of the English Landscape*, Hodder and Stoughton, 1955.

3. For a recent assessment of the English Landscape Movement see Watkin, David, *The English Vision*, John Murray, 1982.

4. Ashworth, William, *The Genesis of Modern British Town Planning. A Study in Economic and Social History of the Nineteenth and Twentieth Centuries*, Routledge and Kegan Paul, 1954.

5. Best, Robin H., *Land Use and Living Space*, Methuen, 1981.

6. This chapter was being written at a time when public perceptions of agriculture and conservation were just beginning to swing in favour of the latter so far as government was concerned. Two useful spurs to this change of heart were: Shoard, Marion, *The Theft of the Countryside*, Maurice Temple Smith, 1980; and MacEwen, Ann and Malcolm, *National Parks: Conservation or Cosmetics?* George Allen and Unwin, 1982.

7. Veblen, Thorstein, *The Theory of the Leisure Class. An Economic Study of Institutions*, MacMillan, 1899.

8. See note 4 above.

9. For an architectural analysis see Kenneth Frampton's *Modern Architecture. A Critical History*, Thames and Hudson, 1982.

10. Colvin, Brenda, *Land and Landscape*, John Murray, 1948; Crowe, Sylvia, *Tomorrow's Landscape*, 1956; *The Landscape of Power*, 1958; and *The Landscape of Roads*, all Architectural Press. There is much geographical literature on the perception of landscape. For a study which looks more deeply into one's own nature within nature, Jay Appleton's book *The Experience of Landscape*, John Wiley, 1975, is a fascinating explanation of our feelings towards landscape.

11. For anyone wishing to pursue the research field, the few examples given here are only a start, but as indicated for reference 3 Chapter 2, the Open University is

an excellent source. The following give a contrast of approaches: Bourne, Larry S. and Simmons, J. W. (Eds.), *Systems of Cities. Readings in Structure, Growth and Policy*, OUP. 1978; Castells, Manuel, *The Urban Question. A Marxist Approach*, Edward Arnold, 1977.

12. Cullingworth, J.B., *Environmental Planning. 1939-1969. Vol. 1. Reconstruction and Land Use Planning 1939-1947*, HMSO, 1975.

13. See reference 4 above.

14. Ebenezer Howard's work was first published in 1898 under the title 'Tomorrow: a Peaceful Path to Real Reform*, but reissued in 1902 as *Garden Cities of Tomorrow*. His analysis of social and financial questions went to the root of many city problems, but the eventual outcome fell well below his argument, especially in questions of land values and community benefit.

15. Henry George published his *Progress and Poverty* in the USA in 1879 and the application of his argument to current economic problems can be found in Fred Harrison's recent book. (Ref 5, Chapter 1).

16. Boardman, Philip, *World of Patrick Geddes: Biologist, Town Planner, Re-Educator, Peace-Warrior*, Routledge and Kegan Paul, 1978.

17. Heilbroner, Robert L., *Business Civilisation in Decline*, pp 9 & 10, Pelican Books, 1977. Joseph A Schumpeter's arguments can be found in *Capitalism, Socialism and Democracy*, Unwin University Books, 1943.

Chapter 4

1. For an early study which unravels some of the complexities of political choice see Friend, J.K. and Jessup, W. M., *Local Government and Strategic Choice: an Operational Research Approach to the Processes of Public Planning.*, Tavistock, 1969. A more recent general exploration into the question of risk and choice can be found in Moore, Peter G., *The Business of Risk.*, CUP, 1983.

2. A discussion on Kondratieff theory can be found in Rostow, W. W., *Why the Poor get Richer and the Rich Slow Down. Essays in the Marshallian Long Period*, MacMillan, 1980. The application of the theory to the problem of land availability and its effect on economic growth and decline can be found in Harrison, Fred., *The Power in the Land. An Inquiry into Unemployment, the Profits Crisis and Land Speculation*, Shepheard-Walwyn, 1983.

3. See reference 18, Chapter 2.

4. Hirsch, Fred., *The Social Limits to Growth*, Routledge and Kegan Paul, 1977.

5. Gershuny, Jonathan, *After Industrial Society. The Emerging Self-Service Economy*, MacMillan, 1978. And, Gershuny, Jonathan and Miles, Ian, *The New Service Economy. The Transformation of Employment in Industrial Societies*, Frances Pinter, 1983.

6. Department of the Environment, *English House Condition Survey, 1981. Part 1. Report of the Physical Condition Survey*, HMSO, 1982.

7. Countryside Commission, *What Future for the Uplands?* HMSO, 1983; and *A Better Future for the Uplands*, HMSO, 1984. For Europe see Commission of the European Communities, *Effects on the Environment of the Abandonment of Agricultural Land*, No. 62, Brussels, 1978.

8. Townsend, Peter, *Poverty in the United Kingdom*, Penguin, 1979.
9. Town and Country Planning Association, *A New Prospectus. Policy Direction for the Next 20 Years*, London, 1984.
10. Jowell, Roger and Airey, Colin. (Eds), *British Social Attitudes. 1984 and 1985 Reports*, Gower, 1984 and 1985.

Chapter 5

1. Barlow, Sir Montague, *Report of the Royal Commission on the Distribution of the Industrial Population*, HMSO, 1942.
2. Scott, Rt. Hon. Lord Justice, *Report of the Committee on Land Utilisation in Rural Areas*, HMSO, 1942.
3. Fothergill, Stephen, and Gudgin, Graham, *Unequal Growth. Urban and Regional Employment Change in the UK*, Heinemann Educational, 1982.
4. The problem in the USA is analysed in Commoner, Barry, *The Poverty of Power. Energy and the Economic Crisis,* Jonathan Cape, 1976, and Goldschmidt, W., *As You Sow: Three Studies in the Social Consequences of Agribusiness*, Allenheld, Osman, 1978. In the UK, two recent indictments are made by Body, Richard, *Agriculture: The Triumph and the Shame*, and *Farming in the Clouds*, Temple Smith, 1982 and 1984.
5. Commission of the European Communities, *The FAST Programme*, Brussels, 1982.
6. Nordhaus, W, and Robin, J., *Is Growth Obsolete?* in *Economic Growth*, National Bureau of Economic Research, New York, 1972.
7. Stone, P. A. *Housing, Town Development, Land and Costs*, Estates Gazette, 1963.
8. Real Estate Research Corporation, *The Costs of Sprawl*, U.S. Government Printing Office, 1974.
   Windsor, Duane, A critique of *The Costs of Sprawl*, Journal of the American Planning Association, Vol. 45, No.3, 1979.
9. Mishan, E. J., *The Costs of Economic Growth*, Pelican, 1969.
10. Burchell, Robert, W. and Listokin, David, *Energy and Land Use*, Rutgers University, 1982.
11. This exposition is best found in the new introduction to the second edition of Unwin, Raymond, *Town Planning in Practice*, Ernest Benn, 1911.
12. The arguments were at their height in the late 1960s and early 1970s. See Needleman, Lionel, *Economics of Housing*, Staples, 1965.
13. Keogh, Geoffrey *The Economics of Planning Gain*, in *Land Policy: Problems and Alternatives*, Barrett, Susan, and Healey, Patsy (Eds.), Gower, 1985.
14. Hall, Peter *et al.*, *The Containment of Urban England*. Vol. 2, George Allen and Unwin, 1973.
15. MacEwen, Ann and Malcolm, *National Parks: Conservation or Cosmetics?* George Allen and Unwin, 1982.
16. Reference has already been made to various writers on these subjects. See Ashworth, William (Chapter 3, 4); Howard, Ebenezer (Chapter 3, 14); Offer, Avner (Chapter 5, 15) and Douglas, Roy (Chapter 5, 15).

17. McAuslan, Patrick, *The Ideologies of Planning Law*. Pergamon, 1980.
18. Franks, Sir Oliver, *Report of the Committee on Administrative Tribunals and Enquiries*. HMSO, 1957; and Skeffington, A.M., *People and Planning. Report of the Committee on Public Participation in Planning*, HMSO, 1969.
19. Analyses of the Cow Green Reservoir and Holme Pierrepont power station cases are contained in Gregory, Roy, *The Price of Amenity*, MacMillan, 1971.
20. Two wide critiques of post-war town planning can be found in Ravetz, Alison, *Remaking Cities*, Croom Helm, 1980, and Eversley, David, *The Planner in Society. The Changing Role of a Profession*, Faber and Faber, 1973.
21. Bowers, J.K. and Cheshire, Paul, *Agriculture, the Countryside and Land Use. An Economic Critique*, Methuen, 1983.
22. Layfield, Frank, *Report of the Committee of Inquiry into Local Government Finance*, HMSO, 1976.
23. The question of simplicity and clarity is discussed by Layfield (22 above). For a full account of the rate support system and its complexities see also Burgess, Tyrrell and Travers, Tony, *Ten Billion Pounds. Whitehall's Takeover of the Town Hall*, Grant McIntyre, 1980.

Chapter 6

1. Wolters, G. J. R., *Standards for Environmental Protection*, in *Planning and Development in the Netherlands*, Vol. XI, No 2, Van Gorcum Ltd., 1979, pp 92/3.
2. For an analysis of the conflict between the aims of the Corporate State and those of Democracy, see Williams, Raymond, *Towards 2000*, Chatto and Windus, 1983.
3. Report from the *Audit Commission for Local Authorities in England and Wales*, HMSO, 1984.
4. For an analysis of why Whitehall has so limited a view of the Country, and hence faulty approaches to expenditure, see Helco, H. and Wildavsky, A., *The Private Government of Public Money*, Macmillan, 1981.
5. A revealing comparison between the British and French balance of central and local power is found in Ashford, Douglas, E., *British Dogmatism and French Pragmatism*, George Allen and Unwin, 1982.

Chapter 7

1. For a comprehensive history of the city see Mumford, Lewis, *The City In History*, Secker and Warburg, 1961. For an attractive historical analysis of design principles see Bacon, Enmund, N., *Design of Cities*, Thames and Hudson, 1967.
2. Pettigrew, C. W., *National and sector balance sheets for the United Kingdom*, in *Economic Trends*, Central Statistical Office, November 1980.
3. Holford, W. and Wright, H. Myles, *Cambridge Planning Proposals*, CUP, 1950.

4. Directorate of Planning and Research, Cambridgeshire.

5. An historical perspective of values attached to local viewpoints as against wider realities of urban growth can be found in Young, Ken, and Garside, Patricia, *Metropolitan London. Politics and Urban Change 1837-1981*, Edward Arnold, 1982. An interesting piece of research by Jeffrey Bishop, School for Advanced Urban Studies, University of Bristol, into perceptions of the new city of Milton Keynes suggests that the attraction lies in the sense of being in a village; for the City has wide open spaces and many small groups of houses.

6. A critique of the 6th Plan was given by B. Ecremont in the proceedings of the International Seminar on *The Management of Metropolitan Regions*, Volume 2, Lille, 1977.

7. See the Layfield Report. (Reference 22, Chapter 5.)

8. Cockburn, Cynthia, *The Local State: Management of Cities and People*, Pluto, 1977.

9. Both the *Royal Commission on Local Government in England*, HMSO, 1969, and the *Royal Commission on the Constitution*, 1973, recommended devolution to the regions. The case of Amsterdam was reported to the Seminar on the *Management of Metropolitan Areas* held in Rome, 1985, by the Organisation for Economic Co-operation and Development.

10. Friend, J. K., Power, J. M. and Yewlett, C. J., *Public Planning: The Inter-Corporate Dimension*, Tavistock, 1974.

11. Hadley, Roger, and Hatch, Stephen, *Social Welfare and the Failure of the State. Centralised Social Services and Participatory Alternatives*, George Allen and Unwin, 1981.

12. Handy, Charles, *The Future of Work. A Guide to a Changing Society*, Basil Blackwell, 1984.

13. The modern 'inner city' problem emerged in the UK after debate in the House of Commons in the late 1960s and the initiation by Government of a special Urban Aid Programme, directed at areas of social deprivation. In 1969 the Home Office set up twelve Community Development Projects, and these were followed in 1972 by three Department of the Environment Inner Area Studies.

14. Lord Scarman, *The Scarman Report*, as presented to Parliament in November 1981, Penguin 1982, pp. 159-60.

15. See reference 12, Chapter 5.

16. Munton, Richard, *London's Green Belt: Containment In Practice*, George Allen and Unwin, 1983.

17. For the study of Hatherleigh see Glyn-Jones, Anne, *Rural Recovery: Has It Begun?*, Devon County Council and the University of Exeter, 1979. The research on migration into Cornwall has been carried out by Bryan Brown *et al*, as part of the programme funded by the Economic and Social Research Council.

18. See Reference 12, Chapter 2.

Chapter 8

1. For an essay on current nationalism, and others relevant to the debate about regional and national characteristics, many insights can be found in Isaiah Berlin, *Against the Current. Essays in the History of Ideas*, Hogarth Press, 1979.

2. Siedentop, L.A., *Viewpoint: The Strange Life of Liberal England,* Times Literary Supplement, August 16, 1985.

3. Large, Peter, *Britain's New People are Top of the World*, The Guardian, February 7, 1986.

4. Reich, Charles, A., *The Greening of America*, Penguin, 1971.

5. Daniels, Thomas, L. and Nelson, Arthur, C., *Is Oregon's Farmland Preservation Programme Working?*, in *Journal of the American Planning Association*, Volume 52, No. 1, 1986.

6. Hall, Peter, (Ed.), *Europe 2000*, Duckworth, 1977.

7. Robertson, James, *The Sane Alternative: Signposts to a Self-fulfilling Future*, James Robertson, 1978. See also: *Future Work. Jobs, Self-employment and Leisure after the Industrial Age.* Gower, Temple Smith, 1985.

Index

235